Neglected Social
Theorists of Color

Neglected Social Theorists of Color

Deconstructing the Margins

Edited by Korey Tillman,
David R. Dickens, and
C. C. Herbison

LEXINGTON BOOKS
Lanham • Boulder • New York • London

Published by Lexington Books
An imprint of The Rowman & Littlefield Publishing Group, Inc.
4501 Forbes Boulevard, Suite 200, Lanham, Maryland 20706
www.rowman.com

86-90 Paul Street, London EC2A 4NE

British Library Cataloguing in Publication Information Available

Library of Congress Cataloging-in-Publication Data Available

ISBN 978-1-7936-4318-6 (cloth)
ISBN 978-1-7936-4320-9 (pbk.)
ISBN 978-1-7936-4319-3 (electronic)

For Chance Herbison

Contents

Acknowledgments

We are deeply grateful to all the authors who contributed to this project: Tirth Bhatta, Moushumi Biswas, Marcus Brooks, Manisha Desai, Robert J. Durán, Simon Gottschalk, Julien Grayer, Amanda D. Hernandez, Heather A. O'Connell, Moushumi Roy, Rianka Roy, Maya Singhal, Sonia Valencia, and Daniel R. Wildcat. Not only did they agree to be part of this project, they all were extraordinarily patient and cooperative at every step of the way. It was our goal to introduce readers to the work of a wide variety of neglected theorists of color and thanks to all the hard work of our contributors, we feel that we have achieved our objective.

We would also like to thank Drs. Marta Soligo and Josiah Kidwell, who provided invaluable assistance in putting together the manuscript. Also, Angelique Dickens, Connie Dye, and Pam Weiss were extremely helpful at various stages of the project, and Jonathan Jiménez played a major role in getting the whole thing off the ground. Last but not least, we want to thank our fabulous editor, Courtney Morales, for her expert guidance and enthusiasm for what we were trying to do.

Introduction

In all scholarly disciplines, the existing body of work is narrowed to construct an academic canon (David and Zald 2009). However, as the famous historian of science Thomas Kuhn points out in his classic book *The Structure of Scientific Revolutions,* "an apparently arbitrary element, compounded of personal and historical accident" (1962, 4) often plays a significant role in shaping the accepted views of a particular scientific community. Nowhere is this more evident than in contemporary sociology, given the highly politicized nature of the discipline (see Frisby 1972; Fay and Moon 1977; Lemert 2017). As a result, many scholars whose work may hold significant potential for contributions to contemporary debates in social theory go unrecognized. Still others, while not completely ignored, have fallen victim to a cultural and political climate not receptive to their work (Conner, Baxter, and Dickens 2019).

Feminist scholars have been in the forefront of those arguing that many insightful social theorists have been ignored because of their gender and, to a lesser degree, their race or sexuality, highlighting the noticeable absence of women, people of color, and other marginalized groups within the discipline (Clough 1993; Weinstein 2006; Sprague 2007; Thomas and Kukulan 2014). Many who teach courses on sociological theory make light of this fact by referring to the theory canon as consisting of "dead, white males." At the heart of the matter is whether or not the canon should be more diverse. To address this concern, some theory book authors and editors have begun to include the work of a select few female (such as Charlotte Perkins Gilman) and African American male (including W. E. B. Du Bois) theorists in their texts. While these persons have indeed played a largely unrecognized role in the development of social theory, adding a couple of individuals at the end of a theory course does little to resolve the larger issue—and potentially undermines a broader, more radical critique of the sociological theory canon.

A few (very few) studies of significant marginalized theorists of color have appeared recently, including Aldon Morris's (2015) excellent book on W. E. B. Du Bois and Marcus Hunter's (2018) fine study of those he calls "the new black sociologists." In the present text we extend this approach to

1

include not only African American scholars, but those from Afro-Caribbean, Latinx, Asian, Asian American, and Native American backgrounds as well.

Equally important, there are many authors who come from academic fields outside of sociology, such as philosophy or history, or who are not academics at all but are instead journalists, independent writers, or activists, whose work also has been marginalized. We consider them social theorists nonetheless, as they too have made significant contributions to the analysis of issues of concern in contemporary American society. While our perspective here is unorthodox, it is not unprecedented (see Lemert 2017). Most famously, Karl Marx, while he did earn a doctorate in philosophy, never held an academic post of any sort, but he is today universally considered to be a "founding father" within the sociological theory canon.

An additional feature of the present text is its unique format. Most previous work similar to ours focuses primarily on intellectual biography. Each chapter here contains three parts: an overview of the individual's intellectual life; an in-depth analysis of their theoretical work; and, finally, a discussion of the contemporary significance of their work. In so doing, we aim to deconstruct the boundaries of the theory canon in American sociology by incorporating, in the broadest possible way, the work of a variety of neglected theorists of color.

ORGANIZATION OF THE BOOK

Following this introduction, the text presents the work of an alphabetically ordered set of neglected social theorists of color. Each chapter includes a brief biographical sketch, an examination of the selected theorist's work, and a discussion of their contemporary significance.

In chapter 1, Maya Singhal examines the work of Suzanne Césaire, born Jeanne Aimèe Marie Suzanne Roussi in Martinique on August 11, 1915. After moving to France to study literature in the 1930s, she met and married the famous revolutionary theorist Aimé Césaire, with whom she, along with others, founded the literary review *Tropiques* after returning to Martinique. During this time, Singhal points out, Césaire wrote the only seven essays and poems she ever published, masking her radical criticism in commentaries on aesthetics, ethnology, surrealism, and travel writing. Singhal notes that much of the mystery surrounding Suzanne Césaire's life and thought is due to a lack of published writings, but that she may be understood best as a "theorist mother," matriarch of Black Caribbean feminist thought, and a "founding mother" of all postcolonial critics.

In chapter 2, Julien Grayer provides a detailed overview of the life and work of Oliver Cromwell Cox, a Trinidadian-born scholar who earned his doctorate in sociology at the University of Chicago. Cox spent most of his academic career at historically Black colleges and universities. Grayer points out that while Cox's work on racism and "race relations" is most often the focus of commentaries on his work, more central to his sociological research is his analysis of capitalism and capitalist development, especially his view of capitalism as a globally interconnected system. Another important component of Cox's theory is his argument that capitalism was the progenitor of modern racist social systems. Cox may thus be seen as anticipating both Wallerstein's World-System Theory and the theory of racial capitalism. Grayer also perceptively argues that Cox has been marginalized in American sociology not only due to the color of his skin, but also because he was a Marxist and a harsh critic of the dominant form of scholarship on race.

In chapter 3, Daniel R. Wildcat provides a comprehensive presentation of the vast intellectual output of the Native American philosopher-historian Vine Deloria Jr. Wildcat argues that four major themes run throughout the entirety of Deloria's work. First, Deloria maintained that the ultimate cause of the more-than-five-century-long conflict between American Indians and the white Western European settlers was a fundamental collision of very different worldviews, especially regarding religion. Second, that one of the most distinguishing features separating American Indian and Western worldviews was their respective notions of history and its meaning, with American Indians understanding history primarily through a spatial lens and white Euro-Americans in a linear, temporal fashion. Third, Deloria placed a heavy pragmatist emphasis on experience relative to knowing and doing. Finally, Wildcat claims that Deloria's most explicit exercise in theorizing was his suggestion that the fundamental axiom of American Indian metaphysics could be represented as power plus place equals personality, what Wildcat refers to as the Deloria 3P principle.

In chapter 4, Marcus Brooks examines the life and work of Augustus Granville Dill. The career path taken by Dill was an unconventional one. Dill enrolled in the W. E. B. Du Bois–led department of sociology at Atlanta University in 1902, at a time when the Atlanta Sociological Laboratory was making major contributions to history, methods, and philosophy, establishing the first American school of sociology, a distinction, Brooks points out, traditionally misattributed to the University of Chicago. After earning a second bachelor's degree at Harvard in 1908, Dill ultimately returned to Atlanta University as head of the sociology department and coedited several volumes on African American life. Most important, Dill soon resigned from his academic post and moved to New York to become business manager for *The Crisis*, the official magazine of the NAACP, where he worked for the next fifteen years. After a series of controversies, including Dill's arrest during a gay sex sting, he left the organization, but reemerged within a few years to become a prominent practitioner of what Brooks calls "Black public sociology." Here Brooks argues that Dill's erasure from the sociological canon was not primarily because of racism or queerphobia, though he points out that these certainly existed, but because of his role as a Black public sociologist.

In chapter 5, Heather A. O'Connell focuses on a neglected aspect of Charles S. Johnson's sociological research. Johnson earned his doctorate at the University of Chicago under the mentorship of Robert E. Park. After completing his doctorate, Johnson remained in Chicago to complete a major project on the 1919 race riots in the city, later published as *The Negro in Chicago*. Johnson then moved to New York where he served as research director for the National Urban League. He then moved to Fisk University, where he started the first think tank at a predominantly Black institution and later became the first Black president of the university. While all of these accomplishments earned him well-deserved accolades, O'Connell focuses on the research Johnson conducted on Black experiences in the South while he was at Fisk, where he argues that all aspects of life for rural Black residents were shaped by their connections to the plantation, emphasizing the significance of social structures emanating from slavery.

In chapter 6, Robert J. Durán rightly points out that there is an increasing recognition of the contributions of African American sociologists, such as W. E. B. Du Bois, but that a similar appreciation for the work of Latinx sociologists is also needed. Toward that end, Durán provides a comprehensive overview of the intellectual life and work of the contemporary sociologist, Alfredo Mirandé. He outlines four strands of what he calls Mirandé's evolving scholarship. First is his assimilation into traditional sociology. Second is his development of what Durán calls a Chicana/o sociology. Third is Mirandé's application of the law to advocate on behalf of the underdog, and fourth is his examination of topical themes in the relationship between the United States and Mexico. Durán also explores the question of why Mirandé's work has not received the recognition it deserves and examines the significance of his work for the analysis of contemporary society.

In chapter 7, Amanda D. Hernandez and Sonia Valencia provide a comprehensive overview of the work of Cherríe Moraga, who is currently Professor of English at the University of California, Santa Barbara. They point out that, while Moraga is best known for her collaboration with Gloria Anzaldúa on the 1981 feminist classic, *This Bridge Called My Back: Writings by Radical Women of Color*, this was just a starting point for her scholarship. They also note that her work spans many different genres beyond women's and gender studies, touching on key issues of identity, the environment, and heteronormative white supremacy and patriarchy, all important topics for contemporary social theory. Hernandez and Valencia discuss Moraga's work thematically rather than chronologically or by genre to counter the ways that conventional social science has marginalized poetry, drama, and creative nonfiction as not a part of social theory. The themes they cover range from issues of identity around race, ethnicity, sexuality, and motherhood to those concerning working-class struggles, the environment, and indigeneity. They then discuss why Moraga's work has been marginalized in contemporary social theory and suggest ways her work can be more fruitfully incorporated.

In chapter 8, Rianka Roy and Manisha Desai examine the work of Savitribai Phule, a nineteenth century women's activist and social reformer in India. They point out that Savitribai's work has been sanitized as mere reform rather than as a radical theoretical intervention in the understanding of the caste system in that country. Here they compare her work to that of both Mary Wollstonecraft, as she, like Savitribai, emphasized women's ability to reason and the significance of the public school system, and Jane Addams in her work at Hull House in Chicago. Both Savitribai and Addams challenged social injustice regarding gender, race/ethnicity and class, working extensively for the well-being of immigrants and working-class families. Their theoretical work, however, has always been downplayed. Roy and Desai end their discussion of Savitribai's work by emphasizing her intersectional approach to social inequality as well as her parallels with the decolonial/ postcolonial turn in contemporary social theory.

In chapter 9, Moushumi Roy, Tirth Bhatta, and Moushumi Biswas provide a biographical and theoretical sketch of the work of the Indian historian and radical journalist, Vijay Prashad. Although Prashad earned a doctorate in history from the University of Chicago and taught for two decades at Trinity College in Connecticut, he is perhaps best known for his journalistic work. He is a cofounder of the Forum of Indian Leftists, a correspondent for the *Globetrotter*, and a columnist for *Frontline*. A prolific writer, Prashad has written thirty books, in which he focuses primarily on the economic exploitation and cultural suppression of what he calls "the darker nations," from a Marxist point of view. Prashad's critical scholarship is multidimensional, as he identifies both the economic and political misdeeds of capitalist neoliberalism and their practices of ideological mystification in order to maintain their hegemony over the rest of the world. Roy, Bhatta, and Biswas also importantly point out that Prashad emphasizes the need for close collaboration between intellectuals and progressive social and political movements to criticize and overcome hierarchies of class, race, gender, and sexuality.

In chapter 10, Simon Gottschalk provides a critical examination of Tamotsu Shibutani's contributions to contemporary social theory. At the beginning of his chapter, Gottschalk expresses some reservation about whether or not Shibutani can be considered a neglected social theorist yet, as he concedes, Shibutani's name barely appears in the *Handbook of Symbolic Interaction*. As the prize student of Herbert Blumer, the founder of the theoretical school of symbolic interaction, Shibutani made significant contributions in his books on social psychology, ethnic stratification, and general sociology. Gottschalk focuses especially on two aspects of Shibutani's work: the first concerning the irrational dimension of self-concept, and the second on the role of rumors in the digital era.

REFERENCES

Clough, Patricia. 1993. "On the Brink of Deconstructing Sociology: A Critical Reading of Dorothy Smith's Standpoint Epistemology." *The Sociological Quarterly* 34 (1): 311–33.

Conner, Christopher, Nicholas Baxter, and David R. Dickens. 2019. *Forgotten Founders and Other Neglected Social Theorists.* 2019. Lanham, MD: Lexington Books.

David, Gerald F., and Mayer N. Zald. 2009. "Sociological Classics and the Canon in the Study of Organizations." In *The Oxford Handbook of Sociology and Organization Studies*, edited by Paul Adler. Oxford: Oxford University Press.

Fay, Brian, and J. Donald Moon. 1977. "What Would an Adequate Philosophy of Science Look Like?" *Philosophy of the Social Sciences* 7 (3): 209–27.

Frisby, David. 1972. "The Popper-Adorno Controversy: the Methodological Dispute in German Sociology." *Philosophy of the Social Sciences* 2 (1): 105–19.

Hunter, Marcus A. 2018. *The New Black Sociologists: Historical and Contemporary Perspectives.* New York: Routledge Press.

Kuhn, Thomas. 1962. *The Structure of Scientific Revolutions.* Chicago: University of Chicago Press.

Lemert, Charles. 2017. *Social Theory: The Multicultural, Global and Classical Readings, Sixth Edition.* Boulder, CO: Westview Press.

Morris, Aldon. 2015. *The Scholar Denied: W. E. B. Du Bois and the Birth of Modern Sociology.* Oakland: University of California Press.

Sprague, Joey. 1997. "Holy Men and Big Guns: The Can[n]on in Social Theory." *Gender & Society.* 11: 88–107.

Thomas, Jan E., and Annis Kukulan. 2004. "'Why Don't I Know About These Women?': The Integration of Early Women Sociologists in Classical Theory Courses." *Teaching Sociology* 32 (July): 252–63.

Weinstein, Jay. 2006. "The Marginalization of Application in U.S. Sociology" *Journal of Applied Sociology* 23 (2): 20–23.

Chapter 1

Suzanne Césaire

Maya Singhal

Jeanne Aimée Marie Suzanne Roussi was born in Rivière Salée, Martinique, on August 11, 1915. In the early 1930s, she moved to France to study literature at the University of Toulouse. There, she was introduced to Aimé Césaire by his sister, who was one of her classmates. The couple married soon after in 1937 and had six children over the next fifteen years. In 1939, the Césaires returned to Martinique, taking teaching jobs and, two years later, they founded the literary review *Tropiques* with René Ménil and Aristide Maugée. The review ran from 1941 to 1945, during which time Suzanne wrote the only seven essays and poems she ever published (Wilks 2008; Rabbitt 2013).

They are short, mysterious texts—often masking radical critiques in meditations on aesthetics, surrealism, travel writing, and ethnology. Writing under strict Vichy censorship from 1941 to 1943, the *Tropiques* authors had to "find the right dosage of opposition to Vichy's doctrines . . . without however, provoking the censors to ban the publication," as Ménil reflected (Jennings 2018, 187). Aimé Césaire noted, however, that the authors were "emboldened" over the years (Jennings 2018, 188), and the journal was actually banned briefly towards the end of Vichy rule in September 1944. In a letter denying the journal's request for paper, which was being rationed in Martinique during the war, naval lieutenant Bayle, the head of censure on the island, wrote that he had "no objection, quite the contrary, to a literary or cultural journal" but that he had "formal" objections to "a revolutionary, racial, and sectarian" one. He went on, "Freedom? Certainly, but not the freedom to poison minds, to sow hatred, to ruin morals." Reminding the *Tropiques* editors that they were French, beneficiaries of France's "policy of racial equality," he warned them, quoting a Jean de La Fontaine fable, "As for the ingrates, there is none who does not finally die miserable." Finally, he argued that he imagined *Tropiques* would celebrate the "regionalism" of Martinique, but he found the journal to be something quite different. Instead, he wrote, "For you, you believe in the power of hatred, of revolt, and you set your goal to be the free unleashing of all instincts, of all passions; it is the return to pure and simple barbarism" (*Tropiques* 1978, xxxvii–xxxviii; my translation).[1] In response, Suzanne Césaire penned a short letter on behalf of the editorial team:

> "Racists," "sectarians," "revolutionaries," "ingrates and traitors to the Fatherland," "poisoners of souls," none of these epithets are essentially repugnant to us.
>   "Poisoners of souls" like Racine, according to the gentlemen of Port-Royal.
>   "Ingrates and traitors to our good country" like Zola, according to the reactionary press.
>   "Revolutionaries" like the [Victor] Hugo of *Castigations*.
>   "Sectarians," passionately like Rimbaud and Lautréamont.
>   "Racists," yes. Like the racism of Toussaint Louverture, of Claude McKay and of Langston Hughes—against that of Drumont and Hitler. (*Tropiques* 1978, xxxviv; my translation)[2]

This defiant passage perhaps helps to explain why, as her daughter Ina recalls, some of Suzanne Césaire's students called her "the Black Panther" (Césaire 2012, 65).

When *Tropiques* was again able to publish a few months later, Suzanne Césaire bragged that surrealism was the tool the journal used to sustain "the image of freedom," "in the eyes even of those who thought they had destroyed it forever. Blind because they were ignorant, they failed to see it laughing insolently, aggressively, in our pages. Cowards later, when they did understand, fearful and ashamed" (Césaire 2012, 37). Most people, following these claims by the Césaires and Ménil, argue that the "camouflage" of the writing in *Tropiques* is what allowed the journal to evade the Vichy censors for so long. Yet, as Bayle alludes in his letter, in some ways, the project of *Tropiques* also aligned with the goals of the Vichy government's propaganda machine: to celebrate national heritage and to emphasize the distinctiveness of different regional peoples and cultures (see Jennings 2018). Suzanne Césaire's writing in *Tropiques* is not only a "camouflage" of radical ideas; it is also a kind of "cannibalism," a reappropriation of racial and gendered stereotypes and essentialisms to present a more complicated argument for decolonization and revolution.

After World War II, the Césaires moved to Paris, where Aimé was elected mayor of Fort-de-France and deputy to the French National Assembly representing the department of Martinique. While taking care of the children, Suzanne also spent her Sundays selling communist newspapers and wrote a play called *Youma, aurore de la liberté*, based on Lafcadio Hearn's novel *Youma, the Story of a West-Indian Slave*. Set during the slave rebellion in Martinique in 1848, Hearn's novel is the story of a "da" who saves the white child she nannies. No mere slave in the familiar sense of chattel, Hearn explains:

> The *da*, during old colonial days, often held high rank in rich Martinique house-
> holds. The *da* was usually a Creole negress,—more often, at all events, of the
> darker than of the lighter hue,—more commonly a *capresse* than a *mestive*; but
> in her particular case the prejudice of color did not exist. The *da* was a slave; but
> no freedwoman, however beautiful or cultivated, could enjoy social privileges
> equal to those of certain *das*. The *da* was respected and loved as a mother: she
> was at once a foster-mother and nurse. (Hearn 1890, 1)

Unlikely to be content with highlighting the privilege the *da* enjoyed relative to other enslaved people, Suzanne's project was probably much more ambitious. "If you go by the title," Suzanne Dracius speculates, "the addition of 'aurore de la liberté" to Suzanne Césaire's play, to the simple eponymous title [*Youma*] promises to emphasize the beginnings of the emancipation of slaves more than the servile devotion of the 'da' saving a little *béke* from the fire" (Dracius 2010, 157). In 1952, an amateur theater company performed *Youma*, though the play was never published and the text has since been lost (Rabbitt 2013).

The Césaires returned to Martinique in 1956, after Aimé split from the Communist Party. In 1963, the couple separated, at Suzanne's request, and she returned to Paris to teach. Suzanne had long-standing health issues, and she died at the age of fifty on May 16, 1966.[3]

Suzanne Césaire's contributions as a theorist have been, at worst, dismissed outright as simply derivative of Aimé's and, at best, relegated to cursory citations (see Condé 1998; Curtius 2016; Magloire 2018). She was also judged harshly by her contemporaries—even those she arguably influenced. According to Maryse Condé, "Michel Leiris, the French anthropologist who spent several years in Martinique, complained of her aggressiveness in putting forward Communist-oriented ideas and did not believe that it went well with her duties as a mother" (1998, 62). Chauvinism aside, Condé has, meanwhile, persuasively argued that Suzanne was really *Tropiques*'s resident theoretician (Rabbitt 2013, 51 n. 20).

Much of the mystery surrounding Suzanne Césaire's life and thought is simply due to a dearth of her published writing. Ina Césaire recalls her mother saying, "Yours will be the generation of women with choices" (Césaire 2012, 65)—choices, options, opportunities. In an essay memorializing Aimé and Suzanne Césaire after their deaths, Dracius describes reproaching Aimé for not opening more doors for Suzanne—in particular for never publishing her play, *Youma*:

> The great man had no memory of it. I put the question to him frankly: What happened to the text of that play? Why wasn't it published? In a very small voice, the great man told me that at the time, it was very difficult, for a woman, to be published. It did me no good to speak to him about de Beauvoir, who had come, at the very same time, into that France of the beginning of the twentieth century, with the help and support of Sartre, certainly, with greater difficulty and much later than Sartre, perhaps, but even so, with success. . . . From all evidence, what was good for Simone was not good for Suzanne.
>
> Couples are not all alike, all couples do not have the same pacts. Not all couples are safe from "contingencies."
>
> All women belong to the "second sex" but all don't write *Le deuxième sexe*. Moreover, the problems for a Martinican woman, a woman "of color," a "daughter of the *islands*," are doubtless increased (Dracius 2010, 156).

So, Dracius instead sets out in search of Suzanne Césaire's garden, paraphrasing Alice Walker. Yet, Walker's "mother's garden" is the place where she sees her mother "radiant, almost to the point of being invisible—except as Creator: hand and eye. She is involved in work her soul must have" (Walker 1983, 408). Setting out to find Césaire is more like Walker searching for Zora Neale Hurston, another now-celebrated Black woman theorist unappreciated in her time. We can follow the writings she left behind, scraps of people's memories, in the course of conducting a kind of archeology, piecing together the vestiges with history, context, and hunches.

Dracius's (2010) "search for Suzanne Césaire's garden" also highlights another theme in recent work on Césaire: the adoption of her as a theorist mother and matriarch of Black Caribbean feminist thought. Condé describes Césaire as "the founding mother of all the postcolonial critics who denounce, as Sara Suleri puts it, 'the simple pieties that the idiom of alterity frequently cloaks'" (1998, 66). Jennifer Wilks describes Césaire as Negritude's "Madonna: its singular feminine presence, related to the Trinity but unquestionably separate" (2008, 109).[4] Kara Rabbitt takes up Dracius's essay explicitly in her article "In Search of the Missing Mother," in which she argues that Césaire's use of "us" pronouns and the presentness of the land of Martinique in her writing make her a particularly engaging, inspiring theorist, easy to recuperate as a "genealogical/theoretical ancestor" (Rabbitt 2013, 37). Yet, as Rabbitt also notes, one limit of these maternal claims is the lack of attention to gender in most of Césaire's writing. Rabbitt lists the "few" yet "significant" (2013, 42) "women" in Césaire's work: her feminine personifications of lifeforces and land (Africa, Martinique), her often quoted description of "hummingbird women, tropical flower-women, women of four races and dozens of bloodlines" (2013, 40) in her critique of exoticism in the Caribbean, and André Breton's nameless muse "whose love serves to link man to the cosmos" (2013, 42).

Blunting the force of these theoretical gems, scholars have often focused more squarely on Césaire's contribution as a feminist corrective to masculinist tones in surrealism and Negritude, likely in part because of her work as a feminist activist. Wilks (2008) and Marina Magloire (2018), for instance, criticize surrealists, particularly André Breton, for exoticized and feminized writings about the Caribbean. Breton, Wilks argues, writes of Césaire's beauty in such a way that the description of the woman is conflated with the land of Martinique.[5] Similarly, she criticizes the presumed male subject of Negritude. Magloire also argues, "The persistent sexual metaphors of the Negritude poets depend upon the recumbent female body of Antilles-Africa, whose passive sensuality must be reclaimed by and for the black male" (2018, 108). Wilks (2008) further argues that, while most Negritude writers offer an essentialist vision of Blackness, Césaire's work is more carefully historicized.

Beyond a simply feminist corrective to racist or patriarchal work, Césaire's critical approach is characterized by a method of appropriating problematic tropes to highlight the importance of marginalized classes in society, from the Black person figured as primitive to the fetishized woman to the overlooked child. Daniel Maximin and Keith Walker draw from Césaire's essay, "The Great Camouflage," to talk about this method as a powerful technique for "camouflaging" her radical ideas (Césaire 2012). Magloire combines the Creole word "doudou," referencing a sweet, gentle woman, and Caribbean folklore centered on shapeshifting witches to argue, "The ever-present suggestion of magical and supernatural power within colonial narratives of the doudou runs counter to their representations of gendered submission and compliance, constantly unsettling the image of the woman of color as a welcoming hostess to her colonial guests—an irony upon which . . . Césaire . . . capitalize[s] in [her] own self-representation" (2018, 109). Condé meanwhile cites the last line of "Poetic Destitution" ("Martinican poetry will be cannibal or it will not be" [Césaire 2012, 27]) to term Césaire's approach "literary cannibalism," in other words, "a rewriting and magical appropriation of the literature of the *other*" (Condé 1998, 62). This "cannibalism" makes Césaire's work challenging to read: She criticizes exoticized poetry about the Caribbean as being made for tourists—too sweet, easy, and sentimental (*Tropiques* 1978 [1942], 50), and yet, Césaire also mimics these rhetorical styles. She takes up essentialized race theory to critique universalism and discrimination. She refigures feminized landscapes and infantilized people as camouflaged revolutionaries. Césaire's method encourages us to reread, rethink, and look again at things we think we know or take for granted.

In the first issue of *Tropiques*, Césaire takes up the work of Leo Frobenius, an anthropologist preoccupied with African civilization, to argue for the importance of people stereotyped as "primitive" and the problems of European colonialism. Césaire explains Frobenius's theory of "Paideuma," a sort of "life force," separated into two opposite "civilizations": Ethiopian, which was connected to the plant, and Hamitic, which was connected to the animal (Césaire 2012, 5). According to Frobenius, in Africa, "Primitive society displays in abundance features [these essences] of a kind which, in Europe, have disappeared or been overlaid by the accumulation of knowledge and an excessive preoccupation with 'scientific' fact" (Frobenius 1973, 23). As Césaire writes, Frobenius admired the "remnant of a very ancient greatness" in Africa and argued that studying Africa would provide an insight into Europeans' knowledge of themselves, too (Césaire 2012, 6–7).

While Frobenius's arguments are essentialist and troubling,[6] Césaire is careful to note that she does not treat him as a social scientist. Instead, she takes him as a kind of religious guide who, rather than divining the nature of an individual's soul, divines the soul of civilizations in the vein of Jung's collective unconscious. She writes:

> The study of the manifestations of the Paideuma life force constitutes a new science that Frobenius calls the Morphology of Cultures. The Morphology of Cultures is neither primitive history, pre-history, nor modern history. It does not accumulate facts or dates. It is not to be confused with archaeology, nor is it ethnology, or ethnography—No. What it seeks to study is "the organic being" of civilization. Civilization itself conceived of as "a metaphysical entity." (Césaire 2012, 4)

For Césaire, then, the utility of Frobenius's theories is the idea that different kinds of people have different motivations and change in different ways at different points in time. History is not teleological, and "Humanity does not have a will to achieve perfection" (Césaire 2012, 7). Instead, she uses Frobenius to theorize the affective forces motivating the actions of the colonizer during certain moments of history that she calls "shocks" or "surges" of Paideuma:

> It seems that the Euro-American man in the nineteenth century has been seized with a veritable madness for science, technology, machines, the result of which has been the creative imperialist thought of the world economy and its encircling of the globe. This veritable madness for power and domination, which turned humanity upside down during catastrophes as horrible as the wars of 1914 and 1939, is the symptom of a new surge of the Paideuma. (Césaire 2012, 9)

Meanwhile, the "Ethiopian," plantlike, does not have the desire to dominate (Césaire 2012, 5). Drawing from the theories of Negritude, Césaire turns these stereotypes of the "primitive" on their head, arguing that the qualities that Black people have been criticized for are crucial characteristics for connecting with what is "real": "It is now vital to dare to know oneself, to dare to confess to oneself what one is, to dare to ask oneself what one wants to be" (Césaire 2012, 10).

In a later essay, Césaire goes further to historicize the condition of Black people in Martinique. Explaining why there is not more art by Black Martinicans, she writes:

> Let's allow the imbeciles to blame it on the race, on its so-called predisposition to laziness, to thievery, to wickedness . . .
>
> If this lack in Black character is not to be explained by the harshness of the tropical climate to which we have adapted, and still less by I don't know what inferiority, it can in fact be explained, believe us, by:
>
> 1. the horrific conditions of transplantation onto a foreign soil . . .
> 2. coerced submission, under pain of the whip and death, to a system of "civilization," to a "style" both even stranger to the new arrivals than the tropical land itself.
> 3. finally, after the emancipation of people of color, through a collective error concerning our true nature, an error born of this idea, . . . from centuries of suffering: "Since the superiority of the colonizers comes to them from a certain life-style, we shall gain strength only by dominating in our turn the technique of this 'style.'" (Césaire 2012, 29)

Césaire continues, again invoking Frobenius's characterization of Black people as "plant-humans," to argue that Martinicans trying to imitate European society are doomed to failure: it is a "disastrous confusion" to equate liberation with assimilation (Césaire 2012, 31). It was these kinds of statements, Eric Jennings (2018) has argued, that led *Tropiques* to be accepted by Vichy censors, also fighting against the assimilation of African people into French society. Yet, this call to be true to oneself is not, for Césaire, a call for Black people to return to Africa or an essentialized Black culture. Instead, "it is about the mobilization of every living strength brought together upon this earth where race is the result of the most unremitting intermixing; it is about becoming conscious of the incredible store of varied energies until now locked up within us" (Césaire 2012, 33) in the service of decolonization:

> The most unsettling reality is our own.
> We shall act.
> This land, ours, can only be what we want it to be. (Césaire 2012, 33)

As many scholars note (e.g., Rabbitt 2008), Césaire's theories about Martinicans' relationship with their land use language that becomes remarkably personal, developing what can only be read as calls to action. Her use of Frobenius's essentialist race theory, then, draws from the idea that Black people are more closely related to the land ("plant-humans") to make an almost genealogical argument for Black people's control over their *own land*, figured as decolonization.

Césaire's "camouflaged" work also reappropriates and refigures tropes of the Antilles as exotically feminine, and the inhabitants as unruly children, less to contradict them than to consider the erotic power of femininity and the fearlessness of children's engagements with the world. In "The Great Camouflage," she describes the Antilles's perilous natural disasters—volcanoes, hurricanes, earthquakes. Then, she describes its manmade disasters: the historical violence of colonization and the slave trade and the ongoing violence of capitalism with its constant competition, its need for progress and new technologies, and its attendant waste, its forms of wage slavery. Césaire appropriates the language of the tourist literature she reviles, describing the islands from the perspective of a Pan American Airways plane[7] as "seashells." From the air, she says that it is impossible to see the islands' "hummingbird-women, tropical flower-women, the women of four races and dozens of bloodlines" (Césaire 2012, 40). The view from the aircraft takes on the perspective of a map—erasing people and nature in favor of a cold, colonial distance. Yet, Césaire writes from the perspective of the plane porthole, implicating herself in this colonialism, even as she fights against it. And perhaps, the view from the plane is in some ways better than the view on the ground, where one can get swept away by the beauty of the islands and miss their troubles and their dangers.

Césaire then takes up the tropes of people of color as "children" by describing the colonial officials who come to the islands and see mixed-race people who share their European blood. It scares them, she explains, to have to contend with their "heirs," their children, who seem to want to claim Europe as their father. "One will have to deal with these unanticipated boys, these charming girls," she warns (Césaire 2012, 43). Taking up these stereotypes of Antilles-Africa as feminine land for conquest and colonized people as childlike or primitive, Césaire turns the tropes on their heads. The feminized island, with its volcanoes and hurricanes, is as dangerous as it is beautiful. In her essay about André Breton, Césaire cites the Surrealist Manifesto to argue that childhood best approximates freedom: "It is perhaps childhood that comes closest to one's 'real life'; childhood beyond which man has at his disposal, aside from his laissez-passer, only a few complimentary tickets; childhood where everything nevertheless conspires to bring about the effective, risk-free possession of oneself" (Breton 1924). In "The Great Camouflage,"

Césaire appropriates the trope of the Antillean as child to suggest the figure of the child as a revolutionary actor. These feared children are Europe's true heirs, made ingenious by struggle. Césaire declares women and children as powerful revolutionary forces, especially because they are unexpected, camouflaged. If the islands seem beautiful, she warns in the last line of "The Great Camouflage," it is only because the viewer cannot see them clearly.

It is probably appropriate and certainly tragic that Césaire, who so powerfully theorized "cannibalism" and "camouflage," was so overlooked and dismissed during her life. Her essays consider Blackness, colonialism, and psychology, clearly in conversation with the better-known work of Aimé Césaire and Frantz Fanon. Her approach to the Caribbean as a central site for understanding the production of modernity prefigures the scholarship of Michel-Rolph Trouillot. Her theorization of race as mixing and the closeness of Caribbean, African, and American geographies precedes the work of Édouard Glissant. Yet Césaire's work is more than all of this, too. Most powerfully, she modeled how to write both courageously and cautiously under fascist rule: she did not simply uncover prejudice masquerading as scholarship—she showed how even the most oppressive rhetoric can be mimicked, satirized, and cannibalized to develop a revolutionary theory.

REFERENCES

Breton, André. 1924. "Manifesto of Surrealism."

Césaire, Suzanne. 2012. *The Great Camouflage: Writings of Dissent (1941–1945)*. Daniel Maximin, ed. Translated by Keith L. Walker. Middletown, CT: Wesleyan University Press.

Condé, Maryse. 1998. "Unheard Voice: Suzanne Césaire and the Construct of a Caribbean Identity." In *Winds of Change: The Transforming Voices of Caribbean Women Writers and Scholars*, edited by Adele S. Newson and Linda Strong-Leek, 61–66. New York: Peter Lang.

Curtius, Anny Dominique. 2016. "Cannibalizing *Doudouisme*, Conceptualizing the *Morne*: Suzanne Césaire's Caribbean Ecopoetics." *South Atlantic Quarterly* 115 (3): 513–34.

Dracius, Suzanne. 2010. "In Search of Suzanne Césaire's Garden." *Research in African Literatures* 41 (1): 155–65.

Edwards, Brent Hayes. 2001. "The Uses of *Diaspora*." *Social Text* 66 (1): 45–73.

Frobenius, Leo. 1973. *Leo Frobenius: An Anthology*, edited by Eike Haberland. Wiesbaden, DE: Franz Steiner Verlag GmbH.

Hearn, Lafcadio. 1890. *Youma: The Story of a West-Indian Slave*. New York: Harper & Brothers.

Magloire, Marina. 2018. "Witchcrafts of Color: Suzanne Césaire, Mayotte Capécia, and the Shapeshifting Doudou in Vichy Martinique." *Meridians* 17 (1): 107–30.

Rabbitt, Kara. 2008. "The Geography of Identity in Suzanne Césaire's 'Le grand camouflage.'" *Research in African Literatures* 39 (3): 121–31.

———. 2013. "In Search of the Missing Mother: Suzanne Césaire, Martiniquaise." *Research in African Literatures* 44 (1): 36–54.

Tropiques, 1941–1945: Collection Complète. 1978. Paris: Jean-Michel Place.

Walker, Alice 1983. *In Search of Our Mothers' Gardens.* Orlando, FL: Harcourt.

Wilks, Jennifer. 2008. *Race, Gender, and Comparative Black Modernism: Suzanne Lacascade, Marita Bonner, Suzanne Césaire, Dorothy West.* Baton Rouge, LA: Louisiana State Press.

NOTES

1. "Lorsque Madam Césaire m'a demandé pour un nouveau numéro de *Tropiques* le papier nécessaire, j'ai tout de suite acquiescé, ne voyant aucune objection, bien au contraire, à la parution d'une revue littéraire ou culturelle.

J'en ai, au contraire, de formelles vis-à-vis d'une revue révolutionnaire, raciale et sectaire. . . .

Liberté? Certes, mais pas la liberté d'empoisonner les esprits, de semer la haine, de ruiner la morale.

Mettons de côté ce qu'il y a de choquant à voir des fonctionnaires, non seulement salariés de l'Etat français, mais ayant atteint un haut niveau de culture et une place de premier rang dans la société, prétendre donner le signal de la révolte contre une patrie qui a été précisément pour eux une si bonne patrie. Mettons aussi de côté que vous êtes professeur et chargé de former les jeunes, ceci ne me regarde en effet pas directement, et retenons seulement le fait que vous êtes Français.

Le Villageois et le Serpent s'imposerait invinciblement à l'esprit. . . . Permettez-moi cependant de vous rappeler que cette fable se termine par: "Quant aux ingrats, il n'en est point qui ne meure enfin misérables." . . .

Depuis Schœlcher, la France s'est engagée dans une politique d'égalité raciale qu'elle n'a pas seulement proclamée, mais qu'elle a plus profondément mise en pratique que n'importe quel pays: de cette politique, vous constituez un vivant témoignage. . . .

Une centralisation excessive, mal dont ont souffert toutes les provinces françaises, a risqué d'étouffer la personalité, de lui substituer un être conventionnel et uniforme, de tuer l'art en tarissant la source de la verité. . . . J'avais cru voir dans *Tropiques* le signe d'une régionalisme non moins vigoureux et tout aussi souhaitable.

Je constate que je me suis trompé et que vous poursuivez un but tout différent . . . Pour vous, vous croyez au pouvoir de la haine, de la révolte, et vous vous fixez comme but le libre déchaînement de tous les instincts, de toutes les passions; c'est le retour à la barbarie pure et simple" (*Tropiques* 1978, xxxvii–xxxviii).

2. "«Racistes», «sectaires», «révolutionnaires», «ingrats et traîtres à la Patrie», «empoisonneurs d'âmes», aucune de ces épithètes ne nous répugne essentiellement.

«Empoisonneurs d'âmes» comme Racine, au dire des Messieurs de Port-Royal.

«Ingrats et traîtres à notre si bonne patrie» comme Zola, au dire de la presse réactionnaire.

«Révolutionnaires» comme l'Hugo des "Châtiments."

«Sectaires», passionnément comme Rimbaud et Lautréamont.

«Racistes», oui. Du racisme de Toussaint Louverture, de Claude McKay et de Langston Hughes—contre celui de Drumont et de Hitler" (*Tropiques* 1978, xxxviv)

3. Many of the details of Suzanne Césaire's life are contested, including her birthdate, the dates of various important life events, and the age at which she passed.

4. The "Trinity" being Senghor the Father, Aimé Césaire the Son, and Damas the Holy Spirit (Wilks 2008, 109). Wilks borrows this Trinity from Léon-Gontran Damas, so she is not entirely responsible for the implications of these metaphorical relationships.

5. In a poem for, it is implied, Suzanne Césaire, Breton writes:

With an eye to what ultimate balance, to what lasting equilibrium between day and night—as one dreams of retaining the exact second when, in very calm times, the sun in sinking into the sea realizes the phenomenon of the "green diamond"—this search, at the bottom of the crucible, for feminine beauty much more often accomplished here than anywhere else and which has never appeared to me more brilliant than in a face of white ash and embers. (*Tropiques* 1978 [1941], 41; my translation).

En vue de quel dosage ultime, de quel équilibre durable entre le jour et la nuit—comme on rêve de retenir la seconde exacte où, par temps trés calme, le soleil en s'enfonçant dans la mer réalise le phénomène du "diamant vert"—cette recherche, au fond du creuset, de la beauté féminine ici bien plussouvent accompli qu'ailleurs et qui ne m'est jamais apparu plus éclatante que dans un visage de cendre blanche et de braises. (*Tropiques* 1978 [1941], 41)

6. In his introduction to an anthology of Frobenius's work, Léopold Sédar Senghor wrote, "Of course the situation of Africanism has evolved since Leo Frobenius and great discoveries and important progress have been made. We shall no longer carry his works with us like a Bible or the Koran when we journey. Nevertheless the two authoritative works [*History of African Civilization* and *The Destiny of Civilizations*] are always in my library and I consult them often" (Frobenius 1973, xiii).

7. This argument anticipates Brent Edwards's (2001) use of aviation imagery to conceptualize diaspora.

Chapter 2

Oliver Cromwell Cox

Julien Grayer

LIFE AND WORK

Oliver Cromwell Cox was born on August 24, 1901, in Port of Spain, Trinidad to a stable middle-class family. His father and uncle, a customs officer and schoolmaster respectively, had a great deal of influence on his temperament and aptitude for study (Hunter 1983). After emigrating to the United States in 1919, he completed his high school diploma and then attended Northwestern University for library science and law, receiving a law degree in 1928. He intended to go back to Trinidad but after a debilitating bout of polio, he instead decided to pursue and enroll in a career in academia. He then matriculated at the University of Chicago in 1930, receiving a master's in economics in 1932.

Fueled by his disillusionment about what he'd described as inadequate explanations for the Great Depression provided by his economist peers, he then moved to sociological theory, receiving his Doctor of Philosophy in sociology from the same university in 1938. The department of sociology at the University of Chicago, known as the "Chicago School," founded in 1892 by Albion Small, was at the peak of its influence during the 1920s and 1930s. Notable for its role in the development of urban sociology, the Chicago School was also quite famous for its studies of race relations. The department and its growth and influence cannot be separated from several simultaneously interconnecting issues, including the increasing urbanization of the United States and the Great Migration of African Americans from the South to the urban centers of the North like Chicago (Baldwin, 2004). Cox's dissertation, "Factors Affecting the Marital Status of Negroes in the United

States" used a sizeable amount of quantitative data on demographics, sex ratios, and employment, among other measures, to determine factors that affected marital rates. Following in the footsteps of many Black academic professionals prior to desegregation, being limited to seeking employment in Black universities and colleges, he then accepted a position as professor of economics at Wiley College, a small historically Black college in Marshall, Texas, from 1938 to 1944 (Hunter 1983; 1985).

While Cox had formed many academic friendships, the small Texas college had resources that were more meager than he had desired for his work, so he then moved to Tuskegee Institute in Tuskegee, Alabama. It was during his tenure at Tuskegee that he published one of his most widely known works, *Caste, Class, and Race* (1948), earning a George Washington Carver Award from Doubleday and Company. Despite his rising and increasing accomplishments, Tuskegee was primarily a vocational school, so Cox had little opportunity to mentor students for graduate work in sociology. It was a situation that was not helped by his critical reception of Booker T. Washington's legacy, something that was not appreciated by the more conservative members of the Tuskegee administration (Hunter 1983). Having applied for a faculty position at Lincoln University in 1949, he then moved to Jefferson City, Missouri, where he would stay until his retirement in 1970. Described as a serious and demanding professor, it was in this period that his scholarly contributions would grow even more. He published a trilogy on the history of capitalism: *The Foundations of Capitalism* (1959), *Capitalism and American Leadership* (1962), and *Capitalism as a System* (1964).

After his retirement from Lincoln University, he accepted a position as Distinguished Visiting Professor at Wayne State University in Michigan. However, controversy and conflict would still follow Cox to Detroit. His antipathy to Black nationalism would sometimes put him at odds with Black Marxist students in his classes on capitalism (Hunter 1983). Cox died on September 4, 1974 with one manuscript in progress, *Race Relations: Elements and Social Dynamics*, being published posthumously in 1976. The vast majority of his career took place in historically Black colleges and universities. And it is in these environs that he would produce some of his most notable contributions to sociology. Despite his relative obscurity, in his lifetime, he was consistently held by his colleagues to be a man who took his scholarship seriously and expected it of his students and peers as well. His dedication to his scholarship had taken him down paths that strayed into theoretical controversies that often placed him at odds with his contemporaries.

ANALYSIS OF THEORY

World Systems Theory and Capitalism

When discussing Cox's contributions to sociological thought and subsequent marginalization, his work on racism and "race relations" is often what's focused on. But what is less discussed is that what is central to Cox's sociological analysis is capitalism and capitalist development. In the 1950s and 1960s his trilogy on the history of capitalism was published and would help give rise to the infrastructure of what would come to be known as "world systems theory." This theoretical approach to world history viewed capitalism as a global interconnected system that was characterized as "a large axial division of labor with multiple political centers and multiple cultures. In English, the hyphen is essential to indicate these concepts. 'World system' without a hyphen suggests that there has been only one world-system in the history of the world." (Wallerstein, [1987] 2004).

In his own series of texts, Wallerstein (1974, 1980, 1989) posited that most nation-states are part of an interconnected and stratified division of labor and resource allocation that may be divided into what he called core nations, semi-periphery nations, and periphery nations, the core nations being those most dominant in the world-system, having numerous benefits and advantages over the semi-periphery and periphery states. For Wallerstein, there have been two types of systems in the course of human history: mini-systems, described as smaller self-contained units and networks, and world-systems, composed of multiple interconnected units within a larger web of multiple regions. These world-systems are further divided between world-empires and world-economies; the former is characterized by a centralized focus of power like a capital city, whereas the world-economy is characterized by multiple foci of social/cultural/economic power, described as "world cities" (Hier 2001; Wallerstein 1974). Arguing that mini-systems no longer existed and that the world-system is the ideal form of analysis, Wallerstein placed the roots of the modern day world-economy in sixteenth-century Europe. It is at this particular point in history that Wallerstein and Cox's arguments about the roots of capitalism as a world-economy converged.

Cox's first book on capitalism defined it as a "system of organizations constituted by a particular economic order and institutional organization" (1959, 15). Building his argument, he used Venice as a prototype for its many sugar colonies throughout the Mediterranean in the early modern era (McAuley 2000). The existence of large-scale territorial operations bound by commercial and exploitative relationships characterized by Venice facilitated the rise of the modern capitalist system. Cox also established quite clearly that capitalism requires a state to be actively involved in the interests of capitalists and not necessarily in the interests of its people, albeit with some concessions (1959, 45). In this regard, for Cox, three factors needed to be present for the growth and sustained prosperity of a capitalist social system: (1) dependence on a capitalist system, (2) a government that facilitated the demands of the capitalist class, and (3) a conflict between the church and state that necessitated tolerance by the state (Cox 1959, 1964).

This point was explored in detail in *Capitalism and American Leadership* as Cox argued that the United States was at the forefront of the capitalist world-system in the mid-twentieth century: "We do not look to America for an understanding of the basic nature of capitalist institutions or their social organization. These have been inherited, accommodated, and perfected here in America" (Cox 1962, 20). Two underlying themes guided his thesis: (1) the political-economic relationship that the United States had with "backwards" periphery countries and (2) the implications of domestic race relations for American capital's political and ideological positions. By developing trade associations and lending programs, America was able to dominate foreign markets in an effort to acquire raw materials as well as export markets. But the domestic racist policies and practices of America threatened its efforts to effect market dominance as well as to export democracy during the Cold War, in an argument that had nascent themes further developed by the "interest convergence theory" proposed by Derrick Bell (1980).

While often considered a Marxist, Cox did break with Marx on several key features, such as prioritizing the nation-state over the city-state and industrial capital over merchant capital (McAuley 2000). Perhaps most important, he went beyond traditional class analysis to adopt a world-system analysis of capitalism (Hunter 1983). This had an effect on Marx's scholarship as it arguably prevented a deeper analysis of the imperialist natures of capitalism that could also help explain capitalist leadership in current world-systems (Hunter 1983). Cox also saw the industrial revolution not as beginning capitalism, but as emerging out of a particular context in which capitalism was already practiced. And it was capitalism, he argued, that was the progenitor of modern racist social systems.

Caste and Race Relations

Published in 1948, *Caste, Class, and Race*, Cox's most widely recognized work, directly confronted the then-popular interpretation of America's racist social order as a caste system. This was, however, not new territory for the scholar, as he'd published "The Modern Caste School of Race Relations" in *Social Forces* in 1942. The crux of this school of thought, Cox argued, is that in the South there existed a caste system not unlike the Hindu caste of India where white Americans were the superordinate caste and Black Americans made up the subordinate caste (1942). Notable scholars who promoted the caste framework, such as Lloyd Warner, held that this caste system was also determined by a lack of intermarriage, social etiquette that adhered to maintaining differences, and deterministic lifelong membership in a group. Cox contended that, while social divisions were evident in caste systems, a caste-like definition does not make a caste system, nor does the existence of said inequalities make a caste system. This was made worse, Cox argued, by the often vague definitions of caste that proponents of the theory employed when they used definitions at all. He further noted:

> Hinduism or the caste society of India is a powerful form of social organization which may go on self-satisfiedly, so to speak, forever. It carries within itself no basic antagonisms. But the social aims and purposes of whites and Negroes in the South are irreconcilably opposed. If such a situation could be termed a society at all, it must be a society divided against itself. (1942, 223)

Cox essentially argued that the caste analogy also ignored how the caste system in India was reliant on some form of common consensus among the populace as something that had predetermined that particular order and had only recently begun to be challenged by figures such as Bhimrao Ambedkhar. Meanwhile the white supremacist system in the United States had always been contested by those racially stigmatized, therefore no consensus was ever built.

It was in his magnum opus that he continued his critique of the caste system framework and further solidified his theoretical contributions to the scholarship on racism and race. It was also at this time that discussions about racism in the United States were dominated by *An American Dilemma: The Negro Problem and Modern Democracy* (1944), written by the Swedish sociologist Gunner Myrdal. Commissioned by the Carnegie Corporation of New York, Myrdal produced an encyclopedic study of the state of African Americans in the years leading up to World War II. At the center of his thesis, Myrdal noted an essential conflict between "American Creed" and American reality:

> Though our study includes economic, social, and political race relations, at bottom our problem is the moral dilemma of the American—the conflict between his moral valuations on various levels of consciousness and generality. The "American Dilemma," referred to in the title of this book, is the ever-raging conflict between, on the one hand, the valuations preserved on the general plane which we shall call the "American Creed," where the American thinks, talks, and acts under the influence of high national and Christian precepts, and, on the other hand, the valuations on specific planes of individual and group living, where personal and local interests; economic, social, and sexual jealousies; considerations of community prestige and conformity; group prejudice against

particular persons or types of people; and all sorts of miscellaneous wants, impulses, and habits dominate his outlook. (1944, xlvii)

In other words, how can a society that values life, liberty, and the pursuit of happiness also be in a position to deliberately deny that to its Black population? *An American Dilemma* enjoyed a prominence in American sociology for several decades, though it was not without its critics. Cox dedicated a full chapter in *Class, Caste, and Race* to a thorough response to and rebuke of Myrdal's assessment of American race relations. Calling Myrdal's work mysticism that reinforced the aforementioned caste framework, he accused Myrdal of ascribing a variety of social problems to caste as though caste were natural. Cox also criticized Myrdal's primarily framing race relations in America through a moral framework rather than a materialist framework: "If the 'race problem' in the United States is preeminently a moral question then it must naturally be resolved by moral means, and it is precisely the social illusion which the ruling class has constantly trying to produce." (1948, 538). And it was also this ruling class that Myrdal effectively sidestepped in his assessment, Cox argued. The caste system analysis placed Blacks and whites into mutually exclusive and oppositional camps, neglecting the commonalities in oppression and exclusion that poor whites faced.

His assessment of racial prejudice was based less on forms of social intolerance and moreso as an aspect of political-class relations (Klarlund 1994; Thompson 1989). Cox primarily defined racial relationships on three levels: ethnocentrism, social intolerance, and racism. While ethnocentrism is a common phenomenon across societies, it is the contact between groups and the meanings they attach to these contacts that should interest the social scientist the most. Holding his position that racial prejudice is primarily the result of capitalist exploitation, he argues that the dominant group exploits the minority and that racism is the ideology necessary to justify continued exploitation (Cox 1948, 1976).

Cox begins his assessment with the Greek and Roman empires, which extended to primarily non-European and "colored" populations but did not have the sort of racializing stigmas that we would identify as racism, but did feature processes of in-out group boundary work. From there he traces modern racialization schemes to European colonization in the fifteenth century, in particular the Portuguese need for trade and labor necessitating traveling to the coasts of West Africa and the expansion of African chattel slavery and plantation systems throughout the Caribbean and the United States. Essentially arguing that, while in-out group frameworks have always been common, the specific phenomenon of contemporary racism is extremely modern and is inextricable from colonialist practices. It is worth noting that Cox, due to his upbringing in the West Indies, was as a youth far removed from the racial discrimination that colored the contexts of his contemporaries. That said, the West Indies are a prime example of the consequences of the ties between racialization and colonialism that he discussed.

SIGNIFICANCE OF WORK AND MARGINALIZATION

A long winding thread at the heart of Cox's theories regarding race held it as intimately tied to capitalism. In particular, that "racial exploitation and race prejudice developed among Europeans with the rise of capitalism and nationalism, and that because of the world-wide ramifications of capitalism, all racial antagonisms can be traced to the policies and attitudes of the leading capitalist people, the white people of Europe and North America" (1948, 322). His form of materialist analysis at the heart of racist exploitation has placed Cox as a contemporary and forebearer of similar works on racism, colonialism, and capitalism by C. L. R. James, Walter Rodney, Cedric Robinson, and Manning Marable. His world-system analysis of capitalism as requiring an active state can also be key for understanding the relationships of neocolonial projects embedded in the missions of Western institutions such as the World Bank and the International Monetary Fund, which force periphery countries to open up to "free trade" often at the expense of their own well-being and resources (Ramsaran 2014). For example, the disastrous capsizing of a state-run ferry in Senegal in 2002 can be traced to the "free trade" loan practices of institutions like the World Bank that altered the social, economic, and political structures of the country in such a way that made adequately funding the ferry much more difficult (Rothe, Muzzatti, and Mullins 2006).

However, despite connecting these threads long before it was popular, Cox was marginalized by the department of sociology at the University of Chicago and sociology at large. Robert Park was a major figure of both the Chicago School and the scholarship on race and racism that it produced, being the person credited with developing the "race relations" paradigm (Turner 1978; Johnson 2004). Cox, however, was highly critical of Park's scholarship, stating that it conflated racial prejudice and racism with immemorial human association. His open critique of such a towering figure in the department and the discipline did not endear him to many and, as a result, he and his work were marginalized and not given the same level of prestige and support (Johnson 2004; Hunter and Sameer 1987)

The department of sociology at the University of Chicago was also associated with two early Black sociologists: Cox himself and E. Franklin Frazier. However, of the two, Frazier has enjoyed a level of mainstream recognition in American sociology that Cox has never achieved in either life nor death, as Frazier became the first African American president of the American

Sociological Association in 1948. Receiving a doctorate from the University of Chicago in 1931, Frazier, in his two most known works, *The Negro Family in America* (1939) and *Black Bourgeoisie* (1957), showed not only how the Chicago School influenced him but demonstrated his commonality and difference from Cox. In *The Negro Family*, Frazier studied the dynamics of the African American family and traced the evolution of these dynamics and culture as a result of contact with mainly white counterparts. Enslavement, for Frazier, was a reconstruction that stripped away West African cultural practices with serious implications for family dynamics (Cheeseboro 1999; Semmes 2001). He did, however, address issues of class and materialist analysis much more explicitly in his second book, *The Black Bourgeoisie*. In this later work, the enslavement of West Africans and the decades following emancipation that were discussed in *The Negro Family* gave rise to a Black middle class similar in attitudes and aspirations to their white middle-class counterparts.

Frazier's acceptance into the mainstream of American sociology, as opposed to Cox's fate, could thus be attributed to Cox's open reputation as a Marxist and that much of his best-known work was dedicated to deconstructing what was then the dominant form of race relations scholarship (Cheeseboro 1999). As noted earlier, Cox saw racism as concurrent with capitalism, and his conclusion that the eradication of capitalism was necessary to bring about a more democratic society would not have made him especially popular with Cold War–era audiences. Much like the marginalization of W. E. B. Du Bois from the sociological canon as detailed in *A Scholar Denied* (Morris 2015), Cox has been largely absent from contemporary sociological discussions.

In 2020, Cox's work received new attention via the publication of *Caste: The Origins of Our Discontents* by American journalist and author, Isabelle Wilkerson. Already famous for her Pulitzer-winning book detailing the Great Migration, Wilkerson analogizes the white supremacist social order of the United States to that of a caste system. Embarking on a comparative endeavor comparing the classical caste system in India, the racial order in the United States, and antisemitic fascism in Nazi Germany, Wilkerson identified several pillars of caste: belief in divine will, heritability, endogamy, belief in purity versus pollution, occupational hierarchy, dehumanization, stigma and cruelty, and belief in inherent superiority versus inferiority (2020, 99–164).

This sort of focus on caste would trigger an engagement with Cox's *Caste, Class, and Race*, albeit cursorily. Describing it as a "cantankerous critique," Wilkerson claims that Cox's arguments regarding the stability of the Indian caste system and the consent of the Dalits were misinformed and misguided, especially considering the activism of various Indian figures at the time of his writing and even before (2020, 255). She goes on to argue: "A caste system persists in part because we, each and every one of us, allow it to exist-in large and small ways, in our everyday actions . . . if enough people buy into the lie of natural hierarchy, then it becomes the truth or assumed to be" (2020, 380). Thus, changing social conditions must entail the changing of social attitudes and actions, arguably falling into the very trap that Cox accused Myrdal of falling into over seventy years ago. Cox, however, squarely associates the eradication of racism with the eradication of capitalism.

In 2006, the American Sociological Association renamed its DuBois-Johnson-Frazier Award the Cox-Johnson-Frazier Award (Wright and Shin 2009). Despite this honor, Oliver Cromwell Cox remains a largely misunderstood, if not obscure, sociologist. His insights led him to connect various threads of thought long before they became popular or recognized in mainstream academia.

REFERENCES

Allahar, Anton, and Lewis Linden. 2014. "Situating Oliver Cromwell Cox (1901–1974)." *Canadian Journal of Latin American and Caribbean Studies* 39 (3): 339–44.

Baldwin, D. L. 2004. "Black Belts and Ivory Towers: The Place of Race in U.S. Social Thought, 1892–1948." *Critical Sociology* 30 (2): 397–450.

Bell, Derrick. 1980. "Brown versus Board of Education and the Interest Convergence dilemma." *Harvard Law Review* 93 (3): 518–33.

Cheeseboro, Anthony. 1999. "Conflict and Continuity: E. Franklin Frazier, Oliver C. Cox and the Chicago School of Sociology." *Journal of the Illinois Historical State Society* 92 (2): 150–72.

Cox, Oliver. 1942. "The Modern Caste School of Race Relations." *Social Forces* 21 (2): 218–26.

———. 1948. *Caste, Class, and Race: A Study in Social Dynamics.* New York: Doubleday and Company.

———. 1959. *The Foundations of Capitalism as a System.* New York: Philosophical Library Inc.

———. 1962. *Capitalism and American Leadership.* New York: Philosophical Library Inc.

———. 1964. *Capitalism as a System.* New York: Monthly Review Press.

Frazier, E. F. 1939. *The Negro Family in America.* Chicago: University of Chicago Press.

Hier, Sean. 2001. "The Forgotten Architect: Cox, Wallerstein and the World Systems Theory." *Race and Class* 42 (3): 69–86.

Hunter, Herbert. 1983. "Oliver C. Cox: A Biographical Sketch of His Life and Work." *Phylon* 44 (4): 249–61.

Hunter, Herbert, and Sameer Abraham. 1987. *Race, Class, and the World System: The Sociology of Oliver Cox.* New York: NYU Press.

Johnson, Yolanda Y. 2004. "Oliver C. Cox and the Chicago School of Sociology: Its Influence on His Education, Marginalization, and Contemporary Effect." *Journal of Black Studies* 35 (1): 99–112.

Klarlund, Susan E. 1994. "The Origins of Racism: The Critical Theory of Oliver C. Cox." *Mid-American Review of Sociology* 18, no. 1/2 (Winter, Spring): 85–92.

McAuley, Christopher A. 2000. "Oliver C. Cox's World System: Insights, Omissions, and Speculations." *Review* (Fernand Braudel Center) 23 (3): 313–408.

Morris, Aldon. 2015. *The Scholar Denied: W. E. B. Du Bois and the Birth of Modern Sociology*. Oakland, CA: University of California Press.

Myrdal, Gunner. 1944. *An American Dilemma: The Negro Problem and Modern Democracy*. New Brunswick, NJ: Transaction Publishers.

Ramsaran, Dave. 2014. "Capitalist Development through the Eyes of Oliver Cox with Some Insights for Caribbean Development." *Canadian Journal of Latin-American and Caribbean Studies* 39 (3): 403–19.

Rothe, Dawn, Muzzatti, Stephen, and Christopher Mullens. 2006. "Crime on the High Seas: Crimes of Globalization and the Sinking of the Senegalese Ferry Lejoola." *Critical Criminology* 14: 158–80.

Semmes, Clovis. 2001. "E. Franklin Frazier's Theory of the Black Family: Vindication and Sociological Insight." *Journal of Sociology and Social Welfare* 28 (2): 3–21.

Thompson, Richard. 1989. *Theories of Ethnicity*. New York: Greenwood Press Inc.

Turner, James. 1978. "The Founding Fathers of American Sociology: An Analysis of Their Sociological Theories on Race Relations." *Journal of Black Studies* 9 (1): 3–14.

Wallerstein, Immanuel. 1974. *The Modern World-System I: Capitalist Agriculture and the Origins of the European World-Economy in the Sixteenth Century*. New York: Academic Press.

———. 1980. *The Modern World-System II: Mercantilism and the Consolidation of the European World-Economy 1600–1750*. New York: Academic Press.

———. 1989. *The Modern World-System III: The Second Era of Great Expansion of the Capitalist World-Economy*. New York: Academic Press.

Wilkerson, Isabelle. 2020. *Caste: The Origins of Our Discontents*. New York: Random House.

Wright III, Earl, and Jean Shin. 2009. "The Significance of the Cox-Johnson-Frazier Award." *ASA Footnotes* 37 (8).

Chapter 3

Vine Deloria Jr.

Indigenous Iconoclast

Daniel R. Wildcat

It is impossible to discuss the philosophical and intellectual legacy of Vine Deloria Jr. in a book chapter. However, it is possible to sketch a broad outline of some contributions Deloria made to the practice of Indigenous philosophy and social theory. I will outline four contributions that stand out for their presence throughout the incredible body of work Vine Deloria Jr. produced over five decades.

At least four ideas emerge throughout Deloria's books. First, Deloria maintained that the ultimate cause of the five-century-long conflict between American Indians and the Western European settlers of the United States and their government was a collision of very different worldviews, especially as they relate to religion. We shall see that much of Deloria's work embodied a comparative worldview analysis. Second, Deloria suggested that the most distinguishing features separating American Indian and Western civilization–shaped American worldviews were their respective views of history and its meaning: American Indians understand history primarily through a spatial lens and Euro-Americans conceptualize history in an ideological progressive linear, temporal fashion. Third, Deloria established experience, both individual and collective, as the touchstone for all his work. While one is tempted to see Deloria as an Indigenous phenomenologist, a better comparison might be to the pragmatic emphasis John Dewey (1959) placed on experience relative to knowing and doing. Finally, Deloria's most explicit exercise in theorizing was his suggestion that the fundamental principle or axiom of American Indian metaphysics could be represented as power plus place equals personality, or what I will refer to as the Deloria 3P principle or axiom.

These four ideas do not represent the only contributions Deloria made. No claim is made here for a comprehensive review of his contributions. Rather, Deloria's legacy in many respects lies in the incredible breadth and depth of his knowledge and contributions. David Wilkins's (2018) book *Red Prophet: The Punishing Intellectualism of Vine Deloria, Jr.* is an invaluable source for a more comprehensive examination of Deloria's intellect. Few scholars today can match Deloria's impressive range of interests and scholarship across so many fields and disciplines. The contributions discussed in this chapter are the result of a modest survey of his published books. Despite the token commitment to interdisciplinary and transdisciplinary studies in the increasingly corporatized academy, it is hard to imagine anyone researching and writing about everything from the law and treaties (Deloria and Lytle 1983; Deloria and Lytl 1984; Deloria and Wilkins 1999; Deloria and Wilkins 2011), religion/theology (Deloria 1973; Deloria 1999; Deloria 1999a; Deloria 2004; Deloria 2009), philosophy (Deloria 1972; Deloria 1979; Deloria and Wildcat 2001; Deloria 2004; Deloria, 2009), history (Deloria 1971; Cadwalader and Deloria 1984) education (Deloria 1991; Deloria and Wildcat 2001), and science, e.g., biology, earth science, physics, and social science (Deloria 1979; Deloria 1997) receiving tenure today.

Before I launch into Deloria's intellectual output, let us deal with an obvious issue. I parse my words here carefully. Deloria never thought of himself as a social theorist. In fact, the most enduring feature of his work is a general suspicion of those who undertook their work under the aegis of social theory. It would be an overstatement to say he was anti-theory, but toward social scientists, especially anthropologists, he was highly critical. The inclusion of Vine Deloria Jr. in a book about unrecognized or forgotten social theorists of color would no doubt earn, if he were living, a witty objection to the effect that only social scientists could think he was unrecognized for something in which he never engaged. But here is the catch: while never explicitly seeing himself as a social theoretician, one does find in his writings four features of his thought and practice of scholarship that are fundamentally relational in character.

In toto, Deloria's Socratic questioning of received views on so many topics certainly makes him an iconoclast of the first order. After all, who would undertake a relentless critique of the science supporting a Bering land bridge thesis for the arrival of American Indians to the Americas (Deloria 1997)? Who would question the efficacy and strategies for creating unity among the First Peoples of this land (Deloria 1969)? Who would suggest that the real hegemony of the modern Western world and its most dangerous feature is not political economy but the Christian tradition (Deloria 1972)? Who would propose that scientists and thinking people outside scientific disciplines need a shared ordinary language to discuss what we think we know (Deloria 1979)?

And, finally, who was bold enough to suggest that the fundamental feature of American Indian metaphysics could be summarized in a simple axiom: power plus place equals personality (2001)?

Consider the following an invitation and one guide, no doubt among many that could be offered, but one suggesting four major features of the Deloria mindscape and scholarly practice that will be useful to those looking for ways to understand Deloria's work as a complex totality. I doubt that those wanting a grand Deloria theory will find one. But for those willing to settle for some inspiration to tackle intellectual work more critically than ever, the following will be useful.

CONTRIBUTION ONE: A CRITIQUE OF WESTERN CULTURAL HEGEMONY

Deloria's view of Western civilization, regardless of whether those immersed in modern American society know it or not, was that many of the problems modern humankind presently faces are shaped by ideas that have deep roots in the tradition now denominated as the Western tradition. Consequently, Deloria (1973) maintained that since 1492 American Indians and Euro-American settlers have been speaking from two very different worldviews; consequently, considerable misunderstanding and miscommunication have occurred. In his 1971 "Introduction" to the republished edition of Jennings C. Wise's, *The Red Man in the New World*, which Deloria revised and edited, Deloria states:

> Until the fundamental differences in cultural outlook, in part inspired by differ-
> ent religious world views, are understood by the people with power who make
> decisions affecting the lives of a million American Indians, little of lasting value
> will be accomplished. Thus the perennial studies to find the "key' to understand-
> ing American Indians, while motivated by a genuine concern, do not begin to
> fathom the deep gulf that exists between Indian tribes and the rest of America.
> (1971, ix)

Deloria was hardly a postmodernist. If anything, he was a non-modernist Indigenous tribalist. He basically understood the Western tradition as civilized only for those situated in the United States and either ideologically or physically insulated from the often violent and oppressive character of Western civilization by the institutions of education, religion, and, of course, a privileged place in the economic system of modern America. In short, civilization exists in the minds of those blind to its corrosive character and who embrace the Christian religion as the guarantor of civilization, most typically expressed in a naive Panglossian belief that this is the best of all possible worlds.

This "best of all possible worlds" thesis embodies Whitehead's (1933) concept of *misplaced concreteness* that Deloria was fond of invoking in his critique of the Western tradition and which he summarized as "after they reached the conclusions to which their premises had led them, they came to believe they had accurately described ultimate reality" (2001, 2). In short, the power of the Western tradition resides in the hubris that produced the nineteenth century, still lingering notion of Manifest Destiny found today in American claims of exceptionalism. In his hugely popular first book, *Custer Died For Your Sins*, Deloria observed that young Indians were refusing to accept white values and US narratives of exceptionalism: "Such anomalies as starvation in the midst of plenty indicate to them that the older Indian ways are probably best for them" (1969, 239).

Deloria's critique of Western civilization is clear in his seminal work, *God Is Red* (1973). Chapters 5 through 8 in *GIR* constitute the foundation of a critique he would build on throughout his scholarship. His American Indian spatial view of history, a response to the abstract and universalizing temporal Western view, deserves a discussion of its own and will be treated as the second major theme in Deloria's scholarship. Nevertheless, a few key points must be made about the basis of his radical, i.e., fundamental, critique of the Western worldview as informed by Christian teachings.

In his discussion of "The Religion Question" in *God Is Red*, Deloria suggested that a host of national and international social problems America faced in the sixties should be framed as the culmination of "a tragic breakdown," predicted by Nietzsche and Kierkegaard, "in both the vision and values of Western man" (1973, 57–74). He also made clear that the job confronting us today, regardless of "race," nationality, or ethnicity, is "the necessity of renewing our vision for the totality of our existence, our understanding of the universe, and the paths by which we can move forward as diverse peoples upon the continent" (1973, 69–70). While it is important to avoid romanticizing the American Indian past, Deloria consistently maintains that a comparison of American Indian worldviews to those of the European immigrants to America will yield the realization that American Indians' deep spatial- and place-based experiential knowledge offers a more consistent view with current scientific thinking than the entrenched Western worldview and also provides more useful suggestions on how we might improve our situation.

Given Deloria's education in theology, it is not surprising that his examination of Western civilization starts with the fundamental role he ascribes to Christian thought in shaping the Western tradition. Interestingly, Deloria concurs with those who argue that the foundation of the modern Western worldview is the Judeo-Christian tradition, but he identifies a very different telos or set of consequences than those championed by political or philosophical conservatives. Instead, Deloria's central discussion in *GIR* draws on his analysis of the destructive role Christianity plays in the dominant attitudes toward nature, humanity, and the very meaning of history itself. In "The Problem of Creation" (chapter 6, *GIR*), Deloria discusses the dangerous features of the story of a fallen or corrupt humankind that also entails an alienation from the natural world. This alienation, when combined with the Christian idea that man was given dominion over the rest of creation, sets up the logic for the perpetual struggle with nature that Christians promulgate. Deloria's argument is that, if Genesis provides a lens through which Christians understand their relationship to the balance of creation, then we should be prepared for ecological disaster. As he sees it, "It is bad enough to consider a Genesis as a historical account in view of what we know today of the nature of our world. But when we consider that the Genesis account places nature and nonhuman life systems in a polarity with us, tinged with evil and without hope of redemption except at the last judgment, the whole idea appears intolerable" (1973, 101).

In chapter 7 of *GIR*, "The Concept of History," Deloria analyzes the abstract presentation of world history once the creation story of the ancient Hebrews, a tribal people, became the creation story for all humankind. The result is the expropriation of a distinct Hebrew people's "Genesis" creation story for service as the creation story and beginning of history for all humankind:

> We are faced today with a concept of world history that lacks even the most basic appreciation of the experiences of mankind as a whole. Unless other cultures and nations have some important relationship with the nations of Western Europe, they have little or no status in the interpretation of world history. Indeed, world history as presently conceived in the Christian nations is the story of Western man's conquest of the remainder of the world and his subsequent rise to technological sophistication. (1973, 122)

By treating history chronologically with only regard to one group of peoples abstractly identified in a fuzzy and largely ideological sense as Western time becomes the convenient tool for post-facto constructions of superiority and "progress."

In short, finding the one true religion and god creates a mindset where the creation story told in that religion marks the beginning of all humankind and the one true world history. The Biblical second coming of Jesus, or judgment day, is the end of history. Never mind that the reign of religion over humankind and life of the planet is relatively quickly eclipsed in the eighteenth and nineteenth centuries by another Western narrative of the reign of science and technology. What is important is that, although the narrative of world history is modified, the narrator and the idea of a Western telos representing the inexorable movement toward a final reward or reckoning as an end, remains.

Deloria's critique of Western civilization was not wholly negative, however. In virtually all his works he challenges Western cultural hegemony with Indigenous counterpoints: e.g., an abstract time-oriented universal history vs. a tribal spatial conception of history, the world as machine vs. the universe as a living moral domain; a world populated with resources vs. a world full of relative scarcity; a reality preoccupied with individual rights vs. one focused on responsibilities, etc.

From his first book, *Custer Died for Your Sins*, to the last, *The World We Used to Live In*, finished shortly before his death, Deloria remained hopeful Indians would recognize the power in their own worldviews. In the final chapters of *Custer,* Deloria expressed optimism in what he surmised as young Indians' willingness to embrace their tribal cultures without shame or a colonial imposed sense of inferiority. Deloria's admiration of Clyde Warrior and other young Indians of the National Indian Youth Council in the late 1960s no doubt shaped this view. Deloria's perspective here was encouraged by what seemed a growing awareness by many—not just Indians—that the institutions and values of American society were morally bankrupt and seemed to only be about what one could literally put in the bank.

Deloria saw an opportunity for change led by Indigenous intellectual activists: "This country could be greatly influenced by any group with a more comprehensive philosophy of man if that group worked in a non-violent and non-controversial manner" (1969, 256). He maintained that Indians should not follow the political route Black militants advocated. Overall, given American society's love of violence, he considered taking a militant position against the dominant society as an invitation to bring violence upon oneself.

Instead, Deloria surmised, "It would be fairly easy, however, with a sufficient number of articulate young Indians and well-organized community support, to greatly influence the thinking of the nation" (1969, 257). Not surprisingly, he concluded, "So it is vitally important that the Indian people pick the intellectual arena as the one in which to wage war" (1969, 257). As American society and the so-called advanced countries of the world face growing crises in their social institutions, our work to make better lives for our own First Peoples requires that we do serious thinking about how we express tribalism in this crisis-ridden world. Deloria's suggestion was to ground—literally and figuratively—modern expressions of tribalism where they began: in the land.

CONTRIBUTION TWO: A COLLISION OF THE WESTERN EUROPEAN TEMPORAL WORLDVIEW WITH AMERICAN INDIAN SPATIAL WORLDVIEWS

American Indians hold their lands—places—as having the highest possible meaning, and all their statements are made with this reference point in mind. Immigrants review the movement of their ancestors across the continent as a steady progression of basically good events and experiences, thereby placing history—time—in the best possible light. (Deloria 1973, 75)

Deloria understood the division between how Western European immigrants and American Indians understood domestic political ideologies as one of great philosophical importance: "When one group is concerned with the philosophical problem of space and the other with the philosophical problem of time, then the statements of either group do not make much sense when transferred from one context to the other without the proper consideration of what is happening" (1973, 76).

His *GIR* chapter, "Thinking in Time and Space" (1973), is one of the most important radical Indigenous responses to the Western view of history. Deloria makes clear that the power of the Western view of history is its linear, temporal logic, where Western colonizers understand themselves as at the front of the line moving history forward in the march of civilization. In *GIR* and *The Metaphysics of Modern Existence* (1979), Deloria explicitly ties this Western notion of history to Christian theology: "History became such a dominant form of interpreting the human experience that Western peoples ascribed a reality to it in itself, particularly when it was expressed in Christian theological concepts. All human existence had meaning because a divine plan was coordinating each and every event preparatory to a grand, climatic judgment. Thus rather than negate daily existence, Western peoples became frantically concerned that every human act had cosmic significance that would be revealed at the Last Judgment" (1979, 32).

Deloria's example of the Vietnam War in his critique of the Western conception of history is telling: "Without venturing further into the field of foreign affairs, it may be well to note in passing that the determination of two American presidents, fighting in Vietnam, not to be the 'first to lose a war,' when winning that war in any final sense would have meant the total destruction of a land and a people, would seem to indicate the extent to which Western peoples—and particularly Americans—have taken the dimension of time or history as an absolute value" (1973, 76–77).

Deloria's point is that the largely abstract universalizing character of Western history leads Western leaders, military and civilian, to exercise their power with a hubris that discounts the importance of place and geography in their ventures at home and abroad. In the most chilling passage of this chapter, written in the early seventies, nearly three decades before 9/11, Deloria, clearly with the Middle East in mind, seems to predict the deadly attack on the World Trade Center and the advent of non-state military organizations: "The world, therefore, is not a global village so much as a series of non-homogeneous pockets of identity that must be thrust into eventual conflict, because they represent different arrangements of emotional energy. What these pockets of energy will produce, how they will understand themselves, and what mini-movements will emerge from them are among the unanswered questions of our time" (1973, 78). Deloria's fundamental principle of American Indian metaphysics, power and (plus) place equals personality, lies pregnant in his words, "non-homogeneous pockets of identity . . . represent different arrangements of emotional energy" (1973, 78).

Extremist non-state military movements that emerged contra-Western hegemonic influence in the Middle East and central Asia continue to pose unanswered questions that are too often shaped by an uncritical ideological war between the West and the rest of the world. The eternal struggle between civilization and barbarism or, in its most contemporary expression, civilization vs. "the other,"—those other-than-civilized peoples by a Western conception of "civilization," continues.

Woe unto those who stand in the way of this abstract, linear view of history, progress, and of course, enlightenment. For, as Indigenous peoples around the world can testify from past and present experience, the power of this, dare I say, totalizing idea of history becomes the justification for acts of injustice and destruction toward anyone who challenges this view. The affirmation of a different spatially and place-shaped history serves, in the eyes of the modern civilized man, as an ex post facto demonstration that those who oppose progress must be either too primitive and uncivilized to understand why the flooding of their homelands and the clearing of their forests are necessary in the march to civilization and for their "own good"; or, worse yet, those who fight the destruction of and removal from their homelands and refuse to accept the march of progress, without the excuse of uncivilized ignorance, warrant the most extreme measures, including even death.

Deloria makes clear that what is missing in the Western view of history is the reality of the experiences of those who see their histories as shaped by places, an insight now widely embraced by social theorists, earth scientists, and scholars throughout the humanities. As he stated in 1973: "Who will find peace with the lands? The future of mankind lies waiting for those who will come to understand their lives and take up their responsibilities to all living things. Who will listen to the trees, the animals and birds, the voices of the places of the land? As the long-forgotten peoples of the respective continents rise and begin to reclaim their ancient heritage, they will discover the meaning of the lands of their ancestors. That is when the invaders of the North American continent will finally discover that for this land, God is Red" (1973, 301).

CONTRIBUTION THREE: A COMMON LANGUAGE OF EXPERIENCE FOR SHARING UNCOMMON EXPERIENCES

In *The Metaphysics of Modern Existence*, Deloria (1979) affirms that a unified view of human knowledge must begin with a metaphysics grounded in experience. As we shall see, Deloria's fourth intellectual contribution situates experience in a multidimensional formula: power and place equals personality. Indigenous peoples, he argues, always "privileged" experience—all experiences, including dreams and visions. For this reason, Deloria's third intellectual contribution is his exploration of experience as the touchstone for knowing. For Deloria, all experiences matter.

Deloria states, "The best description of Indian metaphysics was the realization that the world, and *all its possible experiences,* constituted a social reality, a fabric of life in which everything had the possibility of intimate knowing relationships because, ultimately, everything was related. This world was a united world" (2001, 2, emphasis added). This is "the world, which we experience as a unity" that Capra (1996) and Mohawk (1988) refer to as the "web of life."

In his essay, "If You Think About It You Will See That It Is True," Deloria defended an American Indian view of epistemology which understood "knowledge was derived from *individual and communal experiences* in daily life, in keen observation of the environment and in interpreting messages which they received from spirits in ceremonies, visions and dreams" (1999, 44, emphasis added). Oral traditions, ceremonies, customs, and habits, all were rich with information about the world. The combination of individual and communal experience, including dreams and visions, produced the advantage of seeing all experiences as having value and creating a fuller more comprehensive or wholistic understanding of the world in which we live.

I call this view an unbounded epistemology and ontology. The more experiences we collect, the more we know what we know (epistemology) and better understand the world we live in (ontology). As Deloria states: "The fundamental premise is that we cannot 'mis-experience' anything; we can only misinterpret what we experience" (1999, 45–46).

Deloria understood modern science could deal with the physical, mechanistic features of the world, but he argued that experimental science was epistemically precluded from addressing the difficult social, spiritual, and living systems questions that caused the most pain and suffering in the world. With its supposed rigorous objectivity, Western experimental science also forfeited the ability to address questions of morality and ethics. To this day, the tension between science and religion continues to plague modern societies imprinted with the invidious dichotomies and dualisms of the Western worldview. In place of this divided vision, Deloria argued for a unified metaphysics that understood, "The world is constantly creating itself because everything is alive and making choices which determine the future. There cannot be such a thing as an anomaly in this kind of framework: Some things are accepted because there is value in the very mystery they represent" (1999, 46).

Deloria's portrayal of the world we live in required "two basic experiential dimensions that, taken together, provided a sufficient means to making sense of the world. These two concepts were place and power, the latter perhaps better defined as spiritual power or life force" (2001, 2).

While Deloria (1979) was certainly aware of the important role theoretical activity plays in science, his increasing interest in reading the work of scientists and philosophers was the way in which many were expanding their understanding of the physical world beyond the Newtonian clockwork universe. Deloria understood how the science of the controlled experiment explains the mechanics of the world, but saw its declared objectivity as coming at the cost of being able to say anything about the experiential world we live in, a far cry from a controlled experimental setting.

For Deloria, experiences are a neglected realm of study because of their particularity and uniqueness. For a view of science that understood its work to be the establishment of universal laws and principles, individual, subjective experiences were considered a dead end. This division runs deep in Western traditions, Deloria (1979) contended, and was one of the major stumbling blocks to establishing a coherent system of metaphysics.

It was this divided vision, the eternal and real vs. everyday experience Deloria thought posed a significant barrier to humans ever having a genuine understanding of our human place in what scientists call space-time. A host of dualisms emerge in this view, e.g., ultimate reality over and above the transitory experiences of daily life, man (history) vs. nature, religion vs. science, etc. In *The Metaphysics of Modern Existence*, Deloria (1979) attempts to disabuse all who want a simplistic either/or solution to an abstract problem, by promoting a unified vision of the world that must be built on, or part of, a fundamentally experience-based worldview.

Deloria claims that the advantage of listening to American Indians is that, as Indigenous peoples, their knowledge and recollections seldom make distinctions among their experiences by placing them in one category or another—they simply share their experience. In Deloria's last book, completed shortly before his death, *The World We Used to Live In* (2006), his argument concerning the accounts of the works of spiritual leaders is that experience matters and that those accounts of actions and events, when offered by people present, even non-Indians, ought to be taken as truthful: "Knowing how little superstition exists in Indian communities, I have always considered these accounts as truthful remembrances of past events. Medicine men, for the most part, performed their healings and predictions in front of large Indian audiences that were saying, 'Show Me' long before Missouri adopted that slogan for itself" (Deloria 2006, xix).

Throughout his work, Deloria points out the tight-knit social fabric of tribal relations shaped by shared experiences in a shared place illustrates why American Indian religions needed no preaching or, for that matter, theologies, and why he believed oral traditions were likely to be just as reliable in their substantive meaning. As religious ceremonies and oral traditions were practiced in communal settings with a mindful attentiveness, both were continually vetted for accuracy and reliability.

Deloria's chapter, "Our Social Groupings," in *The Metaphysics* (1979), is his most explicit social theory-informed piece and, although he does not explicitly say so, it clearly draws on American Indian experiential ways of knowing. Influenced by the work of the German Protestant theologian, Gerardus van der Leeuw, Deloria states: "There is no distinction between sacred and secular; everything is permeated by a central vision of meaning, and life is not divided into categories" (1979, 157).

Deloria's solution to this dualism was an appeal to American Indian traditions that simply recorded events as they were experienced, without thinking of dreams and visions as somehow less real or more real than everyday experiences. The difference was in the context or situation in which they were experienced, not in any supposed ontological status:

> The old Indians, as Rising Sun noted, were interested in finding the proper moral and ethical road upon which human beings should walk. All knowledge, if it is to be useful, was directed toward that goal. Absent in this approach was the idea that knowledge existed apart from human beings and their communities, and could stand alone for 'its own sake.' In the Indian conception, it was impossible that there could be abstract propositions that could be used to explore the structure of the physical world. . . .
>
> In formulating their understanding of the world, Indians did not discard any experience. Everything had to be included in the spectrum of knowledge and related to what was already known. Since the general propositions which informed the people about the world were the product of generations of tradition and experience, people accepted on faith what they had not experienced, with the hope that during their lifetime they would come to understand. (1999, 43–44)

This becomes very clear in Deloria's (2006) book, *The World We Used to Live In,* where he contends that the witnessed accomplishments of "medicine" men and women observed by others should not be discounted carte blanche as nonsense. Quite the contrary, Deloria's point is that, logically speaking, these should be considered as credible. On this front Deloria was quite consistent.

CONTRIBUTION FOUR: POWER AND (PLUS) PLACE EQUALS PERSONALITY, OR DELORIA'S 3P PRINCIPLE

Deloria (2001) proposed power and place equals personality as an axiom or fundamental principle of Indigenous metaphysics, or "Indian forms of knowledge," about how the world works. He viewed our world and the broader cosmos as all about power, power that surrounds us and permeates the world in which we live: "Here power and place are dominant concepts—power being the living energy that inhabits and/or composes the universe, and place being the relationship of things to each other" (2001, 22–23). Personality, the third concept, is the result of power plus place. Knowledge, or wisdom, according to Basso's (1996) terminology, sits in places. The 3P formula: p_1 (power) + p_2 (place) = P(personality), constitutes Deloria's fundamental epistemological premise about what we know and who we are.

It would be a mistake, however, to view this principle as a simplistic, mechanistic formula rather than a mnemonic device. Like all great insights that capture genius in parsimonious expression, $p_1 + p_2 = P$, what I call the 3P principle, articulates a reality and knowledge system of deep space/place complexity. While power and place are directly and explicitly defined, personality is insinuated and obliquely addressed. In semiotic terms, personality is merely a sign. Personality signifies the particular, the unique, that which by virtue of the existential concepts of power and place, and their melded and conjoined character, remind us that, while the only constant in a living universe is change, our human situations in an experiential sense are always the embodiment of the unique character of power and place.

Personality, as I have developed the concept following Deloria's use, operates at the level of our individual selves and more broadly at a social and cultural level addressing what tribal people share collectively in their cultural selves (identities). The particularity—the unique character of our human personalities—entails that knowledge or knowing is always personal and, at the most fundamental level, always about relationships: what indigenous, e.g., John Mohawk (1988), and nonindigenous thinkers, e.g., Fritjof Capra (1996), liken to a web of life. The emphasis of the particular produces, as Deloria repeatedly defended, a more realistic view of knowledge than the epistemology Western science promotes, because knowledge is emergent through experience to those paying attention.

Deloria's conceptualization of power is quite consistent with modern physics, for we now know that there is no such thing as empty space in the natural world. Even in the deepest reaches of outer space we find low density elemental particles, electromagnetic radiation, and nanoparticles of energy. For Deloria the universe is alive, including the physical world. And it is this pervasive sense of power, including spiritual power—unseen but felt, i.e., sensed—on which Deloria focused. The power in his power and place equals personality (3P) formula for American Indian metaphysics was not power in a political or economic sense, but in a very fundamental sense the cosmic physical and spiritual medium we live in and move through daily. His 3P axiom suggests that power always expresses itself uniquely in the place where humans experience this power. For instance, you and I are in different places now. You are in a very particular place; it is not the place I am in. Here we see Deloria's emphasis on experience applied: who we are, how we behave, and how we think—our personality—is influenced by those relationships with other aspects of life and features of the natural world we experience. Deloria proposes that the 3P axiom captures the unique combination of relations and relationships we experience in place and consequently shapes the human personality each of us possesses.

Given Deloria's (1973, 75–89) emphasis on place throughout his work, I explicitly extended the 3P axiom to capture the kinds of cultural uniqueness that different peoples on the planet have by specifically understanding the cultural diversity of Indigenous peoples as a function of power plus place. Recently, the Indigenous Peoples Knowledge Community of the National Association of Student Personnel Administrators (NASPA) has critically examined Deloria's 3P axiom to see how it might be useful in achieving justice, equity and inclusion for students in higher education (Wilkinson and Wildcat 2020).

While this application of Deloria's axiom is in its early stages, it appears promising and speaks to another of the major themes in Deloria's work: his critique of the Western tradition's conceptualization and treatment of the world in hegemonic universal abstractions. Student affairs professionals attempting to grapple with the systemic inequality found in higher education will benefit from a critical examination of power and place in the lives of their students and themselves. If nothing else, the 3P axiom encourages those who work in student services and other college/university offices and activities that support students to recognize the uniqueness of every student they serve. This includes the growing recognition that student success has every bit as much to do with the realities of the world our students find themselves in, their realities not ours, before they step into our classrooms, whether a physical classroom or a virtual space. Deloria championed the idea that American Indian student success can be greatly enhanced if they could hold on to their tribal cultural and intellectual traditions, thereby defining success for themselves.

In *Custer Died for Your Sins*, Deloria was optimistic about the prospect of Indian students doing this: "The stage is now being set, with the increasing number of Indian college students graduating from the universities, for a total assault on the non-human elements of white society. Ideologically the young Indians are refusing to accept white values as eternal truths. Such anomalies as starvation in the midst of plenty indicate to them that the older Indian ways are probably best for them" (1969, 235). The refusal of young Indians to fall into what Deloria called the liberal "bicultural trap" gave Deloria hope that if Indian students could hold on to their tribal values, they might actually use Western-inspired techniques to strengthen their own culture. He concluded, "Accommodation to white society is primarily in terms of gaining additional techniques by which they can give a deeper root to existing Indian traditions" (1969, 235).

The interest of student affairs and student service professionals in exploring Deloria's 3P axiom is promising, for we now know student success is a function of understanding and valuing the uniqueness of each student. The 3P axiom emphasizes both the particular needs and the strengths that each student possesses and the importance of understanding both in the context of their history, place, and culture. For professionals working in student services, this power and place lens offers tremendous insight, especially as many in higher education are coming to the realization that student success is often not a function of intelligence, but of the students' life situation.

A constellation metaphor is a useful way to think about the situations both our students and those of us trying to serve them experience inside and outside the classroom. For example, each of us is occupying this one place at this one time and then that will change as we move through life, as we move through our academic careers and as we support students. Our lives are all about relationships; consequently, we must advocate for having the time to build a relationship with a student in order to better understand their life beyond our classrooms or the services we offer. Engagement—relationship building—often offers one window into a student's life situation. Understanding their situation will allow us to be much more successful [competent] in communicating with a student about their success.

We must move away from the deficit model of student learning. When students come into our classroom, they are not empty vessels that we are going to fill with knowledge. Students know a lot based on their life experience. If we begin to appreciate that fact, it allows us to communicate more effectively what we want to share with them.

Although most TCUs (Tribal Colleges and Universities) are less than fifty years old, one of the advantages of being in tribal colleges and universities is they are all about the power of a place and the uniqueness of peoples of these places. Being fundamentally Indigenous or tribal institutions, TCUs never subscribed to the idea of the ideal college student or the best prepared college student. All of higher education is going to be better because many educators are walking away from those prescriptive notions of what an incoming college student must be. TCUs also embody distinct tribal and intertribal personalities. While Dartmouth and other elite institutions talk about a distinct educational experience and culture, most of them would be amazed at the distinctive cultures TCUs embody.

While some basic notions of requisite skills are widely shared, so is the recognition that students are more than an SAT and ACT score. Tribal colleges thrive and are successful because they understand that students have rich life experiential knowledges. Most TCUs draw on what students already know through their life experience to introduce them to new knowledge. A positive feature of TCU institutional culture is their affirmation of tribal culture and the relationships students are involved in outside and beyond the college classroom situation. All of this speaks to the idea that power plus place equals personality and provides a broader lens to view the beauty of diversity that surrounds us.

The 3P axiom also informs the place-conscious practice of land acknowledgments many institutions and organizations are developing. However, if institutions are not careful, they are going to make this a kind of pro forma check-the-box activity and undermine the spirit of the acknowledgment. Institutions must think about the state of the planet and the small part of the biosphere where they sit. The reality of climate change and the continuing destruction of biodiversity in this thin biosphere of our Mother, the Earth, require land acknowledgments that reflect the spirit of the land and the first Earth keepers of those places.

Educational institutions adopting a land acknowledgment must think deeply about what that acknowledgment means, especially for the First Peoples and their ancestors who may have once called the place your institution sits their home. Institutions have an obligation to build a meaningful substantive relationship with those first Earth keepers that goes deeper than what a simple acknowledgment embodies. It is one thing to acknowledge the land and the First Peoples of that place, but an institution must make sure it embodies respectful relationships to the land, air, water, and all surrounding life. We also should use land acknowledgments as a way of enhancing the actions that institutions say they are doing in the area of social justice.

A good example of how the 3P axiom could be applied today is in the Land Back (LB) movement. LB has reverberated with the same kind of power that our relatives had nearly a half century ago when they occupied Alcatraz. When the most recent reincarnation of the Land Back movement was first getting attention, land back simply expressed the idea that stolen lands needed to be returned to the First Peoples of those lands. At this point there is no settled definition of what LB means. The lack of a definition might be a blessing, for it allows the exercise of Indigenuity in establishing a widely shared understanding, while still providing the opportunity for the peoples of a place to give LB a unique expression based on their particular land-relationship.

A host of issues immediately emerge. First, serious questions arise about returning land in a property or real estate sense to peoples who never understood land as private property. Deloria repeatedly emphasized tribes understand the land to represent something much more valuable and qualitatively different, in a cultural and spiritual sense, rather than a purely economic exchange. The idea that any one person could own the land made no sense then and makes no sense now in tribal worldviews. Second, even if a simple kind of tribal trust were developed through which land could be environmentally and ecologically restored and protected, questions would certainly emerge about which tribes should be included in such a trust, particularly in landscapes, like the Great Plains, where many tribes moved through and may have lived there for short periods of time while hunting and gathering. To use the title of Deloria's 2006 book, the world we used to live in was very different than the one we now inhabit. LB is a radical idea and in principle makes good sense, but its realization will require considerable Indigenuity.

Given the colonial interruption of the relationship of the First Peoples to places under consideration for LB, Deloria's 3P axiom could prove useful in the development of a viable LB policy. His primary point would be that the need for a serious, deep spatial understanding about those places and their history (multiple and layered kinds of relationships that have produced what they presently experience) must be developed. Some of this work will be fundamentally restorative in a deep experiential and spiritual sense, e.g., for urban Indians removed from their homelands and wanting to return will take time, possibly the development of new ceremonies to address the constellations of relationships that now shape the unique power of a place. Similarly, those who remained on US government–designated reservations, small parts of what was once a very extensive homeland, may suffer from institutionalized colonization, for example, in education, economics, government, and religion, to name only some of the most prominent.

Therefore, different peoples, places, and histories could produce different expressions of LB. It is unlikely the surviving tribal peoples of the places now known as Los Angeles, Chicago, or Miami will be able to get back the land on which those metropolises sit today returned to them in a trust. But if we take the fundamental idea of the restoration of a symbiotic relationship between a people and a place as central to what Land Back means, we could move beyond a legal, property-based idea of giving the land back to someone in an ownership sense and open the door to imagining LB as the restoration of a place by the persons living there in a respectful and responsible fashion. Imagine what their places might look like if their urban dwellers decided to develop an Indigenously informed sense of kinship and caregiving with the land, air, water and the biosphere surrounding them. Certainly, some might decide to move away from large city landscapes. However, others might take seriously the need to change how they live there. For those choosing to remain, the opportunities to think deeply and reimagine those places as sites for ecological and cultural restoration, the 3P axiom could prove quite useful.

Deloria (1973) thought that humankind needed to be engaged with our eco-environment kin. For that reason, the Dakota access pipeline (DAPL) action at Standing Rock several years ago represents something he would have seen as hopeful. Standing Rock affirmed something deep about our present human condition, inextricably bound up in a complex web of relationships with the land, air, water and the life surrounding us.

By the end of the actions of the "water protectors," there were more non-Native people standing side by side to protect the water than Indigenous peoples and that is not a bad thing. Standing Rock and the Water Protectors represent an incredibly positive statement about what it means to be a water protector. The water protection activities at Standing Rock reminded people of various religions, places, and cultures that, among the complex web of relations connecting us, water literally runs through our bodies and shapes our communities in many ways.

The power plus place equals personality axiom for Indigenous metaphysics may very well serve as a metaphysical principle for the balance of this century. Deloria's theorizing operated at the level of metaphysics, because without setting forth something very different to build upon, he felt it would be impossible to convey what was most valuable in American Indian worldviews. He also sought to articulate a way of working outside the silos of academe, thinking outside of Aristotelian categories or boxes to suggest how to live well in the world, recognizing that reality, such as we can know it, can never be reduced to a single people's understanding of it. While for some, such views might be frightening, for Deloria it provided an argument not for pitting differing peoples with different experiences against one another, but rather for a serious exploration of metaphysics to examine the maxim that "we are all the same, we are different," and then wrestle with what that means.

REFERENCES

Cadwalader, S. L., and Vine Deloria, Jr. 1983. *The Aggressions of Civilization: Federal Indian Policy Since the 1880s*. Philadelphia, PA: Temple University Press.

Capra, Fritjof 1996. *The Web of Life*. New York: Anchor Books.

Deloria, Vine, Jr. 1969. *Custer Died for Your Sins: An Indian Manifesto*. New York: Macmillan

———. 1970. *We Talk, You Listen: New Tribes, New Turf*. New York: Macmillan.

———. 1971. *Of Utmost Good Faith*. San Francisco: Straight Arrow Books.

———. 1973. *God Is Red*. New York: Grosset & Dunlap.

———. 1977. *Indians of the Pacific Northwest*. New York: Doubleday.

———. 1979. *The Metaphysics of Modern Existence*. Golden, CO: Fulcrum Publishing.

———. 1991. *Indian Education in America*. Boulder, CO: AISES.

———. 1997. *Red Earth, White Lies: Native Americans and the Myth of Scientific Fact*. Golden, CO: Fulcrum Pub.

———. 1999. *Spirit and Reason: The Vine Deloria, Jr., Reader*. Golden, CO: Fulcrum Publishing.

———. 2004. *Evolution, Creationism and Other Modern Myths: A Critical Inquiry*. Golden, CO: Fulcrum Publishing.

———. 2006. *The World We Used to Live In: Remembering the Powers of the Medicine Men*. Golden, CO: Fulcrum Publishing.

Deloria, Vine, Jr., and C. M. Lytle. 1983. *American Indians, American Justice*. Austin, TX: University of Texas Press.

———. 1984. *The Nations Within: The Past and Future of American Indian Sovereignty*. Austin, TX: University of Texas Press.

Deloria, Vine, Jr., and James Treat, eds. 1999. *For This Land*. New York: Routledge.

Deloria Vine, Jr., and Daniel Wildcat. 2001. *Power and Place: Indian Education in America*. Golden, CO: Fulcrum Publishing.

Dewey, John. 1959. *Experience and Education*. New York: Macmillan.

Fanon, Frantz. 2004. *The Wretched of the Earth*. New York: Grove Press.

Mohawk, John. 1988. "Animal Nations and Their Right to Survive." *Daybreak*. Summer 19 (2).

Wilkins, David. 2018. *Red Prophet: The Punishing Intellectualism of Vine Deloria, Jr*. Golden, CO: Fulcrum Publishing Co.

Wilkins, David E., and Vine Deloria, Jr. 2011. *The Legal Universe: Observations on the Foundations of American Law*. Golden, CO: Fulcrum Publishing Co.

Wise, Jennings C., and Vine Deloria, Jr., eds. 1971. *The Red Man in the New World Drama*. New York: MacMillan.

Chapter 4

Augustus Granville Dill

Marcus Brooks

"You misjudge us because you do not know us."—W. E. B. Du Bois (1903)

Two decades ago, R. W. Connell described the recovery of neglected socio-logical theorists like W. E. B. Du Bois and Jane Addams as "beginning a kind of affirmative action" (1997, 1512). Since the last millennium, scholars of historical sociology (Aldridge 2009; Brooks and Wright 2020; Hunter 2018; Morris 2015; Wright 2009) have brought to light a range of marginal-ized sociologists and demonstrated that far from being just *affirmative action* additions, their uncovering urges us to consider and reconsider established canon, epistemologies, and ontologies of sociological labor and knowledge production and dissemination. And while uncovering the sociological thought of ignored and forgotten scholars surely benefits the discipline by inject-ing a diversity of intellectual standpoint by which established disciplinary knowledges can be tested, compared, and incorporated, there is also a more human—and fundamentally sociological—reason to engage in the work of providing intellectual reparations (Hunter 2016). That is, that doing the gene-alogical work of uncovering the past is not only often deeply personal work rooted in the aspiration to see oneself represented in the discipline (Lee and Hughes 2018), but it is also a practice in the sociological imagination (Mills 1959), because biographical and historical work helps us to understand our present and gives us new tools to imagine futures.

I say genealogical, because the search for one's intellectual ancestry is a biographically motivated mechanism for marginalized scholars, who often feel unrepresented and underappreciated in the canon and the academy, to write themselves into the foundation of the discipline. For example, Hedwig Lee and Christina Hughes (2018, 20), self-identified women of color, ask "where did we fit in our history as scholars?" as the biographical impetus for reclaiming the work of the scholars denied, Anna Julia Cooper and Zora Neale Hurston. Lee and Hughes make clear, though, that their goal is multi-purpose, personal on the one hand, and a deep examination into the potential losses to the field on the other: "It is hard to quantify the implications that the denial of their scholarship has had on our field" (2018, 29). Marcus Anthony Hunter (2016) reminds us that that claiming intellectual reparations is a means by which we pay our debt to ignored scholars of the past and is also how we begin to address and repair the flawed logics that undergird dominant disciplinary epistemologies. The present volume, and others like it, are part of the process of providing those intellectual reparations. And by uncovering these hidden figures we give respect to their contributions and introduce potentials for novel methodology, theory, and praxis.

I draw from both motivations, biographical and disciplinary, in introducing the reader (hopefully not for the first or last time) to the Atlanta Sociological Laboratory–trained, Black, and queer sociologist Augustus Granville Dill (1881–1956). As a Black, queer sociologist myself, I have taken on the duty of uncovering and sharing Dill's story as one that is affirmative of not just my place in the discipline, but the places of other queer scholars of color who are not represented in the foundational histories of the field. Elsewhere (Brooks and Wright 2020) I used Dill's life and work as the foundation for the conceptualization of a Black public sociology. In this essay I interrogate why Dill was ignored and discuss a contributing factor in his historical negation—his praxis of deploying his sociological labor through subjugated knowledges (Collins 2000). I also refine my conceptualization of Black public sociology by, in effect, arguing against its necessity and problematizing the limiting potentials of conceptualizing community intervention and activist labor within the constraints of sociology as a discipline. I begin though with a brief biography of Dill, highlighting his sociological credentials and multiple modalities of deploying Black public sociology.

AUGUSTUS GRANVILLE DILL: A BRIEF BIOGRAPHY

Dill was born in Portsmouth, Ohio, on November 30, 1881, barely a generation removed from the end of African enslavement in the United States. From an early age the would-be scholar showed an aptitude for education, leadership, and public speaking. At just thirteen years old, he was featured in the local paper, the *Portsmouth Daily Times* (1895), where he was praised for graduating from sixth grade early and moving on to high school. As a young man he was active in multiple arenas as a member of a literary club (*Portsmouth Daily Times* 1896), secretary for the annual Emancipation Day celebration (*Portsmouth Daily Times* 1897a), and member of his high school debate club (*Portsmouth Daily Times* 1897b), and he serenaded audiences with piano performances (*Portsmouth Daily Times* 1897c). Foreshadowing his academic achievements, the young scholar earned his teaching certificate at just fifteen years old (*Portsmouth Daily Times* 1897d). Although he was too young to practice at the time, a few years later he would teach at his alma mater, Portsmouth High School.

After nearly embarking on a military career as a student at West Point (*Portsmouth Times* 1902), Dill made the fateful decision to enroll at the W. E. B. Du Bois–led department of sociology at Atlanta University in 1902 (*The Crisis* 1913). It was during these years that the Atlanta Sociological Laboratory made its seminal contributions to the history, methods, and philosophy of sociology, including establishing the first American school of sociology—a distinction traditionally misattributed to the University of Chicago, institutionalizing methods and theory triangulation, use of insider researchers, routine acknowledgment and disclosure of research limitations, and engagement in criminology and criminal justice (Wright 2009). The sociology curriculum at Atlanta included substantive training in theory and methods, but there was also a focus on engagement and collaboration between faculty, students, and the community (Wright 2002a, 2002b). Undergraduate and graduate students, along with "non-academically trained college graduates," were intimately involved in data collection and reporting for the annual Atlanta University Conference publications (Wright 2002c, 350).

It was in this academic environment, where "science was to produce valid knowledge useful to liberation struggles" (Morris 2017, 11), that Dill honed his raw talents and developed the sociological standpoint that would underpin all of his later activism. Dill graduated in 1906 and, following in the footsteps of his mentor, enrolled in and earned a second BA from Harvard in 1908 (Dill 1914). He returned to Atlanta after his time in Cambridge and was granted an honorary Master of Arts in 1909 (*The Bulletin of Atlanta University* 1909). Dill left Harvard intent on continuing as an educator and was considering job offers from Black high schools in Kansas City (Dill 1908a) and Portsmouth, but he was hesitant to accept these as his, "interests are quite largely in southern work" (Dill 1908b). Dill did return to the South intent on teaching at Atlanta University, but University President Edward Twichell Ware had other plans for him—offering Dill the position as the university's northern secretary. Dill, disappointed, was committed to the work of Atlanta and accepted the offer:

> As you know, I have hoped all along to be in the work and at the University—
> for the cause for which the University stands is the cause for which I shall ever
> labor. I feel that my best work can be done in the classroom and there I hope to

be. Still, I see the need for work in the North and am willing to do what is really
best for the present (Dill 1908c).

As northern secretary Dill was tasked with traveling to the North to spread
awareness about the innovative work being done at Atlanta University and
to secure donations to the school. President Ware understood and made clear
to Dill that his status as a "Harvard Man" gave him a level of social capital
that would not be best used in the position of professor. As an Atlanta graduate, Dill was committed to projects of liberatory science and, as a Harvard
graduate, he could arouse the interests of northerners who otherwise would
not concern themselves with "higher education for the Negroes" (Ware 1908).
Because of his background, Dill was able to secure a letter of introduction (a
common credential at the time given to those seeking the company of people
of higher status) from the Harvard president, Charles William Eliot (Dill
1914). The work was difficult, and at times dangerous (Dill 1909), but Dill
remained in this position for two years until, in 1910, he returned to Atlanta to
succeed Du Bois, who left to New York to cofound the National Association
for the Advancement of Colored People (NAACP), as head of the department
of sociology.

    During his three-year tenure as head of the department, Dill, with
assistance from Du Bois, continued the work of the Atlanta Sociological
Laboratory and the duo coedited four editions of the annual publication: *The
College Bred Negro American* (1910), *The Common School and the Negro
American* (1911), *The Negro American Artisan* (1912), and *Morals and
Manners Among Negro Americans* (1914). These studies, and correspond-
ing publications, maintained the Atlanta Sociological Laboratory tradition
of "systematic and scientific inquiry outlined by Du Bois upon his hiring at
Atlanta University some 12 years earlier" (Wright 2002b, 22). Additionally,
the findings and resolutions in these studies provided the foundational materials Brooks and Wright used to conceptualize Dill's post-institutional work as
"forms of empirically grounded cultural production informed by his knowledge production and carried out via the knowledge dissemination of Black
public sociology" (2021, 319). I will reserve further discussion of this for the
next section, where I examine why Dill has gone unrecognized.

    In summer 1913 Dill resigned his position at Atlanta University and moved
to New York to begin work as the business manager for *The Crisis*, the official magazine of the NAACP (Dill 1914). While his primary role was with the
magazine, while living in New York Dill pursued other forms of engagement,
such as public speaking (*Portsmouth Daily Times* 1919a; *Portsmouth Daily
Times* 1919b), community organizing (*Chicago Defender* 1920), art cura-
tion (*New York Age* 1921), and being a member of Harvard's Intercollegiate
Liberal League (*New York Times* 1921). During his fifteen-year tenure with

The Crisis, Dill and the magazine experienced both great success and trouble. Initially there was growth for the publication: "Our work has been successful, the circulation growing from 25,000 copies per month in 1913 to 105,000 copies per month in 1919" (Dill 1920). Du Bois clearly recognized Dill as an asset to him and his work of racial uplift, and in 1920 the pair established a publishing company, Du Bois and Dill Publishers. They were joined by *The Crisis*'s literary editor, Jessie Fauset, in establishing, under the new publishing company, the first magazine targeted at Black children, *The Brownies' Book* (1920). The importance and contribution of the monthly magazine to young Black children is encapsulated by a parent, Bella Seymour, in just the second issue of the magazine. She wrote: "My little girl has been studying about Betsy Ross and George Washington and the others, and she says: 'Mamma, didn't colored folk do anything?' When I tell her as much as I know about our folks, she says: 'Well, that's just stories. Didn't they ever do anything in a book'" (*The Brownies' Book* 1920, 45)?

The young mother, who describes herself as not having much schooling and being busy with housekeeping, articulates the tension between the Black oral tradition as a necessary "culture kit" for Black people denied access to literacy (Mitchell 1986) and the dominant forms of knowledge transmission (Collins 2000). The young mother offers an affirmation that the trio's goal of creating a magazine designed to inspire racial pride and self-confidence among Black children is not in vain: "I do hope you are going to write a good deal about colored men and women of achievement" (*The Brownies' Book* 1920, 45). Emblematic of Dill's practice of a Black public sociology, the positive propaganda of Negro art (Du Bois 1926) also was a way to counteract false and demeaning cultural codes about what it meant to be Black in America.

Despite the professional successes of *The Crisis* and *The Brownies' Book* during these years, Dill had a reputation for being *eccentric* (Gates and Brooks 2009) and *flamboyant* (Kellner 1984), and often came into conflict with his colleagues at *The Crisis*, especially the magazine's executive secretary, Mary Childs Nenery. After one altercation between the pair, Nenery described Dill as incompetent, insolent, and uncooperative and insisted he be fired (Lewis 1997). In another instance, referencing a decline in circulation and advertising revenue, Du Bois (1923) wrote to Dill explaining how he had contributed to the magazine's difficult circumstance. In the letter he tells Dill of the myriad complaints he had received from colleagues and subscribers and takes Dill to task for his poor, and sometimes antagonistic, attitude. He confesses to Dill that in "silence and isolation" he asks himself: "Can Mr. Dill do this work? Does Mr. Dill want to do it" (Du Bois 1923)? Dill worked at *The Crisis* for another five years. During this time his job performance was erratic, and it's clear that he was managing mental illness (Du Bois 1927a). Dill's occupational difficulties came to a climax in December 1927 when Du Bois wrote a letter to Dill asking for his resignation (Du Bois 1927b). In the letter Du Bois (1927b) urges Dill to "Forget the little incident that has worried you so out of all proportion to its significance." This "little incident" is understood to refer to Dill's arrest during a gay sex sting in a public restroom (Chauncey 1994; Schwarz 2003; Woodard 2014). As a point of historical correction, I will explore this period a bit further.

The little biographical record we have about Dill typically makes two incorrect assertions, either directly or by omission, about Dill's firing. First, is that Du Bois not only fully ended his relationship with Dill but was outright hostile to his former protégé (Gates and Brooks 2009; Lewis 2009). While Dill surely had a difficult time after leaving his post at *The Crisis,* including experiencing homelessness and spending time in a mental health facility, it is not true that Du Bois had abandoned his longtime friend. During the years after Dill's departure Du Bois was in contact with his sister, Mary Dill Broaddus, and members of the local community trying to secure resources and employment for Dill (Du Bois 1930a, 1930b). And while the pair never mended their professional relationship, they maintained a friendship and communication for decades after Dill left the magazine (Du Bois 1950). The second assertion is that Dill "spent the rest of his life in obscurity" (Appiah and Gates 2005, 386). While it is true that he fell upon hard times after his separation from *The Crisis*, Dill eventually reclaimed his mantle as "one of the eminent colored orators in the country" (*Portsmouth Daily Times* 1919a, 10).

I argue that Dill's enthusiastic return to public life and the work of racial uplift is, at least in part, attributable to Du Bois's commitment to his friend. In September 1931, after years of Dill borrowing money, sleeping in public places around Harlem, and chronic unemployment, Du Bois (1931) wrote a harsh letter to his friend describing his behavior as "humiliating to all your friends beyond endurance." In the letter, Du Bois offers to help Dill get back on his feet, but admonished Dill for his behavior: "It is unthinkable that you should continue living on borrowed money and at the expense of those who wish you well" (Du Bois 1931). In prior correspondences, Du Bois (1923) always maintained a commitment to his friend, but always made clear that his primary commitment was to the racial uplift of Black people. Being adept in the optics of positive propaganda, Du Bois (1926) relayed to Dill that the way his actions represented his people was "unfair . . . to the Negro race" (Du Bois 1931). While I cannot be certain that Du Bois's letter was responsible for helping Dill emerge back into public life, Du Bois's reminder that Dill's behavior was hurtful to their larger goals of racial uplift surely would have been received by Dill as a reminder of his duty to his people as an educated Black man and member of Du Bois's (1903) Talented Tenth.

Within a year's time Dill resumed his public speaking (*New York Times* 1932), worked with the 135th street library (*Afro-American* 1932), a central public institution that aided in the growth of Harlem Renaissance artists[1] (Anderson 2003), and opened the Harlem Personal Service Shop at 236 W 135th (Estcourt 1933). Dill's Harlem Personal Service Shop served the community as a space for Black placemaking, a "site of endurance, belonging, and resistance" (Hunter et al. 2016, 32). Through the shop he was able to offer mail and telephone services to those in the community who lacked access to these necessities of civil society (Estcourt 1933). Aside from the practical services offered, the shop gave Dill the opportunity to engage in positive propaganda (Du Bois 1926) and material uplift (Banks 2010) in support of Black artists through his monthly performance showcase, Mr. Dill's Five-Twenties, and displays of work in the shop. The prominent Black journalist, Henry Lee Moon, described Dill's place as, "much more than a shop," it was a "cultural center for Negro Harlem" (1935, 9). As a member of Du Bois's Talented Tenth (1903), Dill understood that leveraging his privileged position in service to his community was necessary to the project of racial uplift, and he funneled most of the shop's revenue into supporting the artists he featured, only keeping enough of the proceeds to keep the shop open (Harrison 1934).

In mid-thirties Harlem, reeling from The Great Depression, riots, and economic divestment (Lewis 1997), Dill, despite his shop's important role in the Harlem community, was forced to shut down in December 1935 (Moon 1935). Dill spent the next several years working as a reporter for the International Negro Press (*New York Amsterdam News* 1936a) and as organist for Reverend John Haynes Holmes's Community Church (*New York Amsterdam News* 1936b). While Dill continued to do some work within the community, he again struggled with poverty and mental illness during these years (Holmes 1942). In 1948 Dill moved back down south, this time to Louisville, Kentucky, to care for his ill sister, Mary Dill Broaddus (*Afro American* 1948). Dill lived out his final years in Kentucky, working various jobs as assistant manager for a local theater chain (Ladd 1951) and then as a florist (Dill 1952). Dill continued his activism and public speaking while living in Louisville and traveled back to New York often (Ladd 1951). Dill passed on March 8, 1956, at seventy-four years of age.

BLACK PUBLIC SOCIOLOGY AS
SUBJUGATED KNOWLEDGE

John D'Emilio, describing the Black, queer Civil Rights leader Bayard Rustin, wrote: "He has become a man without a home in history" (2003, 1). Until now this was true of Dill—but why? He never stopped his sociological work, not during his time at *The Crisis* and not after. Why then is he not more recognized as a sociologist in the discipline's canon? There are two obvious answers: racism and queerphobia. Clearly racism has always been a factor in the negation of Black intellectual thought, particularly within the discipline (Hunter 2016; Watson 1976; Wright 2002c), but there have been significant efforts made to recognize the sociological work of some Black thinkers. Dill has largely been excluded from those efforts (Aldridge 2009; Morris 2017; Wright 2009). Queerphobia gives us an alternative hypothesis considering the lack of queer representation in the canon and the historical erasure of Black queer men from movements of racial uplift due to their perceived threat to the movement (Woodard 2014). This explanation, however, also fails to account for Dill's erasure. As in the tradition of Black sociology, non-sociologists have been incorporated into the canon as lay race theorists (Randolph 2018), not because of their sociological credentials, but on account of their insights on race, racism, and structures of power in society. This has been true of Black, queer thinkers like James Baldwin and Audre Lorde (Randolph 2018). Additionally, as it is related to what we do know about Dill, he is perhaps *most* well-known for his sexuality—in the context of his arrest and subsequent separation from *The Crisis*. If racism and queerphobia do not provide adequate justification for Dill's sociological negation (Wright 2002c), what does?

I propose that Dill has been excluded from the sociological canon, not because of who he is (of course not fully discounting racism and queerphobia), but because of the type of sociological labor in which he engaged. What sets Dill apart from other Black thinkers whose insights have been recovered, whether it be his contemporaries in the discipline (Aldridge 2009; Randolph 2018; Wright 2002a) or the Harlem Renaissance (Schwarz 2003), is that they left behind caches of written work for contemporary scholars to draw from. Aside from the four editions of the annual Atlanta publication, there is a lack of a written record of Dill's intellectual thought. It is easier to recognize the accomplishments of those like Baldwin, Lorde, Rustin, and the Harlem Renaissance writers, because there is thorough documentation of their social, political, and cultural thought. For figures like Dill, we can only search the margins and fill in the blanks. This is a worthwhile endeavor, though, not only because it restores the history of an important Black, queer sociologist, activist, and public intellectual, but also because giving Dill his intellectual reparations (Hunter 2016) benefits the field at large by helping us craft new insights into contemporary disciplinary practices (Lee and Hughes 2018).

It is understandable that one would look at Dill's biography and conclude that he is just an under-recognized activist with a background in sociology, but not necessarily a practicing sociologist. Earl Wright II and I (2020) reject this idea and argue that Dill's post-academic work represents the work of Black sociology that necessitates that liberatory action be taken when empirical research finds inequality and oppression (Watson 1976; Wright and Calhoun 2006). The practice of Black sociology, then, has two components: 1) knowledge creation—accomplished through traditional forms of sociological data collection and analysis, and 2) knowledge dissemination—accomplished by taking those empirical findings and putting them to use outside of the academy, either by influencing public policy via direct legislative engagement or culture via the practice of positive propaganda (Du Bois 1926). We (Brooks and Wright 2020) conceptualize this empirically grounded cultural production as a form of Black public sociology. In the four editions of the Atlanta annual publications Du Bois and Dill coedited, we find resolutions that call for creating self-affirming spaces for Black children (Du Bois and Dill 1911, 1914), endorsing academic and technical education for Black people (Du Bois and Dill 1910, 1912, 1914), fostering a cross-race class consciousness (Du Bois and Dill 1912), investing in cultural training (Du Bois and Dill 1910) and promoting the important role of college educated Blacks in being of service to their communities (Du Bois and Dill 1910). These efforts represent knowledge creation and Dill's Black placemaking, promotion of Black art and artists, and public speaking are examples of knowledge dissemination.

This understanding of the relationship between knowledge production and dissemination and the recognition of nontraditional routes of knowledge transmission is at the core of making sense of Dill's sociological negation. His work has largely gone unrecognized because his sociological output (Gans 2016) did not take the traditional forms of writing, lecturing, or research. Rather than navigating the traditional academic or authorial routes of knowledge dissemination, Dill took the findings from the research he worked on during his time in the academy and used them to inform his public activism via Black placemaking, Black art, and engaging with the public (Brooks and Wright 2020). Borrowing from Patricia Hill Collins in *Black Feminist Thought* (2000), we can understand Dill's practice of Black public sociology as advocacy for subjugated knowledge. Using Collins's framework, but replacing "woman/women," with "queer men," I assert: "Traditionally, the suppression of Black [queer men's] ideas within male controlled social institutions led African-American [queer men] to use music, literature, daily conversations, and everyday behavior as important locations for constructing a black . . . consciousness" (2000, 251–52). Collins's (2000) theoretical framework is useful here as she argues that Black women who engage in these alternative forms of knowledge do so as a result of the struggle in doing academic work that challenges injustice. Because the arbiters of sociological work have been white men within the academy, political work which not only questions their supremacy, but does so in a non-legitimized venue (i.e., public speaking as opposed to a peer-reviewed publication), is summarily dismissed as not valid as it does not fit within the bounds of that which is deemed sociological.

As a method of sociology that is rooted in meeting the needs of Black people, the salience of function is elevated over that of form. Meaning that Dill transcended what are now disciplinary norms and, understanding the particular cultural contours of Black life (Hall 1997), engaged in forms of racial uplift that were legible by and impactful to his community. For example, today we look back at the Harlem Renaissance as an aspirational period where Black novelists and poets changed how Black people were represented in media. And while it is true that the diversity of the Black experience was put on paper through the storytelling of Harlem Renaissance writers, their audience was predominantly white (Schwarz 2003). The Harlem Renaissance period saw increased rates in literacy, but the Black illiteracy rate during this era was still five times higher than that of whites (NCES 2020). With this in mind, Dill's eschewing of academic publications in favor of public speaking can be read as a continuation of the Black oral tradition (Mitchell 1986). In other words, instead of turning to academic publishing as the acceptable form of knowledge dissemination, Dill drew on his situated knowledge as a member of the community and practiced forms of knowledge dissemination that, while not recognized within the power structure of the academy, are commensurate with a tradition of Black knowledge transmission (Collins 2000). It is that cultural awareness that is at the core of Black public sociology.

In considering how Dill's life and work afford insight into contemporary sociological practice, it is in the broadening of epistemology of public sociology and ontology of the public sociologist. While the work being done at the Atlanta Sociological Laboratory centered around active involvement with local publics, it wasn't until 2004[2] that conversations about the role of public sociology as part of the larger discipline began to be debated in earnest. In his address, Burawoy (2005) makes the case that sociology is a steward of civil society and that sociologists should play an active role in protecting it. Burawoy's promotion of an institutionalized public sociology has been criticized from various perspectives: that sociology has no place in the public discourse (Boyns and Fletcher 2005), that public sociology discourse is US-centric and ignores sociological practices historically and in modern times in the Global south (Lozano 2018), and that professionalization would create a second class of sociological practitioners (Collins 2013), to name a few. Gans, reengaging in the debate he helped start, lamented that all the discourse debating the merits of public sociology "virtually ignore[ed] the public and the role it plays in the realization of public sociology" (2016, 3). Building on Gans's criticism, Douglas Hartmann highlights the plurality of publics and argues that "sociologists [need to] do a better job of engagement, acting in the social world; figuring out who our various constituent publics might be and what kind of information, knowledge, perspective, and assistance they are in need of; and being clear about using our knowledge, information, and perspectives properly" (2017, 11). Hartmann's call to consider public sociologists' various publics leads him to the conclusion that there should be "many different faces of public sociology" (2017, 9).

These insights shift the focus of the debate from the legitimacy of public sociology as a practice onto the communities with whom public sociologists are engaged, but they fail to conceptualize a typology of practices that are indigenous to and productive for the communities with whom the public sociologist works. This is where the work of intellectual reparations (Hunter 2016) can uncover previously discarded sociological praxes that can inform contemporary debates—in this case, debates surrounding public sociology. In conceptualizing Dill's sociological practice through the framework of Black public sociology, we (Brooks and Wright 2020) move public sociology discourse into the realm of theorizing practices that are formed for and within the communities for which the public sociologist works. Dill, working and living in Harlem in the 1930s, used the resolutions stated in his coedited editions of the Atlanta annual publications and his knowledge as a community and cultural insider to engage in a form of public sociology rooted in empirical data and carried out through culturally legible forms of communication: Black placemaking, promotion of Black art and artists, and conversing with publics. Fundamental to Dill's practice of Black public sociology is the recognition of his skills and standpoint within the community. So, while he may not have been engaged in traditional forms of racial uplift that involve working toward policy and agenda setting, Dill understood how his interests in art and music could be leveraged within the field of cultural production (Bourdieu 1993) to introduce representations of Black people into the culture, visible to both Blacks and whites, that pushed against dominant representations of Black people as lazy, prone to criminality, and uneducated.

CONCLUSION

In situating Augustus Granville Dill as a practitioner of Black public sociology, it is important to account for the conceptual work that *Black* does in imagining public sociological praxis beyond disciplinary debates. Black gives us space to imagine potential avenues for sociological engagement outside the restraints imposed by mainstream, white sociology. This does not mean that we do away with the fundamental principles of doing scientific sociological inquiry, but rather that we recognize the foundational aspects of professional sociology (Burawoy 2005), meaning research and theorizing, while simultaneously holding that professional sociology has often failed to meet the needs of Black (and other marginalized) communities both in areas of research and application. Black sociology arose in response to a mainstream sociology that eschewed liberatory principles and which "seldom advocated the kinds of progressive changes that would insure that Blacks no longer experience the subjugated status in American society" (Ladner 1976, xx). The formation of a Black sociology gave Black sociologists a lane in which to resist disciplinary constraints and to engage in the work they deemed meaningful.

Black public sociology does the same for public sociology. The Black in Black public sociology bypasses standard academic debates and instead shifts the focus to the needs of the people and communities with whom we work. Black public sociology centers theorizing and conceptualizing methods of *doing* public sociology instead of debating whether or not we should be engaging in public sociology. As Patricia Hill Collins notes, public sociology is inherently "a constellation of oppositional knowledge and practices" (2013, 81) and those who are most inclined to engage in public sociology do so out of passion and not necessarily as a route of academic advancement. Black public sociology, then, removes the barriers of disciplinary constraints and, in Behrooz Ghamari-Tabrizi's words, provides a warrant for sociologists to, "transcend their disciplinary loyalties" (2005, 366). Dill engaged in forms of sociological labor which, until now, have been absent in the historiography of the discipline, but which has deep roots in the traditions of subjugated knowledges that are intellectual but not considered to be properly academic (Collins 2000). In conceptualizing a Black public sociology, I am careful to not reproduce restrictive modes of sociological praxis. So, while my conception of Dill's Black public sociology as that which uses data from empirical research to inform his engagement in cultural production to impact dominant cultural codes (Hall 1997) about Black people, to both Black and white people, I am not asserting that this is the *only* way Black public sociology can or must be practiced. Rather than limiting the conception of a Black public sociology within the confines of a typology framed around Dill's work, I return to the important role of standpoint and biography as entrées into sociological theorizing (Clerge 2018).

While my representation of Black public sociology, through the lens of Augustus Granville Dill, highlights the important function of cultural production, this frame is applicable, because this is the type of sociological labor that emerges when Dill's biography as a musician and a skilled orator are placed into conversation with the resolutions of the Atlanta School's annual publications. This unification of personal capabilities and scientific resolutions are at the core of what Black public sociology is. There is no right or wrong way to do Black public sociology; rather, it is a framing device that puts one's talents, skills, and cultural identity in conversation with their research. Black public sociology resists the tendency to rely on conventions of social action, imagining instead how sociologists can meet the needs that their data elucidate based upon their standpoint. A central component of this is a recognition of one's position within a community, as Clerge writes: "If white sociology does not understand our culture . . . how can they be charged with building knowledge about the social problems that plague us and our similarities or differences with other groups?" (2018, 234)

In this sense Black public sociology provides the impetus for *all* activist-minded sociologists to consider the relationship between their work, identity, and community and to take that information to triangulate solutions based on their cultural competency and their skillset. So, while Black gives public sociology maneuverability and agility to envision unique forms of practice, as a liberatory practice, it is not exclusionary. This is what we gain by going, "back through the work of our earliest writers and thinkers and make explicit the implicit contributions" (Hunter 2016, 1382). And Blackness gives us the tools to do this. Black feminist epistemology (Collins 2000) provides the tools to understand why Dill's forms of sociological labor have not been categorized as such and Black public sociology gives us a way to understand how he practiced the work that he did after leaving the academy. As a retrospective biography, there is no way of knowing how Dill thought about the relationship between his professional and public sociologies. So while Dill may not have thought of his public speaking and activism as sociological labor, by drawing on Black epistemologies we can take previously unacknowledged forms of knowledge production and dissemination and use them to "help shape the way we approach research and the forms of knowledge that are valued" (Lee and Hughes 2018, 29). It doesn't matter so much, then, how Dill thought about his work, as how his intellectual progeny can understand his work and use that understanding to inform our own. In this way, Dill's passion for pedagogy lives on. By excavating his legacy and giving him his intellectual reparations (Hunter 2016), Dill teaches us ways to practice public sociology that eschew disciplinary debates and get right to the core of how we conceptualize the relationship between our work, our selves, and our activism.

REFERENCES

Afro-American. 1932. "New York Society." *Afro-American*, May 28, 1932. ProQuest Historical Newspapers.

———. 1948. "News in Tabloid." *Afro-American*, June 5. ProQuest Historical Newspapers.

Aldridge, Delores P. 2009. *Imagine a World: Pioneering Black Women Sociologists*. Maryland: University Press of America.

Anderson, Sarah. 2003. "'The Place to Go': The 135th Street Branch Library and the Harlem Renaissance." *Library Quarterly* 73 (4): 383–421.

Appiah, Kwame Anthony, and Henry Louis Gates, Jr. 2005. *Africana: The Encyclopedia of the African and African American Experience*. New York: Oxford University Press.

Banks, Patricia A. 2010. "Black Cultural Advancement: Racial Identity and Participation in the Arts among the Black Middle Class." *Ethnic and Racial Studies* 33 (2): 272–89.

Bourdieu, Pierre. 1993. *The Field of Cultural Production*. New York: Columbia University Press.

Boyns, David, and Jesse Fletcher. 2005. "Reflection on Public Sociology: Public Relations, Disciplinary Identity, and the Strong Program in Professional Sociology." *American Sociologist* Fall/Winter: 5–26.

Brooks, Marcus A., and Earl Wright, II. 2021. "Augustus Granville Dill: A Case Study in the Conceptualization of a Black Public Sociology." *Sociology of Race & Ethnicity* 7(3): 318–22.

The Brownies' Book. 1920. New York: Du Bois & Dill.

Burawoy, Michael. 2005. "2004 Presidential Address: For Public Sociology." *American Sociological Review* 70 (1): 4–28.

Chauncey, George. 1994. *Gay New York: Gender, Urban Culture, and the Making of the Gay Male World 1890–1940*. New York: Basic Books.

Chicago Defender. 1920. "Lincoln House Items." *Chicago Defender*, March 20, 1920. ProQuest Historical Newspapers.

Clerge, Orly. 2018. "The New Black Sociology: Bringing Diasporic & Internationalist Perspectives." In *The New Black Sociologists: Historical and Contemporary Perspectives*, edited by M. A. Hunter, 219–36. New York: Routledge.

Collins, Patricia Hill. 2000. *Black Feminist Thought: Knowledge, Consciousness, and the Politics of Empowerment*. New York: Routledge.

———. 2013. *On Intellectual Activism*. Pennsylvania: Temple University Press.

Connell, R. W. 1997. "Why is Classical Theory Classical?" *American Journal of Sociology* 102 (6): 1511–57.

The Crisis. 1913. "Men of the Month." *The Crisis* 6 (5): 222.

Dill, Augustus Granville. 1908a. "Personal Correspondence between Ware and Dill." Robert W. Woodruff Library of the Atlanta University Center, Edward Twichell Ware Records, Box 26, Folder 7, June 23, 1908.

———. 1908b. "Personal Correspondence between Ware and Dill." Robert W. Woodruff Library of the Atlanta University Center, Edward Twichell Ware Records, Box 26, Folder 7, July 17, 1908.

———. 1908c. "Personal Correspondence between Ware and Dill." Robert W. Woodruff Library of the Atlanta University Center, Edward Twichell Ware Records, Box 26, Folder 7, July 24, 1908.

———. 1909. "Personal Correspondence between Ware and Dill." Robert W. Woodruff Library of the Atlanta University Center, Edward Twichell Ware Records, Box 26, Folder 7, January 08, 1909.

———. 1914. "Records of the Class." Pp. 92–94 in *Harvard College Class of 1908: Secretary's Second Report*, edited by Guy Emerson. Cambridge, MA: Crimson.

———. 1920. "Records of the Class." Pp. 135–37 in *Harvard College Class of 1908: Secretary's Third Report*, edited by Guy Emerson. Cambridge, MA: Crimson.

———. 1952. "Letter from A.G. Dill to Du Bois, May 8, 1952." Du Bois Papers (MS 312). Special Collections and University Archives, University of Massachusetts Amherst Libraries. Retrieved August 25, 2020. https://credo.library.umass.edu/view/full/mums312-b136-i445.

Du Bois, W. E. B. 1903. "The Talented Tenth." University of Minnesota Digital Archives. Retrieved August 25, 2020. http://moses.law.umn.edu/darrow/documents/Talented_Tenth.pdf.

———. 1923. "Letter from Du Bois to A.G. Dill, April 02, 1923." Du Bois Papers (MS 312). Special Collections and University Archives, University of Massachusetts Amherst Libraries. Retrieved August 22, 2020. https://credo.library.umass.edu/view/full/mums312-b167-i319.

———. 1926. "Criteria for Negro Art." *The Crisis*. Retrieved January 31, 2020. http://www.webdubois.org/dbCriteriaNArt.html.

———. 1927a. "Letter from Du Bois to Mary Dill Broaddus, November 14, 1927." Du Bois Papers (MS 312). Special Collections and University Archives, University of Massachusetts Amherst Libraries. Retrieved August 25, 2020. http://credo.library.umass.edu/view/full/mums312-b175-i310.

———. 1927b. "Letter from Du Bois to A.G. Dill, December 29, 1927." Du Bois Papers (MS 312). Special Collections and University Archives, University of Massachusetts Amherst Libraries. Retrieved August 25, 2020. https://credo.library.umass.edu/view/full/mums312-b176-i632.

———. 1930a. "Letter from Du Bois to Reverend John Haynes Holmes, September 20, 1930." Du Bois Papers (MS 312). Special Collections and University Archives, University of Massachusetts Amherst Libraries. Retrieved August 25, 2020. https://credo.library.umass.edu/view/full/mums312-b054-i150.

———. 1930b. "Letter from Du Bois to Mary Dill Broaddus, October 6, 1930." Du Bois Papers (MS 312). Special Collections and University Archives, University of Massachusetts Amherst Libraries. Retrieved August 25, 2020.

———. 1931. "Letter from Du Bois to A.G. Dill, September 10, 1931." Du Bois Papers (MS 312). Special Collections and University Archives, University of Massachusetts Amherst Libraries. Retrieved August 25, 2020. https://credo.library.umass.edu/view/full/mums312-b058-i079.

———. 1950. "Letter from Du Bois to A.G. Dill, July 26, 1950." Du Bois Papers (MS 312). Special Collections and University Archives, University of Massachusetts Amherst Libraries. Retrieved August 25, 2020. https://credo.library.umass.edu/view/full/mums312-b128-i187.

Du Bois, W. E. B. and Augustus Granville Dill. 1910. *The College Bred Negro American*. Atlanta, GA: The Atlanta University Press.

———. 1911. *The Common School and the Negro American*. Atlanta, GA: The Atlanta University Press.

———. 1912. *The Negro American Artisan*. Atlanta, GA: The Atlanta University Press.

———. 1914. *Moral and Manners Among Negro Americans*. Atlanta, GA: The Atlanta University Press.

Estcourt, Charles, Jr. 1933. "Man Thinks His Way Out of Depression." *Nebraska State Journal* July 2, 1933. https://www.newspapers.com.

Gans, Herbert J. 2016. "Public Sociology and its Publics." *American Journal of Sociology* 47 (1): 3–11.

Gates, Henry Louis, and Evelyn Brooks. 2009. *Harlem Renaissance Lives from the African American National Biography*. New York: Oxford University Press.

Ghamari-Tabrizi, Behrooz. 2005. "Can Burawoy Make Everybody Happy? Comments on Public Sociology." *Critical Sociology* 31 (3): 361–69.

Hall, Stuart. 1997. "Representation, Meaning, and Language." In *Representation: Cultural Representations and Signifying Practices*, edited by Stuart Hall. London: Sage Ltd.

Harrison, Paul. 1934. "In New York." *News Herald*, March 27, 1934. https://www.newspapers.com.

Hartmann, Douglas. 2017. "Sociology and Its Publics: Reframing Engagement and Revitalizing the Field." *The Sociological Quarterly* 58 (1): 3–18.

Holmes, John Haynes. 1942. "Letter from John Haynes Holmes to Du Bois, March 04, 1942." Du Bois Papers (MS 312). Special Collections and University Archives, University of Massachusetts Amherst Libraries. Retrieved August 26, 2020. https://credo.library.umass.edu/view/full/mums312-b098-i084.

Hunter, Marcus Anthony. 2016. "Du Boisian Sociology and Intellectual Reparations: For Coloured Scholars Who Consider Suicide When Our Rainbows are Not Enuf." *Ethnic and Racial Studies* 39 (8): 1379–84.

———. 2018. *The New Black Sociologists: Historical and Contemporary Perspectives*. New York: Routledge.

Hunter, Marcus Anthony, Mary Patillo, Zandria F. Robinson, and Keeanga-Yamahtta Taylor. 2016. "Black Placemaking: Celebration, Play, and Poetry." *Theory, Culture & Society* 33 (7–8): 31–56.

Kellner, Bruce. 1984. *The Harlem Renaissance: An Historical Dictionary for the Era*. Westport, CT: Greenwood.

Ladd, Bill. 1951. "Augustus Granville Dill Will Begin a Sentimental Journey." *The Louisville Courier Journal*, March 23, 1951. https://www.newspapers.com.

Ladner, Joyce. 1976. *The Death of White Sociology: Essays on Race and Culture*. Baltimore, MD: Black Classic Press.

Lee, Hedwig, and Christina Hughes. 2018. "#SayHerName: Why Black Women Matter in Sociology." In *The New Black Sociologists: Historical and Contemporary Perspectives*, edited by Marcus Anthony Hunter, 20–31. New York: Routledge.

Lewis, David Levering. 1997. *When Harlem Was in Vogue*. New York: Penguin Press.

———. 2009. *W. E. B. Du Bois: The Fight for Equality and the American Century, 1919–1963*. New York: Holt.

Lozano, Alberto Arribas. 2018. "Reframing the Public Sociology Debate: Towards Collaborative and Decolonial Praxis." *Current Sociology* 66 (1): 92–109.

Mills, C. Wright. 1959. *The Sociological Imagination*. New York: Oxford University Press.

Mitchell, Ella P. 1986. "Oral Tradition: Legacy of Faith for the Black Church." *Religious Education* 81 (1): 93–112.

Moon, Henry Lee. 1935. "About Books." *New York Amsterdam News*, December 28. ProQuest Historical Newspapers.

Morris, Aldon. 2015. *The Scholar Denied: W. E. B. Du Bois and the Birth of Modern Sociology*. Oakland: University of California Press.

———. 2017. "W. E. B. Du Bois at the Center: From Science, Civil Rights Movement, to Black Lives Matter." *The British Journal of Sociology* 68 (1): 3–16.

NCES. 2020. "120 Years of Literacy." *National Center for Educational Statistics*. Retrieved August 30, 2020. https://nces.ed.gov/naal/lit_history.asp.

New York Age. 1921. "Negro Arts Exhibition Draws Large Number of Sightseers." *New York Age*, August 20, 1921. https://www.newspapers.com.

New York Amsterdam News. 1936a. "See Hall Dedicated." *New York Amsterdam News*, May 30, 1936. ProQuest Historical Newspapers.

———. 1936b. "Singer's Appearance Postponed 3 Weeks." *New York Amsterdam News*, July 25, 1936. ProQuest Historical Newspapers.

New York Times. 1921. "College Liberals Organize League." *New York Times*, April 4, 1921. ProQuest Historical Newspaper.

———. 1932. "Woman Peace Worker Honored." *New York Times*, April 14, 1932. ProQuest Historical Newspaper.

Portsmouth Daily Times. 1895. "A Colored Carrier." *Portsmouth Daily Times*, June 29, 1985. https://newspaperarchive.com.

———. 1896. "A Pleasant Reception." *Portsmouth Daily Times*, December 1, 1896. https://newspaperarchive.com.

———. 1897a. "Emancipation Day." *Portsmouth Daily Times*, August 31, 1897. https://newspaperarchive.com.

———. 1897b. "High School Debaters." *Portsmouth Daily Times*, November 20, 1897. https://newspaperarchive.com.

———. 1897c. "The Boggmek Entertained." *Portsmouth Daily Times*, November 20, 1897. https://newspaperarchive.com.

———. 1897d. "A Youthful Applicant." *Portsmouth Daily Times*, June 23, 1897. https://newspaperarchive.com.

———. 1902. "Appointed Alternates." *Portsmouth Daily Times*, August 2, 1902. https://newspaperarchive.com.

———. 1919a. "You Must Put Your Best in Life if You Are a True American Citizen." *Portsmouth Daily Times*, September 16, 1919. https://newspaperarchive.com.

———. 1919b. "Has Praise for Augustus Dill." *Portsmouth Daily Times*, October 4, 1919. https://newspaperarchive.com.

Randolph, Antonia. 2018. "James Baldwin and the Lay Race Theorist Tradition." In *The New Black Sociologists: Historical and Contemporary Perspectives*, edited by Marcus Anthony Hunter, 42–51. New York: Routledge.

Schwarz, Christa A. B. 2003. *Gay Voices of the Harlem Renaissance*. Bloomington: Indiana University Press.

Ware, Edward Twichell. 1908. "Personal Correspondence between Ware and Dill." Robert W. Woodruff Library of the Atlanta University Center, Edward Twichell Ware Records, Box 26, Folder 7, August 1, 1908.

Watson, Wilbur H. 1976. "The Idea of Black Sociology: Its Cultural and Political Significance." *American Sociologist,* 11 (May): 115–23.

Woodard, Vincent. 2014. *The Delectable Negro: Human Consumption and Homoeroticism within U.S. Slave Culture*. New York: New York University Press.

Wright, Earl, II. 2002a. "The Atlanta Sociological Laboratory 1896–1924: A Historical Account of the First American School of Sociology." *Western Journal of Black Studies* 26 (3): 165–74.

———. 2002b. "Using the Master's Tools: The Atlanta Sociological Laboratory and American Sociology, 1896–1924." *Sociological Spectrum* 22 (1): 15–39.

———. 2002c. "Why Black People Tend to Shout! An Earnest Attempt to Explain the Sociological Negation of the Atlanta Sociological Laboratory Despite its Possible Unpleasantness." *Sociological Spectrum* 22 (3): 336–61.

———. 2009. "Beyond W.E.B. Du Bois: A Note on Some of the Little Known Members of the Atlanta Sociological Laboratory." *Sociological Spectrum* 29 (6): 700–17.

Wright, Earl II, and Thomas C. Calhoun. 2006. "Jim Crow Sociology: Toward an Understanding of the Origin and Principles of Black Sociology via the Atlanta Sociological Laboratory." *Sociological Focus* 39 (1): 1–18.

NOTES

1. I use the term *artists* in a broad sense to include the myriad expressive modes of cultural production (i.e., painters, musicians, poets, novelists) of the people with whom Dill engaged.

2. I recognize that then-ASA president Herbert Gans coined the term "public sociology" in his 1988 presidential address, but disciplinary discourse on the topic was minimal until Michael Burawoy's 2004 presidential address.

Chapter 5

(Re)Emerging from the Shadows

Charles S. Johnson and His Research on the Black Belt

Heather A. O'Connell

Charles S. Johnson was born in 1893 in Bristol, Virginia, a small independent city located in the western tip of the state, close to the Tennessee border. He attended a historically Black university—Virginia Union University—in Richmond, Virginia, for undergraduate studies. He later earned his PhD at the University of Chicago under the mentorship of Robert E. Park.

Johnson stayed in Chicago after graduating, during which time he completed a major project on the causes of the 1919 race riot in the city, which was later published as *The Negro in Chicago* (1922). After completing that project, he moved to New York to serve as the research director for the National Urban League, and founded and edited a professional magazine, *Opportunity*. His work in New York was instrumental in disseminating writing on the Black experience and was part of the larger Harlem Renaissance that aimed to elevate Black artists and perspectives.

His next move was to Fisk University in Nashville, Tennessee—back to the South; back to a historically Black university. Here, he increased his presence in administrative and leadership roles. He received funding from White donors to start the first "think tank" at a predominantly Black institution, and later became the first Black president of the university (for more on the life of Johnson, see Gilpin and Gasman 2003).

He has rightfully received accolades for these accomplishments, but what seems to have received less attention is the research he conducted on Black experiences in the South during his time at Fisk University. That work will be the focus of my discussion, namely *Shadow of the Plantation* (1934).

A (STRUCTURAL) CULTURE OF SLAVERY

Johnson aimed to enhance understandings of Black American culture. This goal was evident in some of his other work, including a later book, *Growing up in the Black Belt* (1941), as well as his earlier role as editor of the magazine *Opportunity*. In *Shadow of the Plantation* (1934), he focuses on the culture of rural Black folk. He uses an isolated community in Macon County, Alabama, as a case study to provide an example of what life looked like for Black people living in the rural South at the time.

There are 612 families—amounting to 2,432 individuals—in his study. He collected qualitative data through surveys and ethnographic observation, and used some census figures to supplement what he learned. The coverage of topics is nearly exhaustive, including family patterns, economic life, education/schooling, religion, social life, and health/mortality. Within each chapter, he describes the dominant trends and elaborates on the experiences of the Black community by allowing the residents to share their stories. In "The Family," we learn that—contrary to dominant trends elsewhere in the city—later rather than early marriage is most common, and children born out of wedlock are not treated as "illegitimate." "Economic Life and the Community" provides detailed breakdowns of White and "Colored" farmers in Macon County in addition to a comparison with the economic position of the individuals participating in the study, which reveals the disproportionate concentration of Black farmers among tenant farmers (discussed further below). Johnson uses the chapter on "The School and the People" to discuss the difficulty of obtaining an education within this community and the subsequently high rates of illiteracy, particularly among the oldest generations—25 percent of male family heads and nearly 20 percent of female family heads were illiterate. The chapter on "Religion and the Church" tells a story that is by now well established within the literature on Black American communities: Johnson finds that the church is the "one outstanding institution of the community over which the Negroes themselves exercise control" and that it serves critical social functions far beyond its manifest spiritual functions (Johnson 1934, 150). Tellingly, the chapter on "Play Life," or the social activities of the community members, is the shortest, and essentially presents a list of activities in which they engage—attending church, taking Saturday trips to town, sports, church suppers, local dances, and "lodges and societies." Finally, Johnson reviews statistics related to health and mortality in the chapter on "Survival," but the primary lesson we learn from this discussion is the tenuous relationship between the Black community and the medical profession, and the subsequently limited understanding we have of the health and mortality conditions associated with this area of the country at the time.

The range of evidence is wide, but Johnson skillfully uses this accounting to paint a picture of Black rural life in the South and connects many of these outcomes to the plantation life that permeates the social structures of the area.

Johnson is squarely focused on Black culture, so he does not include analysis of the neighboring White population. White people only receive mention when they (inevitably) intersect with the lives of the people who were interviewed. Significantly, these mentions appear more frequently in connection to some topics than others—economic life and health/mortality include quite a few, but the religion and social spheres are more clearly separated from the White community.

Broadly construed, Johnson develops an argument to explain what may, at first, seem like peculiarities within the culture of rural Black folk. From his perspective, the isolation of this population is important for understanding their "backwards" culture. "The Negro population of this section of Macon County has its own social heritage which, in a relatively complete isolation, has had little chance for modification from without or within" (Johnson 1934, 16). With limited in- and out-migration, change comes slowly—there is a cultural lag, or a delay in the acceptance of behaviors that are considered the norm in other parts of the country. Moreover, the social and economic structure associated with the context in which they live—that privileges White people and relies heavily on exploitative agricultural practices—constrains their ability to take up some social innovations. It is his attention to the nature of this structure that comprises his more specific theoretical argument regarding the ways in which the history of slavery relates to the culture of rural Black folk.

Johnson argues that all facets of life for rural Black folk (in Macon County, Alabama) are shaped by their connections to the plantation—past and present. Critically, his theoretical development emphasizes the importance of the social structures that emanate from slavery and the persistence of past practices in explaining the present. Throughout the book we find quotes similar to the following:

Once established, custom and routine gave permanence to the structure of relations. (3)

The past is thus kept ever alive, since it is never seriously broken. (25)

The whole of life is bound up with the slow and tedious decadence of the plantation system which . . . formed the industrial and social frame of government in the Black Belt counties, while slavery provided merely the code of laws for the perpetuation of the system. (103)

It has been impossible to escape the force of tradition, as represented in the customs established under the institution of slavery, and adhered to, by the White
population in their relation to the Negroes, and by the Negroes in relation to
themselves. (208)

Despite the overall emphasis on the structures associated with the plantation
system, there are also times when Johnson's argument aligns more, or at least
sympathizes, with an individual focus similar to that promoted by Booker
T. Washington, who was a prominent contemporary scholar. The influence
of his work may not be entirely surprising given Johnson's proximity to
the Tuskegee Institute, which was located within Macon County, Alabama.
References to an individual focus are most evident in early chapters, including the first chapter that Johnson uses to set the stage and develop his argument for the continuation of a "tradition of dependence" among rural Black
folk. He ultimately asserts that the overreliance on White people is not driven
just by "fear" and concludes by linking directly to the work of Booker T.
Washington that suggests Black people lack "a sense of self-dependence"
as a result of being enslaved by White people for centuries. This leaves
readers with the idea that the problem lies within Black folk. However, the
evidence—and even the bulk of the argument developed by Johnson, particularly later in the book—reflects how the economic and cultural systems
that perpetuate White advantage and Black disadvantage are what explain
Black dependence on White people. It is a virtual necessity. In the words of
some of the (Black) interviewees: "You got to be loyal, 'cause you know this
is a white man's country" and "You can't do nothing with white folks agin
[against] you" (Johnson 1934, 27). In the end, it is clear that the structure of
the economic system is the problem. I elaborate on the details of this argument in the paragraphs that follow.

Essentially, Johnson argues that the social and economic dynamics established during slavery remain relatively undisturbed in places like Macon
County, Alabama. Slavery was strongly embedded in the county, as suggested by the concentration of people who were enslaved in 1860, which
was 68 percent (US Census Bureau 1864). Similar to contemporary scholars
(see Molotch et al. 2000), Johnson argued that past decisions—including the
decision to enslave other people—structured subsequent decisions—e.g.,
how to interact with Black Americans—through a reliance on "custom" and
"tradition."

It would take fundamental restructuring to disturb the foundation established after the county was first created by European settlers (who also
asserted their privilege and presumed superiority by driving out the Native
populations). Reconstruction fell short of that fundamental change and, as
Johnson notes, Macon County, Alabama—particularly its rural areas—was

relatively untouched by in- and out-migration. These realities left the population and their culture somewhat stagnant. Despite the centrality of the economic system in his argument, Johnson asserts that all aspects of life have been affected by the shadow of the plantation.

Johnson argues that a key characteristic of this shadow is a sense of "dependence" among the rural Black folk in his study. He suggests "the tenants [are] dulled and blocked in by a backwardness which is a fatal heritage of the system itself" (Johnson 1934, 212). Here, Johnson clearly points to the "system" as the source of the issue. Specifically, he faults the economic system that is centered on cotton production, which can only be profitable under strict circumstances (i.e., the exploitation of others) and results in the exhaustion of the soil. The system is unsustainable, for practical reasons if not for social justice.

This sense of dependence is more than a lingering feeling from slavery. It is continuously re-created by the contemporary system that stems from the historical reliance on slavery in Macon County, Alabama.

> The shell of the past hangs on in the agricultural economy of the community under study. It is present in the high proportion of Negro tenantry [sic], the almost exclusive concentration upon cotton, and the crude unskilled labor in need of land and skilled supervision, the credit system and advances, the tradition of dependence upon planters on the part of the Negro tenants, and the tradition of dependence upon capital on the part of the planters. (Johnson 1934, 103–4)

The dependence of rural Black people on White people is literally built into the economic system and is supported by the limited number of Black people who owned land, and the tenuous nature of that ownership. Johnson finds that only 64 out of the 612 families in his study owned their own farm/land. That is just 10 percent. Moreover, this number has been declining as a result of the deteriorating quality of the soil and small crop yields (which affects their ability to pay on their mortgages) as well as the departure of children, who are then not present to keep the land in the family (also see Gilbert, Sharp, and Felin 2002; Gilbert, Wood, and Sharp 2002).

Johnson also provides evidence of how White people exploit Black people through this system to maintain their relative advantage. Tenants on farms would routinely need to borrow money and buy other goods from the landowner. However, the (White) landowner was the one who kept an accounting of what was owed and paid. The Black rural folk in Johnson's study told numerous stories indicating that White people took advantage of this position of power and took more than what was owed, often leaving the tenant indebted. Even when a Black tenant could prove that the balance had been paid in full, the legal system, too, worked in White people's favor, leaving Black families with no successful means of recourse.

Within the system of loans or "advancements," there are some occasions when a family just cannot pay the tab at the end of the year, be it due to poor crop yields or other circumstances. When this happens, (White) landowners have the option to "close out"—or take everything from—a Black renter. Some do this with ruthlessness; however, others do so reluctantly. Johnson draws upon the interviews and experiences during his research to suggest that some White people engage in this tactic seemingly only because they feel "forced by pressure against themselves to beat down upon the Negroes." This signals the importance of institutionalized racism and a broader culture stemming from that system rather than just individual racists. Moreover, it is not just Black people who are affected by the resulting structural conditions; White people are too. This does not mean that individual racism was not present. It clearly was. This is also not an excuse for the actions of White people, but it is an indication of the power of the system when individual preferences diverge from what is prescribed by the system, especially when the end result aligns with the system and not the individual.

Johnson's work elucidates aspects of Black American culture in urban in addition to rural contexts, most notably in his book *The Negro in Chicago*. This research was commissioned after the Chicago Riot in the summer of 1919. After detailing the events associated with the riot, Johnson provides an extensive set of findings regarding the origins of the Black Chicago population, their experiences with housing, crime, the labor market, race, and Black and White opinions on race relations. This research offers a context for understanding the riot and possible solutions to the underlying racialized tensions, but it is also an important study of Black American urban life. There are other studies that do similar work, many of which also focus on the city of Chicago (e.g., Drake and Cayton 1945; Patillo 1999; Wilson 1978; 1987). The uniqueness of the contributions of his rural life research, particularly at the time of publication, and the parallels with contemporary theories is why I focus my discussion on *Shadow of the Plantation* rather than his body of work as a whole.

WHY THE NEGLECT?

The work of Charles S. Johnson on *Shadow of the Plantation* has been referenced over four hundred times according to Google Scholar. His *Growing up in the Black Belt* similarly has 373. In contrast, *The Negro in Chicago* has only ten. Quantitatively, this suggests he is not a neglected scholar of color and that his rural research has received more attention. However, qualitatively, his work—particularly his theoretical argument—has not received adequate attention.

Taking a closer look at when *Shadow of the Plantation* was referenced, I find that it was not cited by many contemporaries (i.e., only seven references from the 1930s and another seven from the 1940s). The number of citations really did not take off until the 1970s (see figure 5.1), but the peak emerges even later in the 2010s. The delay in attention to his work may, in part, reflect its frequent use for historical context—it often serves as a glimpse into the conditions of the time—rather than for its theoretical argument. Ultimately, I argue that Johnson has been wrongfully excluded from two major lines of research: work focused on the "culture of poverty" and Black disadvantage and the literature on the legacy of slavery.

First, the work of Johnson is, in many ways, similar to the argument later developed by William Julius Wilson in *The Truly Disadvantaged* (1987). Critically, Johnson suggests that the isolation of a disadvantaged people helps contribute to a distinct culture often viewed by outsiders as unintelligible and "backward." Wilson focused more on the concentration of poverty and the factors related to industrialization to explain some of the divergences between Black inner-city culture and that of (White) middle-class Americans, but the theoretical thrust is the same. It seems likely that one explanation for why Johnson's work was not included in these later discussions is due to his indirect reference to concentrated poverty and the later focus on urban rather than rural areas. I further discuss the similarities and differences between these and related works below. However, I emphasize here that I think these

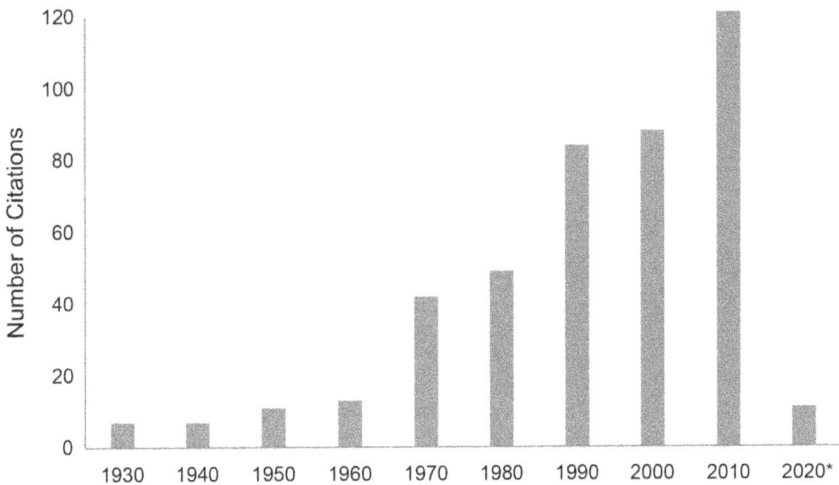

Figure 5.1. Total number of citations identified by Google Scholar in a given decade. Created by author.[1]

works need to be in conversation with one another to provide context for the variety of circumstances under which the proposed processes could occur, and to acknowledge the length of time and historical origins of the (racist) structures that continue to shape the experiences and life chances of racialized minorities in the United States.

Second, there are clear connections between Johnson's work on the *Shadow of the Plantation* and research on the legacy of slavery (e.g., Acharya, Blackwell, and Sen 2016; Kramer et al. 2017; O'Connell 2012; Reece 2020; Reece and O'Connell 2016; Vandiver, Giacopassi, and Lofquist 2006). The legacy of slavery, as understood within this more recent body of literature, reflects the institutionalization of elements of slavery, including the racist ideology—namely the presumed superiority of White people and the inferiority of Black people—used to justify the exploitation of one group by another. Critically, the contemporary legacy of slavery literature emphasizes the structural consequences of this historical institution, much like Johnson in his work. Despite the conceptual overlap, and the eerie similarity between the language Johnson used in some of the selected quotes mentioned above and contemporary research, none of the articles reference his work, including my own (Curtis and O'Connell 2017; O'Connell 2012, 2020; O'Connell, Curtis, and DeWaard 2020; Reece and O'Connell 2016). This omission extends to scholars who focused more broadly on rural places and not just the legacy of slavery (e.g., Duncan 1999; Falk, Talley, and Rankin 1993), which suggests it is not due to an urban bias or differences across specialty areas. Books tend to be less likely than articles to get picked up by later generations if there were not a continuous reliance on the work by scholars in between. However, that explanation still raises the question of why so few of Johnson's contemporaries cited his work. We lost an important theoretical thread that would have helped link historical slavery to contemporary Black-White inequality due to the neglect of theorists of color and an unwillingness to confront the realities of White racism.

Re-centering Structure and Extending the Temporal and Geographic Perspective in Arguments about Poverty and Black Culture

It may seem irrelevant to insert the theoretical perspective from Johnson's work into the now expansive literature stemming from *The Truly Disadvantaged* (Wilson 1987). There are over twenty thousand references to this single book. However, I argue that there are still benefits to remembering *Shadow of the Plantation* within this literature. To situate those contributions, I first review some additional aspects of the literature that attends to Black culture and inequality.

There is a danger in research on Black culture that the reference group will become normalized and seen as unproblematic while seemingly suggesting that any problem lies within the Black population itself. This is a concern I shared at several points when first reading *Shadow of the Plantation*. Yet, as I emphasize above, Johnson repeatedly centered structural elements, including White racism, when explaining the economic and social position of rural Black folk in his study. Despite studying culture, he does not use it to explain the disadvantaged position of Black people.

Unfortunately, we do not see the same careful distinction and ultimate emphasis on structure in Wilson's (1987) work and that of others who endorsed a "culture of poverty" thesis (e.g., Lewis 1966; Moynihan 1965)—or, at least, that is not how contemporaries interpreted these works. Some have argued that the relative emphasis on structure/racism versus the intergenerational, internally propelled transmission of culture is a key distinction between the theoretical development by Johnson and what emerged in later work (Jorgensen 2006). Johnson's research—if inserted into this literature—would provide a stronger foundation for understanding the complex linkages among structure, culture, and life outcomes.

Of course, there have already been several moves to bring the structural elements of "culture of poverty" arguments to the fore. In response to Wilson's (1987) *Truly Disadvantaged* and his earlier book on *The Declining Significance of Race* (1978), Massey and Denton (1993) assert that race is, in fact, still a major axis of stratification in the United States and that residential segregation—i.e., the physical separation of Black people and White people—is the structural driver of that inequality. Subsequent research, after the initial round of responses, has focused more on the consequences of Wilson's arguments for what is referred to as "neighborhood effects," namely the relationship between one's neighborhood context and individual outcomes. However, that literature has been critiqued for an overemphasis on the disadvantage of concentrated poverty that largely affects Black people, and a lack of attention to the advantage of concentrated affluence experienced largely by White people (Howell 2019). Ultimately, this critique is similar to the concerns raised regarding the cultural argument—there is an overemphasis on Black culture while neglecting the role that White racism and the accompanying structures play in generating the perceived deficits within Black culture. Critically, this is a limitation that—as I have argued—is addressed by one of the (neglected) contributions of the work of Johnson.

Social scientists are well aware of the importance of structure, but this often gets lost when discussing aspects of culture, particularly when related to poverty (see especially Williams 2019). Bringing Johnson's *Shadow of the Plantation* into this conversation provides a critical point of reference for ongoing debates regarding how to understand the connections between race and poverty (also see Iceland 2019). Moreover, his work suggests the durability of the factors involved. The structural forces—broadly conceived—that shaped the lives of rural Black folk in the 1930s were also present in the inner city of Chicago in the 1980s. A comparison of these contexts also indicates that the factors involved traverse regions—from the South to the Midwest—and span geographies of different levels of rurality and urbanity. In contrast to the urban-centered approach that emerged from Wilson's work, linking this literature with the work of Johnson provides a broader perspective that incorporates a wider swath of the US landscape. It is the isolation of an already-disadvantaged group and the structures that keep them in that position that leads to the observations made by Johnson and Wilson, not something unique about the rural South or the urban North.

STRENGTHENING THE THEORETICAL FOUNDATIONS OF THE LEGACY OF SLAVERY ARGUMENT

Before describing the contribution Johnson's work makes to the legacy of slavery literature, I first describe some of the evidence from the existing literature and key elements of the driving argument. Similar to the focus of Johnson, the legacy of slavery argument was originally developed in reference to economic outcomes (O'Connell 2012; Ruef and Fletcher 2003), but also processes related to the criminal legal system (Vandiver et al. 2006; for related literature on the legacy of lynching also see, e.g., Messner, Baller, and Zevenbergen 2005). Scholars argue that historical practices become embedded in place (Molotch et al. 2000), and that contemporary institutions reflect aspects of those histories. As Reece (2020) describes, the racialized boundaries and accompanying roles/practices that (White) people created to justify and enforce slavery were reused in the postbellum South because there was still a "need for a permanent labor force" (Reece 2020, 308). Old systems were replaced with new versions that looked different but served the same purposes (also see Bonilla-Silva 1997).

One of the biggest challenges to the legacy of slavery literature is identifying how it persists over time. Overwhelmingly, the evidence offered in support of the legacy of historical institutions is a relationship between a measure of the focal institution in the past and a measure of an outcome at a later point in time. For example, in my original research on the legacy of slavery I focused on the concentration of enslaved people in 1860 and Black-White poverty inequality in the year 2000 (O'Connell 2012). I accounted for contemporary structural factors associated with Southern counties, but I did not consider intervening events that may have occurred, say, in the early 1900s or even 1960s.

This practice of focusing on just the two points in time—or really just how one, earlier point in time is reflected in the contemporary landscape—has been shifting, with greater attention to what happens in between. In particular, Acharya et al. (2016) find that the political legacy of slavery—namely its relationship with contemporary voting patterns—is concentrated in places where the introduction of the tractor was delayed, which maintained a need for cheap labor and, subsequently, the systems used to exploit Black people. Others have examined additional factors, including oppression during the Civil Rights era (Petersen and Ward 2015), population change across the decades (O'Connell, Curtis, and DeWaard 2020), and even Confederate monuments (O'Connell 2020). Finally, Gabriel and Tolnay (2017) develop a theoretical argument suggesting that there are forces that could either facilitate or disrupt the transmission of historically (racialized) histories, which offers a broader framing to guide examinations of the intervening events.

Overall, scholars in the legacy of slavery literature have established greater confidence in our understanding of the persistence (and disruption) of historically racist institutions. Empirical evidence is now starting to reflect the expectation that racist institutions took on new forms over time, but ultimately did not change (also see Alexander 2010; Blackmon 2008). The quantitative studies executed by contemporary scholars are certainly valuable, but *Shadows of the Plantation* provides insight into how counties like Macon County, Alabama, maintained attachments to the plantation system in the critical early decades of the 1900s (also see O'Connell et al. 2020). Contemporary analyses demonstrate there is a link, but Johnson's work articulates the mechanisms.

The work of Johnson is largely consistent with the contemporary legacy of slavery literature, which suggests its contributions at this point may be minimal. However, I argue that it provides a much needed foundation that enhances our understanding of the interrelationships among the various social spheres of life. Moreover, the broad scope of his work speaks to a wider range of topics than currently dominates the literature on the legacy of slavery. The latter point is particularly important when considering the position of more "cultural" outcomes, like marriage and family, within the literature.

Despite some attention to connections between family formation patterns and slavery, there has been limited engagement with the structural elements of the legacy of slavery argument (see especially Moynihan 1965; Patterson 1998; for a partial exception see Bloome, Feigenbaum, and Muller 2017). Instead, scholars have offered a purely individual-level, cultural argument that diminishes Black Americans. Critically, some have argued this is unfounded and misses the structural factors involved in the development and re-creation of Black culture (e.g., Cross 2003; also see Hamilton 2019). Greater attention to the argument and evidence provided by Johnson in *Shadows of the*

Plantation offers a clear foundation from which to develop this increased emphasis on structure and institutions in affecting Black culture, particularly as relates to connections to slavery.

CLOSING THOUGHTS

The move to focus on structure when understanding Black culture is critical to contemporary debates on the sources of Black-White inequality (Hamilton 2019), and strengthening the foundations of the legacy of slavery argument will provide greater clarity regarding the institutional mechanisms involved. However, the perspective offered in *Shadows of the Plantation* is not without its limitations. We need a careful marrying of the work of Johnson and contemporary scholarship.

Of most importance, the focus of Johnson on Black folks leaves the work blind to the role of White people in actively working to reassert their privileged economic and social position (Mueller 2020). We catch glimpses of their involvement, but a theory of the structural, historically rooted factors involved in Black-White inequality would benefit from more attention to the actions and intentions of those supporting those systems of inequality. Howell (2019) has begun this work within the neighborhood effects and segregation literatures by identifying the need to attend to White advantage in addition to Black disadvantage. Similarly, Reece (2020) has urged legacy of slavery scholars to consider the ways in which the systems extending from slavery benefit White people—the original end goal of the institution. However, this kind of theoretical focus will need continued attention as we develop theory regarding the mechanisms involved in generating Black-White inequality, through the legacy of slavery and other means.

In closing, I reflect on how different these and related lines of scholarship could have been had the theoretical work of Johnson received more notice from his contemporaries. It could have—should have—accelerated our understanding of the structural forces shaping (Black) folk ways, the extent to which linkages to slavery are maintained over time, and Black-White inequality more broadly—that is, if we had not neglected the theoretical scholarship of people of color.

REFERENCES

Acharya, Avidit, Matthew Blackwell, and Maya Sen. 2016. "The Political Legacy of American Slavery." *The Journal of Politics* 78 (3): 621–41.

Alexander, Michelle. 2010. *The New Jim Crow: Mass Incarceration in the Age of Colorblindness*. New York: The New Press.

Blackmon, Douglas A. 2008. *Slavery by Another Name: The Re-Enslavement of Black Americans from the Civil War to World War II*. New York: Anchor Books.

Bloome, Deirdre, James Feigenbaum, and Christopher Muller. 2017. "Tenancy, Marriage, and the Boll Weevil Infestation, 1892–1930." *Demography* 54 (3): 1029–49.

Bonilla-Silva, Eduardo. 1997. "Rethinking Racism: Toward a Structural Interpretation." *American Sociological Review* 62 (3): 465–80.

Cross, William E. Jr. 2003. "Tracing the Historical Origins of Youth Delinquency and Violence: Myths and Realities about Black Culture." *Journal of Social Issues* 59 (1): 67–82.

Curtis, Katherine J., and Heather A. O'Connell. 2017. "Historical Racial Contexts and Contemporary Spatial Differentiation in Racial Inequality." *Spatial Demography* 5 (2): 73–97.

Drake, St. Clair, and Horace R. Cayton, Jr. 1945. *Black Metropolis: A Study of Negro Life in a Northern City*. Chicago, IL: The University of Chicago Press.

Duncan, Cynthia M. 1999. *Worlds Apart: Why Poverty Persists in Rural America*. New Haven, CT: Yale University Press.

Duneier, Mitchell. 1992. *Slim's Table: Race, Respectability, and Masculinity*. Chicago, IL: The University of Chicago Press.

Falk, William W., Clarence R. Talley, and Bruce H. Rankin. 1993. "Life in the Forgotten South: The Black Belt." In *Forgotten Places,* edited by Thomas A. Lyson and William W. Falk, 53–75. Lawrence, KS: University Press of Kansas.

Gabriel, Ryan, and Stewart Tolnay. 2017. "The Legacy of Lynching? An Empirical Replication and Conceptual Extension." *Sociological Spectrum* 37 (2): 77–96.

Gilbert, Jess, Gwen Sharp, and M. Sindy Felin. 2002. "The Loss and Persistence of Black-Owned Farms and Farmland: A Review of the Research Literature and Its Implications." *Southern Rural Sociology* 18 (2): 1–30.

Gilbert, Jess, Spencer D. Wood, and Gwen Sharp. 2002. "Who Owns the Land? Agricultural Land Ownership by Race/Ethnicity." *Rural America* 17 (4): 55–62.

Gilpin, Patrick J., and Marybeth Gasman. 2003. *Charles S. Johnson: Leadership beyond the Veil in the Age of Jim Crow*. Albany, NY: State University of New York Press.

Hamilton, Tod G. 2019. *Immigration and the Remaking of Black America*. New York: Russell Sage Foundation.

Howell, Junia. 2019. "The Truly Advantaged: Examining the Effects of Privileged Places on Educational Attainment." *The Sociological Quarterly* 60 (3): 420–38.

Iceland, John. 2019. "Reply to 'A Call to Focus on Racial Domination and Oppression: A Response to 'Racial and Ethnic Inequality in Poverty and Affluence, 1959–2015.'" *Population Research and Policy Review* 38: 665–69.

Johnson, Charles S. 1922. *The Negro in Chicago: A Study of Race Relations and a Race Riot*. University of Chicago Press: Chicago, IL.

———. 1934. *Shadow of the Plantation*. University of Chicago Press: Chicago, IL.

———. 1941. *Growing up in the Black Belt: Negro Youth in the Rural South*. The American Council on Education: Washington, DC.

Jorgensen, Carl. 2006. "Booker T. Washington and the Sociology of Black Deficit." In *The Racial Politics of Booker T. Washington*, edited by Donald Cunnigen, Rutledge M. Dennis, and Myrtle G. Glascoe, 105–32. Oxford, UK: JAI Press.

King, Charles E. 1945. "The Negro Maternal Family: A Product of an Economic and Culture System." *Social Forces* 24 (1): 100–4.

Kramer, Michael R., Nyesha C. Black, Stephen A. Matthews, and Sherman A. James. 2017. "The Legacy of Slavery and Contemporary Declines in Heart Disease Mortality in the US South." *Social Science and Medicine-Population Health* 3 (1): 609–17.

Lewis, Oscar. 1966. *La Vida: A Puerto Rican Family in the Culture of Poverty—San Juan and New York*. New York: Random House.

Massey, Douglas S., and Nancy A. Denton. 1993. *American Apartheid: Segregation and the Making of the Underclass*. Cambridge, MA: Harvard University Press.

Messner, Steven F., Robert D. Baller, and Matthew P. Zevenbergen. 2005. "The Legacy of Lynching and Southern Homicide." *American Sociological Review* 70 (4): 633–55.

Molotch, Harvey, William Freudenburg, Krista E. Paulsen. 2000. "History Repeats Itself, But How? City Character, Urban Tradition, and the Accomplishment of Place." *American Sociological Review* 65 (6): 791–823.

Moynihan, Daniel P. 1965. *The Negro Family: The Case for National Action*. Washington, DC: Office of Policy Planning and Research, U.S. Department of Labor.

Mueller, Jennifer C. 2020. "Racial Ideology or Racial Ignorance? An Alternative Theory of Racial Cognition." *Sociological Theory* 38 (2): 142–69.

O'Connell, Heather A. 2012. "The Impact of Slavery on Racial Inequality in the Contemporary US South." *Social Forces* 90 (3): 713–34.

———. 2020. "Monuments Outlive History: Confederate Monuments, the Legacy of Slavery, and Black-White Inequality." *Ethnic & Racial Studies* 43 (3): 460–78.

O'Connell, Heather A., Katherine J. Curtis, and Jack DeWaard. 2020. "Population Change and the Legacy of Slavery." *Social Science Research* 87 (1): 1–18.

Patterson, Orlando. 1998. *Rituals of Blood: Consequences of Slavery in Two American Centuries*. Washington, DC: Civitas/Counterpoint.

Pattillo, Mary. 1999. *Black Picket Fences: Privilege and Peril among the Black Middle Class*. Chicago, IL: The University of Chicago Press.

Petersen, Nick, and Geoff Ward. 2015. "The Transmission of Historical Racial Violence: Lynching, Civil Rights-Era Terror, and Contemporary Interracial Homicide." *Race and Justice* 5 (2): 114–43.

Reece, Robert L. 2020. "Whitewashing Slavery: Legacy of Slavery and White Social Outcomes." *Social Problems* 67 (2): 304–23.

Reece, Robert L., and Heather A. O'Connell. 2016. "How the Legacy of Slavery and Racial Composition Shape Public School Enrollment in the American South." *Sociology of Race and Ethnicity* 2 (1): 42–57.

Ruef, Martin, and Ben Fletcher. 2003. "Legacies of American Slavery: Status Attainment among Southern Blacks after Emancipation." *Social Forces* 82 (2): 445–80.

US Census Bureau. 1864. 1860 Census: Population of the United States.

Vandiver, Margaret, David Giacopassi, and William Lofquist. 2006. "Slavery's Enduring Legacy: Executions in Modern America." *Journal of Ethnicity in Criminal Justice* 4 (4): 19–36.

Williams, Deadric T. 2019. "A Call to Focus on Racial Domination and Oppression: A Response to 'Racial and Ethnic Inequality in Poverty and Affluence, 1959–2015.'" *Population Research and Policy Review* 38: 655–63.

Wilson, William J. 1978. *The Declining Significance of Race: Blacks and Changing American Institutions*. Chicago, IL: University of Chicago Press.

———. 1987. *The Truly Disadvantaged: The Inner City, the Underclass, and Public Policy*. Chicago, IL: University of Chicago Press.

NOTE

1. The total for 2020 is reflective of the count as of December 2020, and therefore is really only showing the citations in a single year rather than the full decade.

Chapter 6

Alfredo Mirandé

Toward the Development of
Chicana/o/x Sociology

Robert J. Durán

There is an increasing and much needed recognition of the contributions of Black sociologists, particularly W. E. B. Du Bois and the Atlanta School, in shaping sociology as a discipline (Ladner 1973; Morris 2015; Wright 2002, 2009; Wright and Calhoun 2006). A similar appreciation for Latina/o sociologists is also needed and important.[1] The pan ethnic term of Latinos includes population groups such as Mexicans (past and present), Puerto Ricans, Cubans, and residents from other Latin American countries. The mestizo ancestry of Spanish colonizers and indigenous Native Americans has developed into a population group that has encountered various forms of societal discrimination and neglect (Acuña 2000; Moore and Cuéllar 1970; Navarro 2005; Vigil 2012). In the United States, the social construction of race has primarily been viewed as a difference between Black and White, with Latinos encountering discrimination and often encountering difficulty in having those prejudicial barriers removed (Gómez 2007; Haney-López 2003; Perea 1997).

To aid in the correction of these omissions, as is the focus of this book, the scholarship of Professor Alfredo Mirandé (1940–present) will be introduced. In this chapter, I will provide an overview of the intellectual life and work of Mirandé by reviewing forty-five of his articles and ten of his books. This review is a subset of the almost complete written articles and books but is lacking chapters written in edited books and several articles unobtainable through interlibrary loan. The review of Mirandé will outline an intellectual journey shaped by experiences into an evolving scholarship that covers four strands of life (assimilation into traditional sociology, the development of

Chicana/o sociology, applying law to advocate on behalf and in solidarity with the underdog, and examining topical themes between the United States and Mexico). Second, a discussion will be provided to explore why Professor Mirandé's work has not received its full recognition. Finally, an examination of the significance of Professor Mirandé's work for contemporary society, social theory, and social change will be provided, particularly as it relates to the development of Chicana/o/x sociology.

INTELLECTUAL LIFE AND WORK
OF PROFESSOR MIRANDÉ

Alfredo M. Mirandé is a Distinguished Professor of Sociology and Ethnic Studies at the University of California, Riverside. Achieving this success involved a journey between two countries, several academic institutions, the disciplines of sociology and law, and the influence of family. Mirandé (1988, 2000a) was born in Mexico City, and in 1940 he moved to Chicago, Illinois, with his father, who was a bracero, at the age of nine. His interest in sociology was sparked by a sociology class in junior high school, where he encountered a discipline that could study society "with the aim of alleviating societal ills, social inequality, and racism" (1988, 356). It was in graduate school, however, where he realized those interests were more closely aligned with social work or political activism. Sociology was more concerned with objectivity, value neutrality, and conducting detached research. A parallel love of law also occurred in his youth. Mirandé attended Illinois State University, where he earned a bachelor's degree in social science. One of his professors encouraged Mirandé to consider applying to graduate schools, including the professor's alma mater, the University of Nebraska.

Mirandé's application to the University of Nebraska was approved, and he was awarded a teaching assistantship. Mirandé (1988) described his training as based on European scholars (Comte, Durkheim, Spencer, Weber, etc.) in which the department was pushing for a positivist, value-free, sociology. He noted he had teachers who helped and nurtured him for professional development, but he never really felt like he had a mentor with whom he could identify. He earned his doctorate from the University of Nebraska in 1967. Upon graduation, Mirandé (1988) reported being the fourth Chicano to receive a doctorate degree in sociology. The other Chicanos included Julian Samora (PhD in 1953 from Washington University-Saint Louis), Fernando Peñalosa (PhD 1963 from the University of Southern California), and Rudolfo Alvarez (PhD 1966 from the University of Washington). He wrote, "I contend that one of the most important factors shaping the career paths of sociologists is the time when they entered graduate school and received the doctorate"

(1988, 356). He observed that the first pioneers were treated as individuals who "happened to be" of Mexican background, whereas the next generation benefited from the civil rights movement and the Chicano movement of the 1960s and early 1970s. Mirandé describes his experience as spanning both of these two critical periods, but that he was caught between two worlds: the public world was Anglo, and his private world was Mexican.

After Mirandé received his doctorate in 1967, there were four distinct phases of his scholarship. Each of these four phases highlight a change in analysis, methodology, and reflexivity, and each period contributed to his journey as a Chicano sociologist and played a role in the development of Chicano sociology.

Phase I: The Difficulty in Finding an Academic Home in White Spaces (1967–1973)

At the beginning of his academic career, Mirandé's identity appeared to be based on an attempt to assimilate and fit into traditional sociology departments, just as he had in graduate school. In 1967, he joined the University of Kentucky and studied conventional sociological topics, such as occupational aspirations, reference group theory, authoritarianism, and sexual behavior, by conducting surveys in his classes and reviewing the literature (Mirandé 1968a, 1968b). He went by the name Alfred M. Mirande. There was no "o" after Alfred and the accent over the "e" was missing in his surname. He reported: "I began teaching empiricist, value neutral sociology, clean shaven, wearing a suit and tie, and ended with long hair, bearded, in jeans, and participating actively in the events that led to the closing of the campus in the spring of 1970 after Kent State and the invasion of Cambodia" (1988, 359). No other information from these three years in Kentucky were discussed by Mirandé in his writings.

Then, in 1970, Mirandé joined the sociology department at Virginia Tech, which he described as conservative. He utilized previously collected data to analyze kinship ties between rural and urban communities (1970a, 1970b). He reported that, after the first year, he was "terminated" for "'lacking' interpersonal skills, not wearing a tie, and agreeing to serve as the faculty sponsor for the Gay Alliance" (Mirandé 1988, 359). He was then off to the University of North Dakota, where he wrote articles on social mobility and the looking-glass self (1973a, 1973b). His methodology at the time utilized questionnaires to gain information primarily from his students. His research did not stand out as a challenge to the status quo but rather as an attempt to fit into the existing sociological discipline. Nevertheless, his White colleagues lacked the desire to retain him. Moreover, it is very plausible that these predominantly White institutions lacked students of color, particularly those of Mexican and Indigenous descent, to push their departments to recruit and retain a racially and ethnically diverse range of faculty. According to Geolytics, the U.S. Census data for these states in 1970 indicate that they were very White (Nebraska 89 percent, Kentucky 87 percent, Virginia 80 percent, and North Dakota 99.6 percent) and had a miniscule Latino population (Nebraska 2 percent, Kentucky 0.5 percent, Virginia 0.5 percent, North Dakota 0.0 percent). Latina/o scholars, and other academics of color, have occasionally written about the challenges that exist working at predominantly White institutions (PWIs) (Padilla and Montiel 1998; Settles, Buchanan, and Dotson 2019; Stanley 2006).

Phase II: University of California, Riverside, and the Development of Chicana/o Sociology (1974–1989)

For six to seven years after receiving his PhD, Mirandé never seemed to find his groove in academia. He moved from Nebraska, Kentucky, Virginia, and North Dakota, searching for an academic home. That all changed in 1974, at the age of thirty-three, when he was hired for a joint position in sociology and Chicano studies at the University of California, Riverside. His contract involved coming in as a visiting lecturer, and then, after the first year, becoming a tenured associate professor. He writes, "sociology supported my tenure and promotion but Chicano studies did not" because up until that time he had not done very much in that area (1988, 360). In the beginning, he attempted to keep his previous academic routine by collaborating with a master's student named Elizabeth Hammer and writing articles on sexual permissiveness and abortion issues (Mirandé and Hammer 1974a, 1974b).

The more Mirandé began to teach and evaluate the scholarly literature, the more he began to develop a heightened level of critical consciousness to question many of the common assumptions about deviance, gender, and Chicanos. He published his first book, *The Age of Crisis: Deviance, Disorganization, and Societal Problems*, in 1975. In the book, he describes the challenges he encountered teaching courses on social problems and deviant behavior based on the limitations of current textbooks. Mirandé's own textbook was designed to provide, in user-friendly prose, chapters arranged by different authors to help readers gain a more critical perspective of a variety of social issues. Chapters covered topics such as poverty as a social problem, racial and ethnic inequalities, institutional White supremacy, deviance, juvenile delinquency, and crime.

As Mirandé began teaching in Chicano studies, he noticed how there was almost no critical or relevant sociology on Chicanos (Mirandé 1988). Most of the research was written by outsiders. The discipline of sociology at the time was 98 percent Anglo. He began to identify more as Chicano and the more he began to work in this area, the more peripheral he became to mainstream sociology. His academic identity transitioned to adding the accent to his surname and adding the "o" to Alfred. From this moment on, Mirandé's rate of publications increased, as did the prestige of publication outlets, and his desire to develop Chicano sociology. This development of Chicano sociology focused on the family, Chicano and Chicana experiences, and differential treatment of Chicanos by Anglo society.

The Chicano family, especially the roles of mothers and fathers, was one of Mirandé's key focal points. One of his early articles analyzed how the Chicano family had been presented in the literature as either a "tangle of pathology" or "warm and nurturing in a hostile environment" (Mirandé 1977). Although these approaches shared several overlapping themes, Mirandé reexamined the role of Chicano fathers and mothers. He emphasized the colonial context and how benign neglect had left the culture, values, and language of Chicanas/os with no formal legitimate standing in American society. Nevertheless, the Chicano family was an institution that remained resilient despite these negative characterizations. In 1980, Staples and Mirandé teamed up to provide a review and assessment of the past decade's literature on Asian, Black, Chicano, and Native American families. Robert Staples, a sociologist writing about Black sociology and striving to change how the scholarly literature depicted the Black family, was the lead author. Staples and Mirandé provided insights into the complexities of families by race and ethnicity, and it became Mirandé's most cited article. Collaboratively, they reported how there had been an increase in both the quality and quantity of minority family research, but that many challenges remained. Staples and Mirandé urged researchers to provide more balanced accounts of minority families that included both their strengths and weaknesses.

During the third phase of Mirandé career, he set out to build a new paradigm, titled "Chicano Sociology." Several of his articles in the late 1970s and early 1980s (1978, 1982) were a precursor to his 1985 book, *The Chicano Experience: An Alternative Perspective*. In these works, he established how Chicanos, as a historical fact, are a colonized people. Previous sociological approaches were based on existing paradigms such as the assimilationist model, the internal-colony model, and the Marxist model, and simply applying them to Chicanos. To understand and to advocate on behalf of Chicanos required taking the side of the oppressed. Although Chicano sociology was new, it had benefited from early scholars in the 1960s and 1970s, including the work of Octavio Romano, Nick Vaca, Deluvina Hernandez, and Miguel Montiel. Mirandé noted that several contemporary peers were working in the same direction, including Ed Murguia, Maxine Baca Zinn, Robert Blauner, Tomas Almaguer, and Mario Barrera. Mirandé outlined thirteen points that established a base for building Chicano sociology as a distinct theoretical framework.

Developing a Chicano sociology required that Mirandé expand his coverage and insights concerning Chicanas. To accomplish this goal, Mirandé joined with a previous coauthor of several articles in the mid-1970s, Evangelina Enríquez, to collaboratively write *La Chicana: The Mexican American Woman.* The book was published in 1979 and is his second most cited book publication. The authors emphasized how there was an increased focus on Black women, but when sociologists discussed women's issues, they focused primarily on middle-class Anglo women, whereas Chicanas experience triple oppression based on 1) colonization, 2) gender, and 3) a cultural heritage that tends to be dominated by males:

> The oppression of Chicanas, as colonized women, is much more pervasive than that of nonminority women or Chicano men. The effects of this oppression are not additive. Their socioeconomic oppression, as we will see, for example is greater than would be predicted from the cumulative effects of race and gender. (1979, 13)

Such an analysis predates Kimberlé Crenshaw's (1989) groundbreaking work on intersectionality and how oppression was not additive but multiplicative. Mirandé and Enríquez described how little was known about Chicanas and they used the chapters in their book to correct that omission, along with focusing on contemporary issues. By outlining the challenges based on the historical context of colonization, the authors describe the birth of Chicana feminism in the early 1970s, where women carved out a space within the Chicano Movement. Moreover, Chicanas recognized how the Anglo women's movement neglected, and thereby maintained, racism. In conclusion, Mirandé and Enríquez emphasize the importance of liberation for Chicanas by not compromising their principles for self-determination.

Mirandé's third strand of research during this phase was criticizing the Anglo system of justice. His book, *Gringo Justice* (1987), builds on points outlined in *The Age of Crisis* (1975), along with several articles he published in the late 1970s and early 1980s. In an earlier study (1978b), he criticized labeling theory and how not all stigmas identified by Erving Goffman were the same. For example, the stigma experienced by colonized people was different because it was based on an "all-out assault on the culture of the conquered" in an effort to reinforce subordination (Mirandé 1978b, 388). The concept of stigma also failed to account for the role of power and inequality since it was focused too much on societal reaction. *Gringo Justice* (1987) also described the Chicano experience in terms of the conquest that shifted political dominance of the land from Mexico to the United States, where residents of Mexican descent were displaced and labeled as vigilantes, bandits, and revolutionaries. Mirandé also analyzed the beginnings of the border patrol and police and Chicano interactions, along with an examination of gangs in terms of whether these were criminals or barrio warriors, serving to protect the neighborhood. Mirandé challenged popular depictions of Chicano criminality and can be considered one of the early critical criminologists.

During the second phase of Mirandé's career, he found an academic home at the University of California, Riverside, where he served as chair of Chicano studies and found his voice by writing numerous books, articles, and book chapters. His primary methodological approach in the early 1970s began with surveys but he then shifted toward comparative/historical sociology. His identity developed into that of a Chicano scholar: A Chicano sociologist rather than a sociologist who happened to be Chicano. It was a transformation that shaped the remainder of his career.

Phase III: Stanford Law School and Rascuachismo (1990–2011)

Despite all of Mirandé's academic success, the death of his last surviving brother made him question everything about life. He decided to give up his academic appointment and apply to law school to pursue a childhood passion. He was accepted by Stanford Law School in 1990, one of the most elite law schools in the country. This launched the third shift in his academic career. The transition to becoming a first-year law student required an adjustment and several aspects of his background made him unique (being older, Chicano, possessing a PhD, and having a teenage daughter). Some of the challenges he encountered included the difficulty in getting called upon in class, not becoming alienated, adjusting to new hierarchies, and struggling to find his place. He described law school as working to remove previous identities and retraining students toward a hierarchy of an elite, White male culture. He came to learn that many of the students of color had a White parent, which seemed to help improve their assimilation. He kept a journal during this time and captured his experiences in his book, *The Stanford Law Chronicles: "Doin' Time on the Farm"* (2007). Mirandé completed his Juris Doctor degree in 1993. He felt empowered by possessing a JD and a PhD, in a way double-barreled, but he couldn't remove from his thinking or social treatment, that even with all of these fancy degrees, he was still perceived as a "Mexican," a *greñudo*.

Law school had a major impact on Mirandé's scholarship and lived experiences. His interest in law was motivated by a desire to bring about social change. He worked at a law office from 1991 to 1994, which equipped him with an additional skill set. Another point he often alluded to was being bilingual. He worked on developing critical race theory by utilizing the storytelling feature to bring to life the cases he was working on. He did this by creating a fictional character named "Fermina Gabriel" to create a dialogue through the writing of letters. She became a composite of women he had known. The pro bono cases Mirandé handled were "routine cases" with "regular folks" who had "ordinary problems." His 2011 book, *Rascuache Lawyer: Toward a Theory of Ordinary Litigation*, presents a bottom-up view of law, lawyering, and legal practice. In the book, Mirandé shares his philosophy to work on behalf and in solidarity with subordinated peoples. He cited Supreme Court Justice Oliver Wendell Holmes, who stated: "The life of the law has not been logic: it has been experience" (2011, 13). In each chapter, Mirandé outlines the experiences he gained handling different types of cases. The greatest challenge was time management, as he had resumed working full-time at the University of California, Riverside. Being a rascuache lawyer entailed treating people with dignity and respect and in the process forming long-term friendships. The end goal was maintaining a principle of reciprocity and mutual self-help that focused on empowerment and reducing structural forces of inequality.

After his legal training, Mirandé began publishing in law journals. An article in the *New Mexico Law Review* focused on how English-only rules discriminate on the grounds of national origin and race and particularly toward those who are bilingual in English and Spanish. He described a New York Supreme Court decision that allowed a prosecutor to dismiss Latino jurors because they were bilingual, as they were hesitant to accept the official translation provided. Thus, the liberal view of treating everyone equally in this decision, instead perpetuated inequality by removing people who were bilingual and thus primarily Latino. In his critique of critical race theory, Mirandé (2000b) examined Richard Delgado's fictional character, Rodrigo, and called him a nerd. Mirandé questioned why this person of color was transformed into a European who criticized Western culture but was socially and politically isolated from inner cities and barrios. Mirandé encouraged the use of our own histories and experiences to demonstrate that Chicanos exist. After criticizing Delgado, Mirandé set out to create his own fictional character (Fermina) based on narratives and stories of real people and experiences. Subsequent law journal article focus on Mirandé's experiences and correspondence with Fermina including "Alfredo's Jungle Cruise (2000a)," "Alfredo's Mountain Adventure (2001)," and "Alfredo's Caribbean Adventure (2006)." In these articles, written with the use of storytelling, Mirandé describes the challenges within LatCrit in forming a scholarly identity for Latinos and carving out a space within critical race theory.

Not only did Mirandé author two autoethnographic books and several law articles, but he also published *Hombres y Machos: Masculinity and Latino*

Culture (1997). He reported reading Carol Gilligan's book *In a Different Voice*, wherein she describes how women were different from men. In doing so, Gilligan created the term "reasonable man," but Mirandé was pretty sure this "reasonable man" was not Mexican. To explore the topic of Latino masculinity, Mirandé initiated a research study with a team of two bilingual interviewers who conducted 105 interviews with Latino men in northern and southern California, and San Antonio, Texas. In this book he explored several themes, including the genesis of Mexican masculinity, contemporary conceptions and emergent views of masculinity, fatherhood, and the development of Latino men's studies. He found that there was not a single Chicano/Latino masculine mode but rather a variety of Latino masculinities. Most of the men interviewed reported that they placed higher value on internal qualities such as honesty, warmth and kindness, respectfulness, and ethical behavior. The least favorable characteristics were men who were selfish, irresponsible, and did not take care of their families.

During the third phase of Mirandé's career, he used legal analysis and storytelling reminiscent of autoethnography, although he does not use this term to describe his methodological approach. Law school pushed him into the field of Critical Race Theory, particularly the themes of LatCrit. A law school class, titled Lawyering for Social Change, and the professor who taught it, increased his desire for a more humane and empowering form of legal defense. Mirandé emerged as a new man.

Phase IV: Returning to His Roots (2012–2020)

During the fourth phase of his career, Mirandé once again made a shift in his methodological approach, now using ethnography to study topics related to Mexican migration in his book, *Jalos USA: Transnational Community and Identity* (2014a) and sexuality in his book, *Behind the Mask: Gender Hybridity in a Zapotec Community* (2017). In each of these studies he conducted fieldwork by observing the communities he was studying and interviewing residents whose lives were enmeshed in these realities. *Jalos USA* takes us into the lives of migrants living and working in Turlock, California, and coming from the destination community of Jalostotitlán (Jalos), Mexico. Religion played a critical role in the daily lives of these residents, and their relationship with the church provided social, cultural, and human capital. The migrants worked in agriculture, cattle farming, dairies, and service industries. Life was seen as more stable and peaceful in Turlock, yet there was constant scrutiny of whether residents had the proper immigration papers, risking deportation. Life in Jalos was more traditional but it was much harder to find work and get an education there. Mirandé found that living in Jalos instilled residents with a strong work ethic, but this waned over time in Turlock. In addition, time in the United States led some migrants to alcoholism and increased drug use. Mirandé introduced the "Race/Plus Model of Latina/o Subordination" to describe the racialization of Jalos residents in the United States. He argued that Latinas/os "are subjected to discrimination that is not only on race, but on language, culture, and real or perceived alienage status" (2014b, 982). People from Jalos were light in complexion but were not accepted as White or as recipients of White privilege in the United States.

In *Behind the Mask: Gender Hybridity in a Zapotec Community* (2017), Mirandé introduces readers to Los Muxes: indigenous biological males who are a third gender. Los Muxes have existed in Juchitan for centuries, even during pre-Columbian times. Juchitan was considered one of the most culturally, ethnically, and linguistically diverse regions in Mexico. Mirandé conducted 115 open-ended interviews in Spanish and translated these into English. He also documents research challenges he encountered based on insider and outsider statuses. Although he was fluent in Spanish and born in Mexico, it was as if he had on cultural blinders. Reflectively, he recognized how his research had its limitations because he was a non-Zapotec outsider. To reduce hierarchical differences, he attempted to utilize strategies used by other minority researchers, who despite their insider statuses, often lived very different lives from the people they were studying. Overall, his book contributes to developing valuable insights into topics of gender, sexuality, and hybridity.

As the 2010s came to a close, Professor Mirandé revisited his previous work and shared many of the themes and topics developed there with new generations. In his edited book, *Gringo Injustice*, Mirandé put together a team of contributors who were "experts who have not only solid academic credentials but also direct personal experience, inside knowledge of the law" (2020: xvi). Collaboratively, Mirandé and his contributors wrote chapters highlighting key aspects of how Latinos experienced the Anglo justice system. In addition, Mirandé and Maxine Baca Zinn (2020) teamed up to publish an article in the journal, *Sociology of Race and Ethnicity* titled "Latino/a Sociology: Toward a New Paradigm." In this article, Baca Zinn and Mirandé outline the history of Latino/a sociology and explain how it is distinct from the sociology of Latinos. They highlight several defining characteristics of Latino/a sociology, including lived experience, interdisciplinary feminist standpoint theories, critical methodologies, pan disciplinarity, intersectionality, centering of race, challenging the Black-White binary, transnationality, taking a stand against social injustice, and seeking to produce knowledge for social justice. Despite little growth in Latino/a membership in the American Sociological Association since the 1970s, they expressed enthusiasm for the future implementation of Latino/a sociology.

CHALLENGES TO RECEIVING RECOGNITION

It is my opinion that the scholarship of Professor Mirandé has not received the recognition it deserves based on two reasons: 1) the Black-White binary for understanding race in the United States; and 2) sociology's elitism and its lack of racial and ethnic inclusiveness.

As highlighted by the scholarship of several authors, the social construction of race in the United States has primarily operated through the lens described as the Black and White binary (Mirandé 2014b; Perea 1997). As Native Americans were killed through violence and disease or pushed onto reservations, the general ideology of the United States was based on slavery and on viewing Africans as property. After prolonged struggle, the greatest division within the country became the battle to remove slavery in the South and later to enact Civil Rights legislation to provide greater levels of constitutional equality. Through westward expansion the US government incorporated additional Native American tribes and pueblos along with half of Mexico and its residents of mestizo ancestry. However, it was not until 1954 that the Supreme Court ruled that the Fourteenth Amendment was needed to provide equal protection to national or ethnic groups. In the case of *Hernandez v. Texas*, it was established that people of Mexican descent have the right to a jury of their peers. Numerous research studies have examined how Mexicans or Mexican Americans were not treated equally by the law and by societal treatment. In an essentialized conception of race, other racial and ethnic groups beyond Black and White people have been neglected. Mirandé's scholarship focuses on Chicanas/os, a socially constructed ethnic group, which has only recently begun to receive national attention as Latinas/os have now become the largest minority group in the United States. The concepts of Latino or Hispanic, as pan ethnic terms, often hide the heterogeneous complexity of the population described. Mirandé noticed similar challenges in the development of LatCrit when he stated, "We represent some 32 distinct countries, different cultures, and all racial groups" (2001, 525). Thus, despite efforts for national political mobilization, there have been divisions by geographic region, national ancestry, generation status, language, along with class and gender. Generalizations about Latinas/os are themselves complex and do not fit so easily into traditional conceptions of race.

The second obstacle likely impacting the recognition of Mirandé's scholarship is that sociology as a discipline has been dominated by White, male elitism since its foundation. The founding fathers are European (Max Weber, Karl Marx, and Émile Durkheim) and the establishment of sociology in the United States was created during the historical era of separate but equal legislation (Brunsma and Wyse 2019). Thus, the pillar institutions of the University of

Chicago and the Atlanta School produced contrasting visions for sociology, one White and the other Black; one heralded and acknowledged and the other neglected and suppressed. Even one of the most prominent African American sociologists of the time, W. E. B. Du Bois, was largely neglected until Aldon Morris's (2015) book, *The Scholar Denied*, brought to light his many contributions and the many obstacles he faced due to his race. In another publication, Morris describes how the discipline's major professional organization, the American Sociological Association (ASA), has struggled to overcome a lack of racial and ethnic inclusion:

> For 111 years—1906 to 2017—ASA presidents have been overwhelmingly white (over this period, 95 percent have been white). Of that group, 81 percent have been white males and 13.5 percent white women. Only 5 percent of the presidents have been people of color: three black males, one black female, one Asian American female, and one Latino male. (2017, 206)

Relatedly, Baca Zinn and Mirandé (2020) report that probably only 5 percent of ASA's membership is Latina/o. A similar study examined one of the key markers for institutional academic success: publications. Perrucci, Perrucci, and Subramaniam (2019) reported data on the institutional affiliation of editors and authors in four top sociology journals over a fifty-year span and also examined the demographic composition of faculty and graduate students during the same time period. The authors found a clear overrepresentation by faculty from elite departments, both as editors and as authors. They describe this as a cumulative advantage that provides certain faculty enhanced benefits and access to professional networks. The authors question how such a pattern is reflective of meritocracy when elite departments garner most of the resources.

Mirandé did not receive his doctorate at one of these top elite institutions (Nebraska) and he does not work at one (University of California, Riverside).[2] He was born in Mexico to Mexican parents and grew up in Chicago with a father who worked as a bracero. His career and scholarship have thus challenged many of the traditional values held by mainstream (White) sociology. Despite decades as chair of Chicano studies and ethnic studies, his joint appointment in sociology never provided him with the same level of peer support for leadership of that department. Rodolfo Acuña, in his book *The Making of Chicana/o Studies* (2011), also describes the challenges of forming Chicana/o studies programs at universities. Interdisciplinary departments of this sort were largely the product of student efforts to have academic spaces more reflective and inclusive of their own backgrounds. Even many departments and universities that have a large number of Latina/o students do not offer courses related to Latina/o experiences or even faculty from these backgrounds. Acuña reported that "the years 1969–1973 were critical to the formation of Chicano Studies" (2011, 77). Thus, departments including Africana studies, Chicano studies, ethnic studies, and women's studies have been created to increase racial and gender inclusivity at colleges and universities, while conventional departments have been less accepting.

SIGNIFICANCE OF ALFREDO MIRANDÉ'S SCHOLARSHIP FOR CONTEMPORARY SOCIETY AND SOCIAL THEORY

In this chapter I have identified numerous contributions provided by the scholarship of Professor Mirandé that have significantly shaped contemporary sociological work. In conclusion, I will focus upon three themes: 1) the development of Chicana/o/x Sociology, 2) a critique of mainstream conceptions of crime, law, and justice; and 3) developing a more applied and activist form of scholarship to not only study, but to transform contemporary society.

As the Latina/o population has grown to become the largest minority group in the country, its diversity in experiences and backgrounds is an important topic for learning more about this population group and the challenges they experience in the United States. As Mirandé noted:

> Any paradigm that seeks to understand the experience of Mexicans and Latinas/ os in the United States must not only incorporate insider narratives, but also reject monolithic conceptions of Chicana/Latina culture and identity that fail to take into account nationality, gender, sexual orientation, and the regional and generational diversity of the Mexicans and other Latinas/os in the United States. (2014b, 981)

Throughout Mirandé's career, he has given attention to the Chicano experience before and after colonization. His scholarship has provided insight into the lived experiences of Chicanos on various topics, such as the family, gender, identity, law, migration, religion, and sexuality, while challenging the Black-White binary view of race relations. In Mirandé's own words:

> Chicano sociology has given focus and direction to my career and enabled me to bridge the gap between my public and private self . . . by advocating a sociology that is proactive, value committed, and seeks to merge truth and feeling, I have, in a sense, come full circle. These were the reasons why I had first entered the discipline. (1988, 361)

In the creation of Chicana/o or Latina/o sociology, as mentioned previously, Baca Zinn and Mirandé (2020) identified several defining characteristics that make these forms of analysis unique. Mirandé is among a small group of scholars who have worked to develop a space for Latinas/os in sociology and at colleges and universities across the nation in the name of Chicana/o or Ethnic Studies. As the discipline of sociology has been more reluctant to structurally alter its departmental demographics and stance on utilizing research for social justice, many scholars of color have been more welcomed in these broader interdisciplinary departments relating to ancestry (i.e., Africana Studies, Chicana/o Studies, Ethnic Studies, Mexican American Studies, etc.) or more applied fields (i.e., criminal justice, public health, social justice, social work, etc.).

A second important theme is Mirandé's critique of our understanding of crime and how it is applied to Chicanas/os differentially than to White people, such as expanding our conceptions of crime to include conquest and state crime, which were not considered illegal (whereas it was okay to stop people of Mexican descent who were not violating the law simply because of their ethnicity). In addition, issues of language, nationality, and immigration status added a level of complexity for comprehending interactions and misperceptions between people. Mirandé outlined these challenges historically and noted several areas where the law has been applied differentially to Latinos compared to other racial and ethnic groups. For example, he described how prosecutors have used bilingualism to remove Latino jurors and how "looking Mexican" justified exceptions to the Fourth Amendment. Ensuring equity in constitutional protection will be even more important as the Latina/o population continues to increase in size. Responding to unequal treatment also will benefit from increased Black, Brown, and Native alliances.

Finally, Mirandé's scholarship provides an important contribution to how to make sociology more relatable and influential in the lives of those most directly impacted by a variety of social conditions. Mirandé's qualitative research and emphasis upon insider perspectives serves as an important contrast to most academics, who may study marginalized population groups and personally advance in their careers, but provide no investment in the communities they study. While the academic study of sociology is somewhat limited in utilizing research to influence policy and practices, Mirandé's training in law provides him an applied avenue for legally challenging practices and providing advocacy within the US court system. Mirandé has encouraged researchers to take sides and work toward developing knowledge and solutions from the bottom up. To guide such practice, Mirandé's books have not only described his findings but also offered theories to explain what is occurring. By combining both approaches, data and theory, efforts toward social justice can be more pragmatically realized, as expressed by Professor Mary Romero (2020) in her 2019 Presidential Address to the American Sociological Association, emphasizing the importance of social justice for the discipline of sociology. The scholarship of Alfredo Mirandé, as a Chicano sociologist, and his efforts toward accomplishing social justice, remain at the heart of what is needed to address the problems of the twenty-first century.

REFERENCES

Acuña, Rodolfo. 2000. *Occupied America: A History of Chicanos*. New York: Longman.

———. 2011. *The Making of Chicana/o Studies: In the Trenches of Academe*. New Brunswick, NJ: Rutgers University Press.

Baca Zinn, Maxine, and Alfredo Mirandé. 2020. "Latino/a Sociology: Toward a New Paradigm." *Sociology of Race and Ethnicity*. http://dx.doi.org/10.1177/2332649220971326.

Brunsma, David L., and Jennifer Padilla Wyse. 2019. "The Possessive Investment in White Sociology." *Sociology of Race and Ethnicity* 5 (1): 1–10.

Crenshaw, Kimberlé. 1989. "Demarginalizing the Intersection of Race and Sex: A Black Feminist Critique of Anti-Discrimination Doctrine, Feminist Theory and Anti-Racist Politics." University of Chicago Legal Forum, 139–67.

Geolytics. 2010. National Change Database. 1970–2010.

Gómez, Laura E. 2007. *Manifest Destinies: The Making of the Mexican American Race*. New York: New York University Press.

Haney-López, Ian F. 2003. *Racism on Trial: The Chicano Fight for Justice*. Cambridge: Belknap Press of Harvard University Press.

Ladner, Joyce, ed. 1973. *The Death of White Sociology*. New York: Random House.

Mirandé, Alfred M. 1968a. "Reference Group Theory and Adolescent Sexual Behavior." *Journal of Marriage and the Family*. 572–77.

———.1968b. "On Occupational Aspirations and Job Attainments." *Rural Sociology*. 349–53.

———. 1970. "Mental Rigidity and Performance in Sociology." *The Pacific Sociological Review* 13 (1): 62–66.

———. 1970. "Extended Kinship Ties, Friendship Relations and Community Size: An Exploratory Inquiry." *Rural Sociology*. 261–66.

———. 1973. "Mirror, Mirror on the Wall: Another Look Through the Looking Glass Self." *Sociological Focus* (5) 2: 107–11.

———. 1973. "Social Mobility and Participation: The Dissociative and Socialization Hypotheses." *The Sociological Quarterly* 14 (1): 19–31.

———. 1975. *The Age of Crisis: Deviance, Disorganization, and Societal Problems*. New York: Harper & Row.

———.1977. "The Chicano Family: A Reanalysis of Conflicting Views." *Journal of Marriage and Family* 39 (4): 747–56.

———. 1978a. "Chicano Sociology: A New Paradigm for Social Science." *Pacific Sociological Review* 21 (3): 293–312.

———. 1978b. "Deviance and Oppression: The Application of Labeling to Racial and Ethnic Minorities." *International Journal of Contemporary Sociology* 15: 375–96.

———. 1979. *La Chicana: The Mexican American Woman.* Chicago: The University of Chicago Press.

———. 1982. "Sociology of Chicanos or Chicano Sociology?: A Critical Assessment of Emergent Paradigms." *Pacific Sociological Review* 25: 495–508.

———. 1985. *The Chicano Experience.* Notre Dame, IN: University of Notre Dame Press.

———. 1987. *Gringo Justice.* Notre Dame, IN: University of Notre Dame Press.

———. 1988. "I Never Had a Mentor: Reflections of a Chicano Sociologist." *The American Sociologist* 19 (4): 355–62.

———. 1997. *Hombres y Machos: Masculinity and Latino Culture.* Boulder, CO: Westview Press.

———. 2000a. "Alfredo's Jungle Cruise: Chronicles on Law, Lawyering, and Love." *U.C. Davis Law Review* 33 (4): 1347–76.

———. 2000b. "Revenge of the Nerds, or Postmodern Colored Folk—Critical Race Theory and the Chronicles of Rodrigo." *Harvard Latino Law Review* 4: 153–98.

———.2001. "Alfredo's Mountain Adventure: The Second Chronicle on Law, Lawyering, and Love." *Denver University Law Review* 78 (4): 517–52.

———.2006. "Alfredo's Caribbean Adventure: LatCrit Theory, Narratives, and the Politics of Exclusion." *Chicano-Latino Law Review* 26: 207–36.

———. 2007. *The Stanford Law Chronicles: "Doin' Time on the Farm."* Notre Dame, IN: University of Notre Dame Press.

———. 2011. *Rascuache Lawyer: Toward A Theory of Ordinary Litigation.* Tucson: University of Arizona Press.

———. 2014a. *Jalos USA: Transnational Community and Identity.* Notre Dame, IN: University of Notre Dame Press.

———. 2014b. "Light but Not White: A Race/Plus Model of Latina/o Subordination." Seattle Journal for Social Justice 12 (3): 947–82.

———. 2017. *Behind the Mask: Gender Hybridity in a Zapotec Community.* Tucson: University of Arizona Press.

Mirandé, Alfredo, ed. 2020. *Gringo Injustice: Insider Perspectives on Police, Gangs, and Law.* New York: Routledge.

Mirandé, Alfred M., and Elizabeth L. Hammer. 1974a. "Premarital Sexual Permissiveness: A Research Note." *Journal of Marriage and the Family*.

———. 1974b. "Premarital Sexual Permissiveness and Abortion: Standards of College Women." *The Pacific Sociological Review* 17 (4): 485–503.

Mirandé, Alfredo, and Evangelina Enríquez. 1976. "Chicanas: Their Triple Oppression as Colonized Women. *Sociological Symposium* Fall: 91–102.

Moore, Joan W., and Alfredo Cuéllar. 1970. *Mexican Americans.* Englewood Cliffs, NJ: Prentice-Hall.

Morris, Aldon D. 2015. *The Scholar Denied: W.E.B. Du Bois and the Birth of Modern Sociology.* Oakland, CA: University of California Press.

————. 2017. "The State of Sociology: The Case for Systemic Change." *Social Problems* 64: 206–11.

Navarro, Armando. 2005. *Mexicano Political Experience in Occupied Aztlán.* Walnut Creek, CA: Alta Mira Press.

Padilla, Raymond V., and Miguel Montiel. 1998. *Debatable Diversity: Critical Dialogues on Change in American Universities.* Lanham, MD: Rowman & Littlefield.

Perea, Juan F. 1997. "The Black/White Binary Paradigm of Race: The Normal Science of American Racial Thought." *California Law Review* 85 (5): 127–72.

Perrucci, Robert, Carolyn Perrucci, and Mangala Subramaniam. 2019. "Publications in Four Sociology Journals, 1960–2010: The Role of Discipline Demographics and Journal Mission." *Sociological Focus* 52 (3): 171–85.

Romero, Mary. 2020. "Sociology Engaged in Social Justice." *American Sociological Review* 85 (1): 1–30.

Settles, Isis H., NiCole T. Buchanan, and Kristie Dotson. 2019. "Scrutinized but not Recognized: (In)visibility and Hypervisibility Experiences of Faculty of Color." *Journal of Vocational Behavior* 113: 62–74.

Stanley, Christine A. 2006. "Coloring the Academic Landscape: Faculty of Color Breaking the Silence in Predominantly White Colleges and Universities." *American Educational Research Journal* 43 (4): 701–36.

Staples, Robert, and Alfredo Mirandé. 1980. "Racial and Cultural Variations among American Families: A Decennial Review of the Literature on Minority Families." *Journal of Marriage and the Family* 42 (4): 887–903.

Vigil, James Diego. 2012. *From Indians to Chicanos: The Dynamics of Mexican-American Culture.* Third edition. Long Grove, IL: Waveland Press.

Wright, Earl. 2002. "The Atlanta Sociological Laboratory 1896–1924: A Historical Account for the First American School of Sociology." *The Western Journal of Black Studies* 26 (3): 165–74.

————. 2009. "Beyond W. E. B. Du Bois: A Note on Some of the Little Known Members of the Atlanta Sociological Laboratory." *Sociological Spectrum* 29: 700–17.

Wright, Earl, and Thomas C. Calhoun. 2006. "Jim Crow Sociology: Toward an Understanding of the Origin and Principles of Black Sociology via the Atlanta Sociological Laboratory." *Sociological Focus* 39 (1): 1–18.

NOTES

1. In this article, several terms will be used interchangeably, and the particular term used as most appropriate for the author, geographic area, time period, or whether plural or singular. For example, Professor Mirandé uses the term Chicano (plural). In some of his work he focuses specifically on women and thus Chicana will be used. In other instances when applicable Hispanic or Latina/o/x will be used. Questions and debates regarding Latina/o identity and what particular name to use have existed historically. Some identities are self-adopted such as Chicano, whereas others have

been applied by the government (i.e., Hispanic). Currently, Latinx or Chicanx is in vogue, but such an identity has largely been adopted by academics and less so by the community. With the passing of time, new identities and terms will more than likely be adopted or applied to define this population.

2. Perrucci et al. (2019) did note that from 2005 to 2010, Nebraska was considered in the top twenty-three ranked departments. Mirandé graduated in 1967 when it was not included in the top twenty list. The *U.S. News & World Report* ranking of gradu-ate departments in 2017 has it ranked as #63: https://www.usnews.com/best-graduate -schools/top-humanities-schools/sociology-rankings.

Chapter 7

Cherríe Moraga

Amanda D. Hernandez and Sonia Valencia

Cherríe Moraga is best known for her collaboration with Gloria Anzaldúa on the 1981 feminist classic, *This Bridge Called My Back: Writings by Radical Women of Color.* This volume of collected works pushed back on the exclusion of women of color in the broader women's movement and issues around sexuality. While the 1981 publication of *This Bridge* is just a starting point for Moraga's lifelong scholarship, it is often the only work of hers widely known and recognizable. Serving in faculty posts ranging from artist in residence at the Department of Theater and Performance Studies at Stanford University to her current position as professor of English at the University of California, Santa Barbara, Moraga's work spans genres as well as time. Historically, her work is often viewed as strictly under the purview of women's and gender studies. This brief chapter seeks to offer an intervention. We contend that the whole of Moraga's intellectual works touch on key issues of identity, the environment, and heteronormative white supremacy and patriarchy, and that these works are important social theory. Rather than viewing her work purely as artistic commentary, Moraga's body of work offers us theory for making sense of how marginalized individuals navigate our world.

In this chapter we discuss Moraga's work by theme rather than by genre or chronology. Moraga's work includes essays, memoir, poetry, and plays, each circling around the same core themes across the span of her work. As Patricia Hill Collins asserts in *Black Feminist Thought*, we agree that theory produced by those seeking to oppose injustice, such as art, music, and poetry (2000: 9), takes forms that fall outside the academic world's white masculinist standard for theory. By examining Moraga's work thematically, we resist the ways that social science—and academia more broadly—has marginalized poetry, plays, and creative nonfiction as not sufficiently theoretical.

First, we discuss the themes of Moraga's work, from issues of identity around race, ethnicity, sexuality, and motherhood, to the ways working-class struggles, the environment, and indigeneity are explored in her work. Next, we ask what might account for the marginalization and erasure of Moraga's work in contemporary theorizing. And finally, we point to a few ways in which Moraga's work can be applied in contemporary social science research as helpful theoretical framing.

ISSUES OF IDENTITY: RACE, ETHNICITY, SEXUALITY, AND MOTHERHOOD

Much of Moraga's work deals in autobiographical reflection on what it means to live at the intersection of multiple identities. These often included a gender analysis, but more complicated than that are her treatments of what it means to be a woman and Chicana, a woman and a lesbian, a Chicana lesbian mother. All of these identities come together in intimate and inextricable ways, shaping her politics and writing. In "La Güera," first appearing in *This Bridge,* Moraga works through what it means to be "half breed." With her mother, a Mexicana, and her father, an Anglo, Moraga navigates not just two cultures but the ways that she is perceived by others by virtue of her light skin: "No one ever quite told me this (that light was right), but I knew that being light was something valued in my family (who were all Chicano, with the exception of my father). In fact, everything about my upbringing (at least what occurred at a conscious level) attempted to bleach me of what color I did have" (1981, 23). She goes on to discuss how her güera privilege is easily contextual, given her simultaneous identity as "dyke" (1981, 24), and how her choice to identify as Chicana is a deeply political one, given her language, education, and physical appearance. However, she rejects this dichotomizing of her identities, not only as white and Chicana, but the ways those intersect with her other identities: "I am a woman with a foot in both worlds; and I refuse the split" (1981, 29). Rather than compartmentalize her identities or reject that which is socially subordinated, Moraga embraces her identity as it is and how she experiences it at the bodily level: Chicana. Lesbian.

Moraga's lesbianism colors her work. From her own self-identification in essays, to the characters and stories of her plays, Chicana lesbianism is central to her body of work. Articulating race, ethnicity, indigeneity, and gayness in "Queer Aztlán: the Re-formation of Chicano Tribe," (1993) Moraga imagines a space for Chicanx jotería. While feminist spaces had left out women of color, Chicano movement spaces were actively misogynist and exclusionary of women, while *both* movements, the women's and Chicano movements, shunned their queers. Acknowledging the ways that nationalist movements have the danger of sliding into biological essentialism or even fascism, in this essay Moraga is grappling with what a queer/gay acceptance in her own community could look like.

In *Giving Up the Ghost*, Moraga (1994) shows the day-to-dayness of lesbian life as a Chicana, highlighting the dual challenges of violence and love. The play tells the story of Marisa and Amalia, both artists, who find their way to one another despite great losses on both their parts. The play itself only consists of these two women (one, Corky, is a younger version of Marisa). This in itself, being a Chicana play with only two women lovers, disrupts the machismo of Chicano theatre. In "Giving Up the Ghost: Feminist Theory and the Staging of Mestiza Desire," Yvonne Yarbo-Bejarano (2000) suggests this play as a remedy to lesbian exclusion in the broader feminist movement, comparing it to Moraga's essay "A Long Line of Vendidas" from *This Bridge*, where Moraga discusses how her active choice of lesbianism is an act of betrayal against her people—it is to be a vendida, to be la malinche. Yarbo-Bejarano asserts that both in the play and in the essay, Moraga is engaging in feminist theorizing around the nature of the virgin and the whore, the good woman and the fallen woman. This theme of the vendida and the competing expectations of women and how those are shaped by both racial and gendered scripts is consistent throughout her work, including her memoir, *Native Country of the Heart* (2019), where she tells the story of her own mother.

Themes of motherhood and family likewise weave throughout Moraga's work. From grappling with what it means to be white and Chicana in the context of her mostly Chicano family, to asking "What Kind of Lover Have You Made Me Mother?" in *Loving in the War Years* (1983). Two volumes in particular discuss motherhood and her own mother explicitly: *Waiting in the Wings: A Portrait of Queer Motherhood* (1997) and *Native Country of the Heart* (2019). In *Waiting in the Wings,* Moraga outlines her journey into queer motherhood. Moraga and her partner decide to have a child together with the gracious assistance of one of their gay friends. While it could be described as artificial insemination, Moraga rejects the artificialness of her experience. Their child is born prematurely and spends months in a San Francisco hospital on the edge of life and death. Moraga ruminates on the discrimination she and her partner experience from hospital staff as they try to enter the hospital together to see their son—yes, they are *both* the mother. This memoir of early and unsure motherhood stands in contrast to her latest memoir, *Native Country of the Heart* (2019), a self-described love letter to her own mother, where she reflects on both their lives, the way they intertwine, and the geopolitical, gender, and ethnic context of their relationship.

WORKING-CLASS STRUGGLES, ENVIRONMENTAL CONSCIOUSNESS, AND INDIGENEITY

Moraga's first writings depict her reclamation of a Chicana identity and efforts to center the perspectives and experiences of women and queer Chicanas which have been silenced due to heterosexism and homophobia within the Chicano movement. Her later writings—prose and plays—reflect a broad, global critical perspective. Even in Moraga's most personal writing, we contend that she models what Latina theater scholar Tiffany Ana López (2005), theorizes as "critical witnessing." López offers the term "to describe how Latinx authors' creative works bear witness to experiences of pain, violence, and healing and simultaneously position audiences as "critical witnesses" to these stories of survival. Readers and audiences become critical witnesses, López writes, when they undergo "the process of being so moved by a reading experience as to engage in a specific action intended to forge a path toward change" ("Critical Witnessing" 2005, 64). We see this approach in Moraga's essays and plays. In *Giving Up the Ghost*, for example, the audience is a character in the play "The People." López's theoretical framework helps us understand Moraga's keen attention to the sociopolitical experiences of working-class Chicanx families and the ways their experiences of exploitation are directly linked to the exploitation of women, children, communities, and the environment. We can better understand how Moraga engages in a type of writing that pushes us to join her or her characters in coming to consciousness of various issues and taking up collective action.

The United Farm Workers' grape strike and boycott first brought (inter)national attention to the labor exploitation and health effects of pesticide poisoning on the human bodies picking crops. Despite the success of the strike, farmworkers continued to labor under inhumane conditions and exposure to pesticides. Written a decade after the Delano grape strike and boycott, Moraga's *Heroes and Saints* (1994), *Watsonville*, and *Circle in the Dirt* (2002) depict the ongoing effects of environmental violence in Chicanx communities through the lens of gender and desire. All three plays are inspired by the life experiences of cannery and farmworkers in Texas and California. Cerezita, the protagonist of *Heroes*, a limbless head, is inspired by a string of serious birth defects caused by pesticide exposure. *Watsonville* dramatizes the 1985–1987 cannery strike led by women who sought living wages and workers' rights, and *Circle in the Dirt* documents the effects of gentrification in a working-class East Palo Alto community. In all three plays, it is queer people and women who organize the community and lead the fight against agribusiness and "development."

Even in works that do not directly engage the effects of environmental violence, such as *Giving Up the Ghost* (1986) and "Shadow of a Man" (1992), Moraga draws subtle but powerful parallels between gender and environmental violence. In both plays, scenes of violence and trauma to the female body are surrounded by images of abuse to the land. In *Ghost*, for example, the end of Amalia's miscarriage, a long night of bleeding, is marked by sounds of construction work outside her hotel window. Marissa describes how the construction workers are, "tearing up the Mexican earth with steel claws" and she warns that "La Tierra is not as passive as they think. 'Regresaré,' Ella nos recuerda. 'Regresaré,' nos promete" (1986, 25). In these plays, men abuse that which is gendered female for their own personal gain, but through Marissa's words, Moraga challenges the strong/weak and masculine/feminine dichotomies that associate passivity with femininity. In Moraga's plays, women consistently demonstrate unparalleled strength and resilience. Moraga doesn't simply reverse the man/woman and strong/weak dyads but, rather, shows the crippling effect of toxic heteromasculinity on men, which she further theorizes in her writings as she reflects on her father and other male homosocial relationships in her plays.

Chicanx indigeneity and a trans-American ecofeminist consciousness are two major themes in *The Last Generation* (1993), Moraga's second collection of essays and poetry. Throughout this collection, Moraga challenges claims that the Chicanx movement, and by extension Chicanx resistance, is dead. In "Queer Aztlán: The Re-formation of Chicano Tribe," the collection's most oft-cited essay, Moraga reclaims and redefines Chicanx nationalism, a concept in which she finds value and power, as a nationalism in which "la Chicana Indígena stands at the center" (1993, 150). *The Last Generation* marks a paradigmatic shift in Moraga's work, as this is where Moraga first positions herself as a modern Mesoamerican scribe and her work as extension of the *flor y canto* tradition. However, Moraga's earliest writings have included whispers of references to indigenous cosmological symbolism. At the turn of the century, indigenous cosmologies become prominent and distinctive features in her writing, as can be seen in *The Last Generation* (1993) and *The Hungry Woman: A Mexican Medea* (2001), a postapocalyptic play that draws heavily on Mayan and Aztec mythology, La Llorona, and Euripides's Medea to imagine life in the United States following a (failed) revolution.

If *The Last Generation* (1993) and *Hungry Woman* (2001) mark a paradigmatic shift in Moraga's thinking and writing, one in which she centers "la Chicana Indígena" and her own journey toward a Chicana indigeneity, A *Xicana Codex of Changing Consciousness* (2011) bears witness to the full reclamation of that identity. *Xicana Codex*'s title makes highly visible what Moraga notes in the *The Last Generation*'s introduction, that her writing and thinking is informed by and modeled after the Mesoamerican tradition of the codex which seeks to "create a cartography of time and place and of the divine energies that animated through them" (2011, xvi). Moraga adopts the spelling of Xicana/o with an X, "the Nahuatl spelling of the 'ch' sound," she writes, to signal her indigenous identification. She explains that the "X links us as Native people in diaspora" and that it visually signals "a remerging political, especially among young people, grounded in Indigenous American belief systems and identities" (2011, xxi). Moraga notes that the Mayan calendar and symbolism is a framework used to structure her text. That is, *Xicana Codex* rejects a linear format and follows a circular path where the storytelling "returns again and again to the site of origin" (2011, xvii). Following in the tradition of the codex glyphs, Moraga incorporates nine drawings by Celia Herrera Rodríguez, a Xicana/O'dami painter, performance and installation artist, into *Xicana Codex*, that complement the essays and serve as their own stand-alone stories. Moraga glosses over criticisms of Chicanx indigeneity, noting, "from the perspective of some less informed North American Indian activists, Xicanos hold no rights to their indigenous identity by virtue of their Mexicanism" (*Codex* 7). Chicanx indigeneity, metizaje, and the early iterations of Chicanx indigeneity that reified mestizaje tropes are contentious topics even within Chicanx and Latinx Studies (see Contreras 2008; Blackwell 2017; Olguín 2013, Saldaña-Portillo 2001, 2003).

MARGINALIZATION AND ERASURE OF MORAGA'S WORK

We contend that Moraga, an interdisciplinary theorist, playwright, and public intellectual, is largely overlooked in mainstream discourses within our respective fields, sociology and literary studies. Within the fields of Chicanx studies and women's studies, for example, Moraga's early works, in *This Bridge* and *Loving in the War Years*, receive more attention than her subsequent works. In this section, we explore possible reasons why Moraga's larger body of work remains marginalized.

Notable for her juxtaposition of essays, poetry, (dream) journal entries, and drawings, Moraga's writing escapes easy classification and invites us to question genre definitions and function. She also refuses to write exclusively in English and weaves Spanish and Nahuatl into her writing, sometimes without translation. Moraga's prose makes all readers work, something that both undergraduate and graduate students often note when engaging her writing in classes. Genre crossing is not unique to Moraga, but it does challenge Western (read: white) conceptualizations of formal academic writing. Aware of the ramifications of her genre crossing, Moraga observes,

My literary and theater career has been "marred" as much by my politicized cultural essentialism as by my sexualized undomesticated lesbianism, to say nothing of my habitual disregard for the requirements of genre and other literary conventions. (2011, 5)

Those who subscribe to rigid ideas of what constitutes academic or theoretical writing might let the poetry, journal entries, and drawings obfuscate the theoretical advancements in Moraga's writings. Refusing to engage Moraga's work because it crosses disciplinary boundaries or escapes the stranglehold of categorization disregards the performative nature of Moraga's writing. That is, it disregards the way her writing (re)creates the abjection Chicanxs and queer people, specifically lesbians, have experienced and which she theorizes.

Not one to cave into theoretical trends or pressure, Moraga makes various intentional *movidas*, including reviving the concept of nationalism, which some consider outdated and problematic, and rejecting the inclusion of Eurocentric epistemologies, all of which might lead to the exclusion of her work. Moraga raises important questions about the politics and stakes of inclusion with which writers and theorists of color must continue to grapple. She warns against aiming for inclusion and acceptance at the expense of structural change, the latter a goal of various liberation movements including the Chicanx and women's movements (2011, 168). Noting the neoliberal university's ability to absorb and disarm political and epistemological interventions, Moraga interrogates the political economy of concepts like "equity" in the twenty-first century. She contends that within university systems, equity "means integration into the dominant culture, without altering the culture of Euro-American dominance within or outside the university" (2011, *Codex* 169). As we write this essay, universities across the United States have issued public commitments to equity and inclusion in response to the Black Lives Matter movement and their mobilization of the nation against the impunity of white supremacy and murders of unarmed Black men. Rereading Moraga's work raises important questions about the possibilities and limitations of equity and inclusion in relation to structural change and social justice. For Moraga, our fascination with inclusion and desire for "white people, their privileges, and their goodies . . . causes our writing to fall miserably short of the truly revolutionary literature it could be" (2011, *Codex* 5).

Can separatism be a productive strategy in social justice work? Minoritarian scholars often differ on this question. Separatism goes against the grain of our social milieu yet Moraga unapologetically defends this position, one from which she has not wavered throughout her career. In the essay, "The Salt that Cures: Remembering Gloria Anzaldúa," where she gives an account of her relationship with Anzaldúa, including their personal, political, and ideological differences, Moraga defends the exclusion of white and male authors from *This Bridge Called My Back* and notes that their inclusion in Gloria Anzaldúa and AnaLouise Keating's publication of *This Bridge We Call Home* led her to abstain from contributing to the 2002 anthology (2011, *Codex* 122). Lest we dismiss this as a simple, exclusionary practice, Moraga explains that "to be 'inclusive' of (even) queer men and white women . . . would be to suggest that our movement had developed beyond the need for an autonomous dialogue entrenos" (2011, *Codex* 123). Moraga notes that her and Anzaldúa's perspectives on the role of white allies exist within a continuum not to be simplified into a dichotomous structure. She explains that she doesn't disagree with the "spirit of [Anzaldúa's] ideas" but expresses concern over "how the seeming inclusivity of [Anzaldúa's] ideas lends them to appropriation and misinterpretation, especially by white middle-class scholars" (2011, 124; see also Hernandez 2020). In this essay, Moraga asks us to meditate on the contours of collaboration, allyship, and appropriation and to remain alert for the ways these theories are misinterpreted or appropriated in ways that uphold white hegemony. Moraga's writing insists on the need for and liberatory potential of collective movements. Citing Black Panther Richard Aoki, who said, "We didn't lose in the sixties, we just didn't finish the job" (2011, 164), Moraga upholds the radical potential of the people-of-color movements without romanticizing the past. She acknowledges the rampant heterosexism and homophobia that sowed division and violence in these movements but champions the efforts of "Black liberation, El Movimiento, and the American Indian movement" (2011, 165). What do present day identity-based movements look like? Not all scholars or activists working toward the epistemological and material liberation of marginalized peoples will agree with Moraga's approach. However, dismissing Moraga's approach as exclusionary or outdated is too simple: it allows us to evade the difficult questions about goals and methodology that she raises. Not only does Moraga's work remain a theoretically rich site for exploration, it also offers a pedagogical opportunity to engage students in critical theory and theory making.

MORAGA IN CONTEMPORARY THEORY AND SOCIOLOGICAL RESEARCH

Each of the issues and experiences that Moraga addresses remain as relevant as they ever were and continue to shape our current social worlds and circumstances. A cursory search of sociological and social science literature shows little engagement with Moraga outside of the acknowledgment of *This Bridge* as a formative piece that shaped third wave feminist responses to the perceptions of the white middle-class feminism of the second wave.

There are some notable exceptions, however. In "Doing Difference," West and Fenstermaker (1995) engage directly with Moraga's work in "La Güera," quoting her at some length when discussing how feminist scholars must be careful in their applications of intersectional theory to avoid additive "formulas" (see also Sims and Njaka 2020). And in *Female Masculinity* (1998), Judith Halberstam places Moraga's work in *Loving in the War Years* about her Chicana lesbianism and performance of that lesbianism into conversation with other queer thinkers, including Judith Butler, to explore lesbian masculinity, or what Halberstam refers to as the "stone butch" (1998, 124). These engagements provide richness to these scholars' analyses by bringing together gender, sexuality, *and* race and ethnicity in ways similar to that of Moraga. Next, we offer a few interventions of scholarly sites where Moraga's work can be integrated.

Moraga's grappling with and subsequent reconciliation of her racial identity fits into much scholarship on biracial identity, the ways that Latinx are racialized in US society, and the marginal space of Latinx and indigenous peoples in the United States. This work examines who is able to claim a biracial identity and how this often reveals the ways that colorism, class, and language come into play (Golash Boza 2006; Townsend et al. 2012). Moraga's work also offers a historical perspective on theorizing color, class, and language, firmly situated in a feminist of color framework. Shantel Bugg's (2017a, 2017b) and Jennifer Sims's (2016, 2018) work sits directly at the intersections Moraga explores, including mixed race and ethnicity, sexual identity, romantic relationships (particularly interracial ones), and class. Like Moraga, Bugg's and Sims's work is grounded in critical feminist of color scholarship.

Expanding into issues of sexuality, queerness, and lesbian identity specifically, Moraga exemplifies the inability of this part of one's identity to be separated from the other parts of it, such as one's gender or racial identification. Scholars can look to Moraga for examples of a refusal to divorce sexuality from other parts of identity, as Halberstam (1998) does in their analysis of performances of lesbianism. Doing so erases a central part of identity and leads scholars to present only a fractured and inaccurate representation of social actors. We argue that this is not only applicable to those on the margins in a heteronormative society, but also those who identify as straight and/or cisgender. For social scientists theorizing on the performance of gender and sexuality, Moraga's work offers a wealth of insights, especially by adding the concept of racialized performance.

Studies of parenthood and motherhood within social science inquiry often focus on the inequities experienced by mothers, such as the mommy penalty, the motherhood gap, and the second shift. Allowing our focus to shift to dyad-analysis in the style of Goffman or other symbolic interactionists, we can also examine more closely the socialization of mothering as an act of identity formation around "motherhood." Moraga's work provides similar insights into mother-child relationships, the ways this shapes future interactions, and the role of transitioning into (queer) motherhood. Amy Stone (2020) offers a unique dyad-analysis between LGBTQ adult children and their parents. She attributes some of her findings to regional (Southern) difference and briefly teases at the ways these interactions could be racialized. Moraga's work closely aligns with the "comfort work" described by Stone and offers a space to further explore the intersection of race and ethnicity in this type of adult child and parent relationship.

Finally, Moraga's work highlights the ways that colonial imperialism and capitalism have deeply impacted the environment and the ways that this manifests as environmental racism in communities of color, including for migrant and immigrant laborers. As issues around climate change and institutional transnational response to the climate crisis become more pressing than ever, Moraga's work offers important insights for social scientists.

CONCLUSION

Moraga has been writing and producing theory since 1981. Her work has changed over time, both politically and personally. And, of course, the personal is political. The recurring themes in Moraga's work, which we have explored in this essay, shed light on the challenges that continue to plague our theoretical and political interventions even as we achieve hard-fought sociopolitical gains. In a time when our political system and institutions tout multiculturalism and now diversity, equity, and inclusion as the treatment for our social maladies, Moraga insists on asking for more. Almost forty years after her first publication in *This Bridge Called My Back: Writings by Radical Women of Color* (1981), Moraga continues to maintain a radical stance, even as people bristle upon hearing the word radical, advocating instead for compromise. As we strive to create knowledge and movements that highlight our interconnected struggles, Moraga's voluminous writings continue to offer insightful observations, astute cautions, and productive questions that can shape our approaches.

REFERENCES

Anzaldúa, Gloria, and Cherríe Moraga, eds. 1981. *This Bridge Called My Back: Writings by Radical Women of Color*. Watertown, MA: Persephone Press.

Blackwell, Maylei. 2017. "Indigeneity." In *Keywords for Latina/o Studies*, edited by Deborah R. Vargas, Nancy Raquel Mirabal, and Lawrence La Fountain-Stokes, 100–5. New York: New York University Press.

Buggs, Shantel Gabrieal. 2017a. "Does (Mixed-)Race Matter? The Role of Race in Interracial Sex, Dating, and Marriage." *Sociology Compass* 11: 1–13.

Buggs, Shantel Gabrieal. 2017b. "Dating in the Time of #BlackLivesMatter: Exploring Mixed-Race Women's Discourses of Race and Racism." *Sociology of Race and Ethnicity* 3 (4): 538–51.

Collins, Patricia Hill. 2000. *Black Feminist Thought: Knowledge, Consciousness, and the Politics of Empowerment*. New York: Routledge.

Contreras, Sheila Marie. 2008. *Blood Lines: Myth, Indigenism, and Chicana/o Literature*. Austin: University of Texas Press.

Golash-Boza, Tanya. 2006. "Dropping the Hyphen? Becoming Latino(a)-American through Racialized Assimilation." *Social Forces* 85 (1): 27–55.

Halberstam, Judith. 1998. *Female Masculinity*. Durham, NC: Duke University Press.

Hernandez, Amanda D. 2020. "Developing a Mestiza Consciousness Theoretical Framework." *Sociological Spectrum* 40 (5): 303–13.

López, Tiffany Ana. 2005. "Critical Witnessing in Latina/o and African American Prison Narratives." In *Prose and Cons: Essays on Prison Literature in the United States*, edited by D. Quentin Miller, 62–77. Jefferson, NC: McFarland.

Moraga, Cherríe. 1983. *Loving in the War Years: Lo que nunca pasó por sus labios*. Boston, MA: South End Press.

———. 1992. "Shadow of a Man." In *Shattering the Myth: Plays by Hispanic Women*, edited by Linda Feyder and Denise Chávez, 9–49. Houston, TX: Arte Público Press.

———. 1993. *The Last Generation*. Boston, MA: South End Press.

———. 1994. *Heroes and Saints and Other Plays*. Albuquerque, NM: West End Press.

———. 1997. *Waiting in the Wings: Portrait of a Queer Motherhood*. Ithaca, NY: Firebrand Books.

———. 2001. *The Hungry Woman: A Mexican Medea*. Albuquerque, NM: West End Press.

———. 2002. *Watsonville: Some Place Not Here; Circle in the Dirt: El Pueblo de East Palo Alto*. Albuquerque, NM: West End Press.

———. 2011. *A Xicana Codex of Changing Consciousness: Writings, 2000–2010*. Durham, NC: Duke University Press.

———. 2019. *Native Country of the Heart: A Memoir*. New York: Farrar, Straus and Giroux.

Olguín, B.V. 2013. "'Caballeros' and Indians: Mexican American Whiteness, Hegemonic Mestizaje, and Ambivalent Indigeneity in Proto-Chicana/o Autobiographical Discourse, 1858–2008." *MELUS* 38 (1): 30–49.

Saldaña-Portillo, Josefina. 2001. "Who's the Indian in Aztlán?: Re-Writing Mestizaje, Indianism, and Chicanismo from the Lacandón." In *The Latin American Subaltern Studies Reader*, edited by Ileana Rodríguez, 402–23. Durham, NC: Duke University Press.

Saldaña-Portillo, Maria Josefina. 2003. *The Revolutionary Imagination in the Americas and the Age of Development*. Durham, NC: Duke University Press.

Sims, Jennifer Patrice. 2016. "Reevaluation of the Influence of Appearance and Reflected Appraisals for Mixed-Race Identity: The Role of Consistent Inconsistent Racial Perception." *Sociology of Race and Ethnicity* 2 (4): 569–83.

———. 2018. "'It Represents Me': Tattooing Mixed-Race Identity." *Sociological Spectrum* 38 (4): 243–55.

Sims, Jennifer Patrice, and Chinelo L. Njaka. 2020. *Mixed-Race in the US and UK: Comparing the Past, Present, and Future*. UK: Emerald Publishing Limited.

Stone, Amy. 2020. "When My Parents Came to the Gay Ball: Comfort Work in Adult Child- Parent Relationships." *Journal of Family Issues.* http://dx.doi.org/10.1177/0192513X20935497.

Townsend, Sarah S. M., Stephanie A. Fryberg, Clara L. Wilkins, and Hazel Rose Markus. 2012. "Being Mixed: Who Claims a Biracial Identity?" *Cultural Diversity and Ethnic Minority Psychology* 18 (1): 91–96.

West, Candace, and Sarah Fenstermaker. 1995. "Doing Difference." *Gender & Society* 9 (1): 8–37.

Yarbro-Bejarano, Yvonne. 2001. *The Wounded Heart: Writing on Cherríe Moraga*. Austin, TX: University of Texas Press.

Chapter 8

Krantijyoti Gyanjyoti[1] Savitribai
The Light of Revolution and Knowledge

Rianka Roy and Manisha Desai

INTELLECTUAL LIFE AND WORK
OF SAVITRIBAI PHULE

Savitribai Phule was born on January 3, 1831, at Naigaon in Maharashtra's
Satara district. Both her parents, Lakshmi and Khandoji Neveshe Patil,
belonged to the Mali (florist) community. According to the caste system
put in place by Brahmin men over millennia, albeit not without resistance,
the Malis were denied the privilege of education, which was reserved for
those deemed "upper" castes.[2] Besides, as a woman in nineteenth-century
pre-independence India within a rural community, education for Savitribai
would be unattainable had it not been for her invincible spirit and support
from her spouse, Jyotirao Phule. Savitribai was married to the thirteen-year-
old boy Jyotirao (reverentially addressed as Jyotiba) when she was nine years
old, in 1840.

Child marriage in colonial India was a widely practiced social custom.
While the British government had no problem violently transforming economic, political, and social structures for their own benefit, when it came to
cultural practices, they worked with the so-called upper-caste elites to leave
in place oppressive practices that reproduced patriarchal and caste inequalities. Christian missionaries, however, opened schools for Indians, after several phases of negotiation and confrontation with the East India Company.
In 1835, with Thomas Babington Macaulay's recommendations for the
British government to educate Indians, several academic institutions were

established (Chatterjee 1975; Viswanathan 1989). However, these projects often circumvented issues of social injustice related to caste and gender. Like Savitribai, Jyotirao was from the same caste, deemed "lower" by Brahmins, and was forced to leave school. With support from the Persian scholar Ghaffar Baig Munshi and a British official, Lizit Sahab, Jyotirao was able to enroll in a Scottish missionary school. At that time, very few missionary schools in Maharashtra were open to native Indians.

Jyotirao homeschooled Savitribai. Afterward, she completed a teachers' training course at an American missionary institute in Ahmednagar and at Pune's Normal School. Then Savitribai taught girls in Pune's Maharwada, along with Sagunabai, a mentor to Jyotirao. In 1848, the Phules, along with Sagunabai, founded their own school at Bhide Wada. At that time, Jyotirao was twenty-one, and Savitribai was only seventeen. It was India's first school for women started by Indians. While the majority of social reformers in India in that period were from castes deemed "upper" (Anagol-McGinn 1994), Jyotirao and Savitribai broke that mold. The curriculum of their school was different from that of schools run by Brahmins. It included mathematics, science, and social studies, instead of Brahminical texts like Vedas and shastras.

Chakravarti (2005) notes that in the nineteenth-century, Maharashtra witnessed a series of social reformers combating both the inherent prejudices of the Indian society and external colonial forces. However, "Brahman reformers in Maharashtra did not wish to break with Brahmanical traditions and worked within the broad structures of Brahmanical patriarchy and the observance of caste norms" (Chakravarti 2005, 167). The "upper"-caste male reformers in colonial India "wanted to give a face lift to their self-image in comparison to the imperial normative of masculinity" (Bhadwal 2017, 177). Consequently, their efforts were not directed toward diluting the prevalent gender hierarchy.

In fact, reformation led by elite Indian men in colonial India often became a retrospective task—the pursuit of the glorious Indian past outlined in Vedic texts (Chakravarti 2005; Chatterjee 1997). Such reform projects were "skewed in vision" (Bhadwal 2017, 166) and sought to idolize women from castes deemed "upper" according to the life stories of women in mythologies and epics (Anagol-McGinn 1994). These "upper"-caste Indian women "were projected as representatives of a nation's culture and tradition. They were ascribed values of maternity, purity and the willingness to suffer" (Bhadwal 2017, 177).

The Phules, however, did not subscribe to this Brahminical fantasy, and radically undermined such projects with their inclusive work for women and members of castes designated "lower" by the Brahmins, by first and foremost renaming them Dalit or oppressed, thereby rejecting the caste hierarchy.[3] Instead of seeing "lower"-caste persons and "upper"-caste women as objects of charity, the Phules designed curricula and pedagogy to empower them as individuals with critical subjectivities. While the Brahminical pedagogy in its nationalistic fervor attempted to purge education of its colonial influences by integrating the learning of Vedic scriptures, Jyotirao pragmatically felt that "Western education, with its rationalist outlook, could play a key role in the emancipation of the low castes and the concomitant undermining of Brahmin power" (Guha 2010, 76). However, even after adopting Western education, the Phules never veered from the lived realities of the Dalits and oppressed "upper"-caste women. Guha finds that "although his teachers seem to have seen a potential convert, (Jyotirao) Phule resisted the pressure to become a Christian. As with Rammohan Roy, the encounter with missionaries helped him fashion a critique of orthodox Hinduism" (2010, 76).

In 1849, Jyotirao's father banished him and Savitribai from his house, because the couple's social and educational work challenged Brahminical norms. Savitribai and Jyotirao stayed with the family of Usman Sheikh, a friend of Jyotirao's. At that time, Savitribai met Fatima Begum Sheikh, with whom she went to the Normal School. They ultimately graduated together, and Fatima and Savitribai opened a school for Dalits in Usman Sheikh's house in Pune in 1849. In the 1850s, the Phules started two educational trusts—the Native Female School, Pune, and The Society for Promoting the Education of Mahars, Mangs and Etceteras—which eventually sponsored several schools between them. Between 1848 and 1851, Savitribai and Jyotirao founded eighteen schools (Reeta and Raj 2016, 3). By 1851, they had three schools for girls in Pune, with around 150 students. Soon the number of female students enrolled in their schools outnumbered the number of boys in government schools (Kandukuri 2019).

In 1855, Jyotirao wrote his first political play, *Tritiya Ratna*—in which he showed how knowledge, metaphorically identified as the eponymous "third eye," would empower women and all "lower"-caste people to fight Brahminical prejudice. He used this text as a tool for social instruction as well as commentary. Both Savitribai and Jyotirao identified knowledge as an indispensable tool to "understand the system of oppression in order to be able to dismantle it" (Pandey 2019, 97). For them, education had a social purpose and involved the pursuit of truth.

The Phules demanded universal primary education and criticized the colonial government's neglect of it. They criticized the "Downward Filtration" policy of colonial education, which deepened social inequality by favoring "upper"-caste male learners. They even argued that primary teachers should be paid more than regular teachers. They emphasized that the primary school curriculum should be commensurate with the students' needs and contexts; rural and urban curricula should be different, and would include topics such as health and agriculture (Pandey 2019, 97). The Phules initiated the three-language formula in schools, as they recognized the students' need for the knowledge of their mother tongue (vernacular), as well as of Hindi and English. Their schools also offered vocational training.

Independently, too, Savitribai's innovative teaching methods and practices addressed the social realities of colonial India, fraught with caste and gender politics. She gave stipends to her students to minimize drop-out rates. She reportedly encouraged a student to ask for a library for the school at an award ceremony. Savitribai even had dialogues with parents to explain to them the importance of education, so that they would support their children. She introduced "group discussion" into the curricula, having girls discuss the importance of education over household work. The "dialogical form of communication" was an important part of Jyotirao's pedagogical intervention as well (Rege 2010, 93). These practices encouraged rational thinking among students on gender and caste issues. This pedagogical practice also legitimized the agency and voices of marginalized students in educational institutions.

Savitribai encouraged critical thinking and practical knowledge in education, in order to address social problems. According to Pandey, Savitribai's "goal in promoting education for the masses was not simply to raise the temporary standard of living for a few individuals, but to reshape the entire future of the nation" (2019, 97). She stood by Jyotirao, when "he made mass education the focal point of his movement," giving "highest priority to the education of women and low-caste children" (Pandey 2019, 97). Both Savitribai and Jyotirao also extended their pedagogy into social justice work, and contributed toward building the praxis of gender and caste equality that paved the way for the resistance to Brahminical patriarchy and caste hierarchies by another eminent anti-caste social reformer, Bhimrao Ramji Ambedkar's. For Ambedkar (1891–1956), too, the annihilation of castes was dependent on the education and empowerment of Dalits and their recognition of self-worth. In 1942, at the All India Depressed Classes Conference, Ambedkar motivated the audience to "educate, agitate and organize" (Rege 2010). Rege (2010) finds that, in the "Phule-Ambedkarite Feminist pedagogical practice," educators and activists constantly challenged colonial and Brahminical ideas of knowledge, and legitimized marginalized expressions of identity, encouraged Dalit imaginations, while remaining conscious of the power structures that obstruct the formation of Dalit subjectivities.

In 1873, Jyotirao, with support from Savitribai, founded the Satyashodhak Samaj, or the Society of Truth-Seekers. This radical society in Maharashtra focused on educating and empowering women and "lower"-caste groups. The aim of this society was the liberation of society from class, caste, and gender hegemonies through the active involvement of empowered women and Dalit subjects in transforming society. Unlike the Brahminical reformers in colonial India, the Satyashodhak Samaj promoted a horizontal structure of governance, involving grassroots subjects as agents of progress and social change. According to Rege, the Satyashodhak Samaj was "a discursive arena where members of the *shudra* castes invented and circulated counter discourses on the importance of education, the situation of the peasantry and women, the exploitation by moneylenders and brahmans" (2006, 39).

This Society had a well-designed administrative structure. To attain membership, one had to get fifty letters of support and nomination. The Satyashodhak Samaj was open to members from all castes and religions, however. Within one year, the Satyashodhak Samaj had members from many different castes, religions, and professions, i.e., lawyers, peasants, merchants, Malis, Rajputs, "untouchables," Muslims, Brahmins, and government officials (Bhadru 2009). Non-Brahmins, however, were the majority, and Malis were the most prominent. By 1890 a large rural population near Pune and Bombay joined the society. From 225 members in its first year, the number of members increased to 316 in 1876 (Bhadru 2002).

Among the "daringly precocious" (Guha 2010, 77) rules of the Truth-Seekers, members had to actively participate in spreading education among women and the "lower" castes. The curriculum had a pragmatic approach, as it also discussed techniques of improvement in agriculture (Begari 2010). Intellectual development, social upliftment and economic well-being were equally important for the Truth Seekers. Marriages among members of the reform society would take place without the involvement of Brahmin priests. As an administrator, Jyotirao attempted to persuade the British government "to recognize that it was not the Brahmins but the more numerous cultivating castes who were the real representatives of Indian society and the real carriers of its history" (Guha 2010, 77). Additionally, Jyotirao also demanded state intervention in agricultural improvement through the construction of tanks, dams, animal breeding programs, and special education for farmers (Bhadru 2002).

Before cofounding the Satyashodhak Samaj with Jyotirao, Savitribai opened a shelter for widows in 1854, and another large shelter in 1864 for destitute women, including widows and child brides. She offered sanctuary to sexually exploited women with their children, and saved them from social stigma, which had often led women to death by suicide. Savitribai even adopted Yashwant, the son of a Brahmin widow, raised him, and officiated his inter-caste marriage following the rules of the Satyashodhak Samaj (Reeta and Raj 2016). When Jyotirao passed away in 1890, Savitribai defied social conventions by lighting his funeral pyre. Jyotirao's death did not stop her active involvement in social justice work and education. In the nineteenth century, while "upper"-caste men, including Brahminical social reformers, subjected widows to endless deprivation and denial of agency, Savitribai's leadership in social reform even in her widowhood was a remarkable and inspiring exception.

During the bubonic plague in 1897, Savitribai opened a clinic in Pune and worked tirelessly for the victims in the affected regions. While carrying a ten-year-old plague victim in her arms to the clinic, she contracted the disease, and she died on March 10, 1897.

THE POLITICS OF (MIS)RECOGNITION

The question of recognition is fraught with complexities and multilayered. First, it raises the issue of recognition by whom. Savitribai Phule was well recognized in Maharashtra in her time and even later. In her lifetime, she was well known by social reformers and members of her own local and regional communities. Second, is the issue of recognition for what. Many who received help in Savitribai's various organizations and were educated in her schools saw her as a social reformer and an inspiration. Many whom she challenged saw her as a threat and harassed her. Savitribai faced ostracism from her own community, including her father, as we noted earlier. In fact, she would so often be pelted by stones and other debris that she took to carrying a change of clothes with her. Finally, there is the issue of her legacy. How is she remembered today and where is she remembered?

It is important to recognize Savitribai's theoretical contribution in relation to its praxis. Yet, like radical women's work everywhere, her contributions have been sanitized as reform rather than theoretical intervention in the understanding of the caste system. In independent India, Savitribai is known predominantly as a social reformer, primarily in relation to Jyotirao. The dual politics of caste and gender led to her invisibility, because "upper"-caste men designed the pedagogies in both colonial and independent India. More recently, since the resurgence of the Dalit movements in Maharashtra, first in the late 1960s and then again in the 1990s, Savitribai's contributions in her own right, not just as the partner of Jyotirao, have gained prominence. For example, on March 10, 1998, the Indian Postal Service issued a stamp in her honor (India Post 2011). On August 9, 2014, Pune University was renamed Savitribai Phule Pune University. On January 3, 2017, the 186th anniversary of her birth, she even received a Google Doodle (Google 2017).

These cultural recognitions, however, are more tokenistic than actual inclusion of Savitribai's legacy in the theoretical understanding of gender and caste inequality in India. Often the separation between theory and praxis is contrived in ways that privilege "upper"-caste writing as theories above Dalit activism, although the latter certainly has no lack of theoretical merit. The projects of nationalism that shaped the pedagogies in postindependence

India did not eschew caste and gender disparities. Moreover, the postcolonial consciousness did not necessarily reject what Connell (2015) has called the pyramidal structure of theory, in which theory is produced in the Global North from data collected in the Global South. As a result, literature from the Global North and "upper"-caste subjects continued to be recognized as theoretical resources, while writing by Savitribai and her cohort never received much visibility.

It is important to acknowledge the symbiosis of theory and praxis in Savitribai's work. Hence, while one evaluates her as a reformer, her theoretical writing also provides insights into her thoughts and motivation. Unlike the canon of Brahminical male writers, Savitribai's theoretical work includes multiple genres such as poems, letters, and dialogues that challenged the narrative style of "upper"-caste men. Savitribai's writings were meant for Dalit subjects and women, whom she wanted to inspire and educate, and not merely for "upper"-caste scholars who secluded themselves in the ivory towers of caste and gender privilege.

For Savitribai, writing was a part of her activism that foreshadowed feminist and Dalit movements in India. The self-reflexivity in her writing also anticipates Anzaldúa's (1987) identification of writing as the oppressed subject's radical performance of the embodied self. Savitribai's verses were lucid and were influenced by eclectic sources from popular culture. "Her writings demonstrate the influence of folk songs, bhakti, poetry and the *shayari* form (ballad literature). Although she selected "traditional" forms, she consistently "propagated the modern values such as humanism, liberty, equality, brotherhood and rationalism through her writings" (Pandey 2019, 99). But, as Omvedt (2008) eloquently demonstrated, Dalit saints from the fifteenth century onward had sought Begumpura, a utopian place of caste and gender equality, before the arrival of "modern" values via colonization.

In nineteenth-century colonial India, Savitribai's projects aimed at educating and empowering women both socially and intellectually. At the same time, she challenged caste-based hierarchies and social oppression. By opening schools for women and working for Dalit Indians, Savitribai also challenged the hypocrisy of the colonial government that educated Indians to facilitate its administration and not for their own empowerment. Savitribai's projects, therefore, were multidimensional. Pandey (2019) finds that the versatility of Savitribai's education projects for women made her a pioneer feminist in India. In her, Pandey sees the confluence of all three waves of feminism:

> Savitribai's feminism shows shades of first wave of feminism when she talked about ability to reason, self-reliance and public schools. Her feminism showed traces of second wave of feminism when she talked about shelter houses and inter-caste marriages. Her feminism showed some characteristics of the

third-wave feminism also when she talked about treating women with a diverse set of identities and taking *Stree*—Shudra—Atishudra together. (2019, 103)

Pandey also compares her to Mary Wollstonecraft, as both discussed women's ability to reason and the public-school system.

Savitribai's work can also be compared to Jane Addams's work at Hull-House in Chicago. Both worked for the inclusivity and empowerment of women who faced gender-based oppression. Addams's projects, too, challenged the social injustice around race and class. She worked extensively for the well-being of immigrants and working-class families while educating and empowering the women she gave shelter to at Hull-House. Like Savitribai's versatile pedagogy, rooted in praxis, Addams also offered drama classes, music societies, nutrition courses, and skill development opportunities to immigrant workers. Similarly, like Savitribai's sanctuary for widows and destitute women, Addams's Hull-House would also ensure the safety of mothers and their children, as it had day nurseries and clinics. Like Savitribai's institutions, Hull-House became a participatory community center, as it also encouraged its students to present their work at the Hull-House Labor Museum. While industrial exploitation aggravated workers' alienation, "the Hull-House Labor Museum highlighted the skills and talents that immigrants brought from their countries of origin—skills that were otherwise undervalued within Chicago's urban industrial landscape. Addams worked to extend the promise of democracy, and its attendant social, cultural, and economic rights, to all people" (Lee and Lopez 2014, 167).

Like Savitribai, Addams is predominantly noted as an activist, given the patriarchal and elite barriers toward recognizing women as theorists in the nineteenth century. Mentioning how critics always downplayed Addams's achievements as a thinker, Elshtain sees Addams as a "social theorist of underrated power and vitality" (1988, 257). Even her activism is often reductively viewed as "charitable impulses" of a "chaste and maternal" American woman (Elshtain 1988, 257–58). Similarly, popular discourses have woven folkloric narratives about Savitribai as a reformer, but they often tend to reduce her to a stereotypical maternal Indian woman and a teacher, obscuring her theoretical consciousness and contributions that enriched her praxis.

Elshtain (1988) finds that the diverse activities of Hull-House were driven by the theoretical awareness of social heterogeneity, cultural diversity of immigrants, and the need to study diverse social groups using different methods. As an "experiment," Hull-House

was never intended primarily as a charitable institution, nor as a possible solution to the assorted evils of uncontrolled industrialization. Addams' 'subjective necessity' compelled the genesis of Hull-House and precluded any simple account of its purposes or her own. Hull-House aims explicitly to meet the needs of Addams and others like her to put their beliefs into practice, to lead lives of action. (Elshtain 1988, 264)

The women educated at Hull-House were able to write about their understanding of women's empowerment and experience of oppression, much like Savitribai's students. These were voices of insiders, who themselves were victims of discrimination and ostracism, unlike the writing of male reformers, who paternalistically observed the plight of women from their privileged positions. Robbins sees *"writing,* broadly conceived, and supported by shared civic engagement, as the main Archive of the settlement's learning legacy and a means to extend its teachings into social action today" (2017, 81). Collaborative writing practices and various styles of storytelling were dominant among Hull-House residents.

Savitribai's pedagogy similarly involved a keen emphasis on writing and the formation of community. It created subjects, embedded in the community of empowered individuals, who would articulate their feminist and caste experiences, without borrowing from the hegemonic narrative styles of Brahminical patriarchy. They would question the erasure and the censure of caste- and gender-based experiences. Savitribai and her protégés like Muktabai Salve and Tarabai Shinde wrote little, and most of that remained in obscurity. Yet, their compelling candor and polemical edge show new ways of looking at caste and gender problems in colonial India beyond a nationalist framework.

In 1854, when Savitribai was only twenty-three years old, she published *Kavya Phule*—a collection of her reflective poems and short pieces of dialogues. This was before Jyotirao published his first creative work. In 1892, Savitribai published the second collection of poems, *Bavankashi Subodh Ratnakar*—her poetic biography of Jyotirao. In this work, Savitribai writes the history of the slavery and liberation of Dalits and women, in verse form. The use of verse in pedagogy and historiography itself was a theoretical intervention in challenging the esoteric style of Brahminical scholarship. Other than this, Savitribai also wrote several letters to Jyotirao in which she describes the depravity of Brahmins and the plight of women and Dalits and narrates how she would intervene and save the oppressed people from exploitation.

In *Kavya Phule* (1854), Savitribai identifies colonial rule not merely as a problem in India. Challenging the dominant nationalist imagination, Savitribai contends that the colonial education system was an opportunity for the Dalits to break the barriers of casteism. In a poem titled "Mother English," she writes that the English language "lovingly grants the 'shudras' a chance to live." It grants "human dignity" to the 'Shudras,' and

Feeds the "shudras" the milk of human kindness
Nurtures them and gives them confidence
Mother English ends their beastly existence (84)

Savitribai, however, does not uncritically extol colonial rule. Rather, she means only to embrace the opportunity for education that English provided. She declares:

India belongs to none
Iranis, Europeans, Tartars or the Huns
The blood of the natives flows in its veins ("Mother English" 1, 83)

Savitribai's writing in her anthology *Kavya Phule* has both literary and social merit. Her brief verses are clearly aimed at raising awareness about caste and gender identities and unmasking the hypocrisy of Brahminical rituals. She writes on a range of issues—on marriage, agriculture, casteism, and education. Some of her poems also depict the natural beauty of Indian villages, especially her birthplace, Naigaon. Savitribai often uses the dialogic form as an effective and affective method of public engagement and learning. Her rhetoric is exhortative, as she motivates Dalit subjects to pursue education and realize their self-worth. As she asserts in the poem "Golden Chance," without education human life is a "waste" and is comparable to "animal existence." She recognizes that for Dalit learners, colonial education brings an opportunity to stand up to caste discrimination. The learning of English is considered a "golden chance" as

The outcasts can wipe away their woes if they wish . . .
Learn English and do away with caste discrimination
Cast away the tiresome tales of the Brahmins to damnation. ("Golden Chance," 81)

Savitribai also composed verses to be sung by her students, who would be divided into groups—a practice that would build a collective experience of articulation and participation in the classroom. One such poem, titled "Group Discussion," in *Kavya Phule* is meant to be recited by five groups of girls. Among themselves they discuss women's role in the family—whether they should perform household chores, play games, or pursue education. The poem shows how the participants would be seeking their mother's opinion when deciding on their ideal choice. This is an important intervention, considering women's usual status of subjugation in nineteenth-century Indian families.

A significant outcome of Savitribai's pedagogical tradition focused on self-expression was Muktabai Salve's essay, "Mang Maharanchya

Dukhavisatha" (About the Grief of the Mangs and Mahars). In 1855, Muktabai was only fourteen (eleven, according to some sources) when she penned this scathing critique of caste and gender discrimination (Javalgekar 2017). In the same year, Jyotirao's *Tritiya Ratna* was published. Muktabai was among the first eight students in Savitribai's school. Her essay was published in the Marathi journal, *Dnyanodaya* (pronounced "gyanodaya"— meaning rising knowledge) in two parts, on February 15 and March 1, 1855. Being a member of the Mang community, one of the oppressed castes in Maharashtra, Muktabai witnessed the ugliness of caste-based discrimination from a very young age. Her piece is a vivid account of the society she lived in, with historical insights into the condition of the Mangs and the Mahars during the infamous Peshwa rule. By juxtaposing retrospective and contemporary accounts, Muktabai suggests that the Mangs and the Mahars faced discrimination and humiliation for decades.

It is a small essay, but it is replete with profound narratives and reflections. The depictions are deceptively simple, similar to Savitribai's verses, while her observations are actually multidimensional. Muktabai is conscious of how the intersections of caste and class determine the power dynamics in society. She succinctly notes: "Nobody gives us employment because we are Untouchables. No job means no money. We have to endure grinding poverty" (Salve 1855). In the same strain, she reprimands the "upper"-caste reformers for their platitudes, apathy and hypocrisy, and also highlights Dalit women's plight during childbirth.

As a student trained by Savitribai, Muktabai is deeply conscious of the importance of education in the empowerment of oppressed communities. She vehemently criticizes the Brahmins' design to deprive the Mangs and the Mahars of education: "When any Mang or Mahar would learn somehow to read and write, and if Bajirao came to know about this, he would say: education of a Mang or Mahar amounts to taking away a Brahman's job" (Muktabai 2020). Muktabai also observes how the Brahmins monopolized Vedic education as their exclusive property to keep Dalit communities from knowing that the ancient scriptures do not necessarily endorse their malpractices.

Muktabai's piece suggests how actively Savitribai nurtured her students' independent thoughts and expressions. The incandescent spirit and poignancy in Muktabai's writing express that Savitribai the educator had successfully instilled in her students a keen awareness of caste- and gender-based oppression. These reflections, coming from Dalit subjects, rooted in their lived experiences, can be compared to feminist testimonios (Rege 2006). Testimonios not only highlight the agency of individual subjects, embedded in everyday encounters; but also, as an inclusive form, emphasize the collective identity of these individuals within structures of inequality (Gunderson 2010). Together, the dual aspects of testimonios present a consistent yet pluralistic narrative of the oppressed castes and classes. The focus on lived experiences in testimonios lends legitimacy to the voices and narratives that dominant theories and histories tend to exclude.

The recession of these women into invisibility and silence within hegemonic canons, both epistemologically and ontologically, are referred to by Ferrari as "the coloniality of silence" (2019, 3). This represents "operations of power that eviscerate deep silences of their depth and complexity, flattening them to a transparent, mono-dimensional phenomenon indexing ontological absence" (Ferrari 2019, 3). She adds that "the specific historical formation of coloniality relies upon and actively promotes the flattening of deep silence for its perpetration and legitimization—an operation of flattening that is actively concealed through the naturalization of epistemic and ontological inferiority" (2019, 3).

Paik (2014) finds similarities between the 1851 narratives of Sojourner Truth and those of Muktabai Salve (1855), as both raised their voices against gender-based inequality and experiences of caste- and race-based humiliation. Dalits and African Americans have faced similar histories of oppression in terms of the politics of collective identification (from "shudras" and "untouchables" to Dalits, and from Negroes to Blacks to African Americans), negative stereotypes, and demeaning categorizations. Dalit leaders like Jyotirao Phule and Ambedkar also identified the similarities between the plight of Dalits and the slavery of African Americans. Correspondence between Ambedkar and W. E. B. Du Bois in 1946 shows their mutual awareness of casteism in India and racism in the United States. The Dalit Panther Party formed in India in 1972 was modeled on the Black Panther Party. The Dalit Freedom Network has also raised the issue of untouchability in India in the US Congress in recent times.

However, as Paik (2014) notes, most of these initiatives were led by men, and there has not been any distinct effort to form alliances between Dalit and African American women. She also points out the similarities between Black and Dalit women's intersectional writing as a "bridge" connecting these two groups. Collins and Bilge (2016), too, identify how Savitribai's contributions can be studied through the lens of intersectionality. Paik (2014) observes that both groups of women looked upon education as an opportunity for empowerment, which was constantly denied to them. These women also faced gender-based oppression within their own communities. For instance, Dalit men's assertion of rights and social status consolidated patriarchal structures, and the control of women was associated with respectability and dignity for the community as a whole. This created a "fragmented self-identity" (Paik 2014, 86) for Dalit women as they were entrusted with the role of uplifting their race/caste following patriarchal models of respectability.

Paik further points out that, in the twentieth century many middle-class Dalit women were forced to "brahmanize" just as African American women were forced to follow rigid behavioral norms that would "whiten" their cultural practices, body, dress, language and even eating habits (2014, 86). Both groups of women were identified as promiscuous and as sexually available to men of all communities, including their own. Thus, they have been "*doubly exploited*" as women and as members of their communities (Paik 2014, 89).

As a female activist, and an unrecognized theorist in colonial India, who resisted gender and caste hegemonies, Savitribai embodied a spirit of inclusivity, as seen in her "endeavours to foster female consciousness and expression of solidarity and community consciousness" (Anagol-McGinn 1994, 8). This radical inclusivity, however, resulted in her exclusion from the nationalist discourses dominated by the Brahminical patriarchy. In contemporary scholarship, Addams has received some recognition for both her activism and theoretical contribution. Yet, in Global North academia, and even in India, Savitribai as a feminist theorist has remained invisible. Incidentally, Hull-House was established in 1889, while Savitribai and Jyotirao started the first school for women in 1841. Echoing the concerns of Third World feminism (Mohanty 2003) and Transnational feminism (Grewal and Kaplan 1994), Anagol-McGinn explains that

> Eurocentric bias has also affected the charting of protest and self-assertion movements in Afro-Asian women's history. This has been compounded by the lack of an alternative approach to define the experiences unique to women in colonial societies. The use of Western models to explain the Indian woman's situation has resulted in a great hesitancy among sympathetic Indianists to describe even the most radical women as 'feminists' (1994, 3).

SAVITRIBAI'S RELEVANCE TO CONTEMPORARY SOCIETY AND THEORY

Savitribai's contributions take on a particular and poignant significance in the context of the global pandemic and the Black Lives Matter and Dalit Lives Matter protests. India and the United States are both gripped by dual crises: the contemporary global COVID-19 pandemic and the centuries-old Brahminical oppression in India and anti-Black racism in the United States. The global pandemic in both countries has revealed that the virus thrives where the public health care system is threadbare and barely accessible to marginalized Indigenous, Black, and Brown communities in the United States, and Dalits, Bahujans, and poor migrants in India. Women in all these communities are particularly vulnerable as gender divisions of labor and gender-segregated job markets have meant that they are more likely to be employed in low-paid jobs without health benefits. These jobs are also deemed "essential" in the context of COVID-19, raising the question of essential for whom and at what costs to the workers, making them more vulnerable to infection and lack of timely and appropriate care.

In this context, understanding how gender, race, class, and caste intersect to make Indigenous, Black, Brown, Dalits, and Bahujans not only vulnerable but ultimately dispensable, urgently needs the insights of thinkers like Savitribai, who very clearly articulated how the intersections of these social inequalities made all Dalits, and even non-Dalit women, vulnerable to social and even physical death. Savitribai's own tragic death while providing care for the vulnerable during the bubonic plague, demonstrates all too powerfully not just the significance of her work but the necessity of that work for the survival of BIPOC in the United States and Dalits and Bahujans in India, as well as in other parts of the world.

Similarly, Savitribai's focus on Satyashodhak or Truth Seeking, is necessary to our survival as a species, as truth has become a casualty of reactionary politicians all around the world. In the name of economic growth, they enable the greed of corporate capital that brooks no limits to its extractive power to dispossess primarily marginalized communities everywhere, and places a special burden on women's social reproductive labors, not to mention making many parts of the earth inhospitable to life, as climate change refugees demonstrate daily.

Finally, Savitribai's theoretical and pedagogical contributions are key to furthering the contemporary decolonial turn in social theory, which seeks to challenge the epistemic violence that has erased and silenced the knowledges of marginalized communities everywhere, and selectively validated as theory only her writings of elites in the Global North and those from the South who mimic such theorizing. By emphasizing a variety of forms of writings that come from the lived realities of marginalized women and men, encouraging dialogue and deliberation across class, caste, religious, and other backgrounds, Savitribai was part of a radical tradition in social theory that in India dates to the Middle Ages and in the Global North to abolitionists like Sojourner Truth, Harriet Tubman, and Frederick Douglass among others. It is by recognizing such radical theorists everywhere and through a "solidarity-based epistemology" (Connell 2015, 59) that we can ensure an egalitarian society and theory that support the flourishing of all life on earth, rather than perpetuating millennia of systemic oppression.

REFERENCES

Anagol-McGinn, Padma. 1994. "Women's Consciousness and Assertion in Colonial India: Gender, Social Reform and Politics in Maharashtra, c.1870–c.1920." (PhD dissertation). London: School of Oriental and African Studies, University of London.

Anzaldúa, Gloria. 1987. *Borderland/La Frontera: The New Mestiza*. San Francisco: Aunt Lute Books.

Begari, Jagannatham. 2010. "Jyotirao Phule: A Revolutionary Social Reformer." *The Indian Journal of Political Science* 71 (2): 399–412.

Bhadru, G. 2002. "Contributions of Shatyashodhak Samaj to the Low Caste Protest Movement in 19th Century." *Proceedings of the Indian History Congress* 63: 845–54.

Bhadwal, Shelly Parul. 2017. "Words as Weapon: Tarabai Shinde's *Stri Purush Tulana* and Gender Politics in Nineteenth Century India." *Criterion* 8 (3): 165–80.

Chakravarti, Uma. 2005. "Reconceptualizing Gender: Phule, Brahminism and Brahminical Patriarchy." In *Gender and Caste*, edited by Anupama Rao, 164–79. London: Zed Books.

Chatterjee, Kalyan Kumar. 1975. "The Renaissance Analogy and English Education in Nineteenth Century India." *The Journal of General Education* 26 (4): 309–19.

Chatterjee, Partha. 1997. "The Nation and its Women." In *A Subaltern Studies Reader 1986–1995*, edited by Ranajit Guha, 240–62. New Delhi: Oxford University Press.

Collins, Patricia Hill, and Sirma Bilge. 2016. *Intersectionality*. Cambridge, UK: Polity.

Connell, Raewyn. 2015. "Meeting at the Edge of Fear: Theory on a World Scale." *Feminist Theory* 16 (1): 49–66.

Elshtain, Jean Bethke. 1988. "A Return to Hull-House: Reflections on Jane Addams." *Cross Currents* 38 (3): 257–67.

Ferrari, Martina. 2019. "Questions of Silence: On the Emancipatory Limits of Voice and the Coloniality of Silence." *Hypatia* 35 (1): 1–20.

Google. 2017. "Savitribai Phule's 186th Birthday." https://www.google.com/doodles/savitribai-phules-186th-birthday.

Grewal, Inderpal, and Caren Kaplan. 1994. "Introduction: Transnational Feminist Practices and Questions of Postmodernity." In *Scattered Hegemonies: Postmodernity and Transnational Feminist Practices*, edited by Inderpal Grewal and Caren Kaplan, 1–33. Minneapolis: University of Minnesota Press.

Guha, Ramachandra. 2010. "The Agrarian Radical: Jotirao Phule." In *Makers of Modern India*, edited by Ramachandra Guha, 75–78. New Delhi: Penguin.

India Post. 2011. "Commemorative Stamps 1947–2011." https://www.indiapost.gov.in/VAS/Pages/News/Indian_Postage_Stamp_Catalogue_1947-2011.pdf

Javalgekar, Aishwarya. 2017. "Mukta Salve: The First Female Dalit Writer." *Feminism in India*, March 20. Accessed June 20, 2020. https://feminisminindia.com/2017/03/20/mukta-salve-essay/.

Kandukuri, Divya. 2019. "The Life and Times of Savitribai Phule." *Live Mint*, January 12. Accessed June 12, 2020. https://www.livemint.com/Leisure/DmR1fQSnVD62p4D3eyq9mO/The-life-and-times-of-Savitribai-Phule.html.

Lee, Lisa, and Lisa Junkin Lopez. 2014. "Participating in History: The Museum as a Site for Radical Empathy, Hull-House." In *Jane Addams in the Classroom*, edited by David Schaafsma, 162–78. Urbana: University of Illinois Press.

Mohanty, Chandra Talpade. 2003. *Feminism without Borders: Decolonizing Theory, Practicing Solidarity.* Durham, NC: Duke University Press.

Omvedt, Gail. 2008. *Seeking Begumpura: The Social Vision of Anticaste Intellectuals.* New Delhi: Navayana Publisher.

Paik, Shailaja. 2014. "Building Bridges: Articulating Dalit and African American Women's Solidarity." *Women's Studies Quarterly* 42 (3/4): 74–96.

Pandey, Renu. 2019. "Locating Savitribai Phule's Feminism in the Trajectory of Global Feminist Thought." *Indian Historical Review* 46 (1): 86–105.

Phule, Savitribai. 1854 (2012). *Kavya Phule (Poetic Blossoms).* Translated by Ujjwala Mhatre, edited by Lalitha Dhara. Women Development Cell, Dr. Ambedkar College Unit.

Rege, Sharmila. 2006. *Writing Caste/Writing Gender: Reading Dalit Women's Testimonios.* New Delhi: Zubaan.

———. 2010. "Education as 'Trutiya Ratna': Towards Phule-Ambedkarite Feminist Pegagogical Practice." *Economic and Political Weekly* 45 (44/45): 88–98.

Reeta, and Vinit Raj. 2016. *First Indian Women Teacher: Savitribai Phule (Biography of Savitribai Phule).* New Delhi: Educreation Publishing.

Robbins, Sarah Ruffing. 2017. "Collaborative Writing as Jane Addams's Hull-House Legacy." In *Learning Legacies: Archive to Action through Women's Cross-Cultural Teaching*, edited Sarah Ruffing Robbins, 79–134. Ann Arbor: University of Michigan Press.

Salve, Muktabai. 1855 (2020). The Grief of the Mangs and the Mahars. Translated by Braj Raj Mani. *Forward Press*, February 15. Accessed June 14, 2020. https://www.forwardpress.in/2020/02/165-years-ago-first-female-Dalit-writer-wrote-about-the-grief-of-the-mangs-and-the-mahars/.

Viswanathan, Gauri. 1989. *Masks of Conquest: Literary Study and British Rule in India.* New York: Columbia University Press.

NOTES

1. In Marathi, "Krantijyoti" means the light of revolution and "Gyanjyoti" means the light of knowledge.

2. Rather than accept the caste hierarchy as given, to indicate that this hierarchy was put in place by Brahmin men, who deemed some castes as upper or lower, we use quotes around such designations to reject those constructions and use the term Dalit to refer to all those deemed "lower" or "untouchable" by the Brahminical system.

3. Although Jyotirao Phule is popularly known to be the first to use the word "Dalit," Rege (2006) credits Ambedkar with coining the term in his writing and *Bahishkrut Bharat* in 1928.

Chapter 9

Vijay Prashad

A Biographical and Theoretical Sketch

Moushumi Roy, Tirth Bhatta, and Moushumi Biswas

INTRODUCTION AND BIOGRAPHY

Marxist thinker, historian, academic, and journalist Vijay Prashad drew media attention in 1998 when he called Mother Teresa an emblem of the "bourgeois guilt" of Western nations (Najmi and Srikanth 2002). Born in Kolkata, India, on August 14, 1967, Prashad is a notable figure among scholars of—and subscribers to—the Communist movement, both in the East and the West. He continues to believe that socialism can transform society by eliminating the superstructure-substructure stratifications. Towards that end, he offers an alternative explanation for the concept of "Third World," which he says is a political project of the Cold War times and a utopian vision of anti-imperialists (Prashad 2007). In his writings in *The Poorer Nations* (2013), he describes protests against state-backed neoliberal practices of multinational corporations and his critique of the IMF. Fellow writer Amitava Kumar linked Prashad with Frantz Fanon, while historian Paul Buhle calls him "a literary phenomenon" (Bhule 2014).

Prashad's early education was from the Doon School in India, and he went on to earn a bachelor's degree from Pomona College in 1989 and a PhD from the University of Chicago in 1994. His academic career spans over two decades; he taught international studies at Trinity College, Connecticut, from 1996 until 2017. His views on international politics/relations were evident at a 2004 Life After Capitalism conference, where he stated that progressive ideas around the world did not make much of a dent due to a lack of organization on the part of their proponents. Specifically in the United States, he said leftists were not very successful because they were not open to ideas from other parts of the world.

Prashad became interested in Marxism at a young age when he was exposed to the political activism of his aunt, Brinda Karat. As the Communist movement in India celebrated its centenary in October 2020, Prashad coauthored an online article with Karat on the "ruthless abolition" of India's caste system (Prashad and Karat 2020). As a Communist, Prashad's political ideology opposes Israel's policies towards Palestine and calls for an end of U.S. aid to Israel. He is a member of the advisory board of the U.S. Campaign for the Academic and Cultural Boycott of Israel and a former Senior Fellow of the Issam Fares Institute for Public Policy and International Affairs in Beirut. Because of his leadership towards this goal, he was the Edward Said Chair at the American University of Beirut from 2013 until 2014.

As is popularly known, communism cannot coexist with religion, and Prashad's views of embodied religion, such as that of Mother Teresa, originate from Marx's claim that "religion is opium of the people" (Raines 2002, 171). Prashad explained that his purpose behind criticizing Mother Teresa was to show that "her work was part of the global enterprise of imperialism in a practical political as well as in an ideological sense" (Prashad 1998). As a Marxist, Prashad believed it was important to discuss Mother Teresa's "function as mechanism for the alleviation of bourgeois guilt from poverty and suffering rather than a genuine challenge to those very forces that create, produce and maintain that poverty and suffering" (Prashad 1997, 2856). According to Prashad, the Communist movement's approach toward helping the poor is fundamentally different from Mother Teresa's path. The former engaged with "the roots of poverty" rather than providing merely symptomatic relief. Comparing Mother Teresa's charitable activities with that of the Communists, Prashad wrote that the party "does not hand out charity for the few but takes very seriously the task of the devolution of power—democracy—towards the working masses" (Prashad 1997, 2856). He also noted how Pope John Paul II joined Mother Teresa in describing the Bhopal (a city in central India) incident (a poisonous gas leak at the Union Carbide pesticide factory) as a "sad event," resulting from "man's efforts to make progress" (Prashad 1997, 2858). This leak originally affected over 500,000 people, and its after-effects continue to haunt the city. To Prashad, this was a well-orchestrated and "terrifying" attempt to step away from a crime caused by corporate greed. Furthermore, in line with the Communist movement's stand against the "NGO phenomenon," Prashad commented that Mother Teresa, like other "non-political" service organizations that depend on private/non-state funds for sustenance, compromised "her principles for her benefactors" (Prashad 1997, 2857).

Prashad is cofounder of the Forum of Indian Leftists (FOIL) and part of the worldwide Boycott, Divestment and Sanctions movement. He is also a former George and Martha Kellner Chair of South Asian History and Director of International Studies at Trinity College in Hartford, Connecticut, and has thirty books to his credit (as of 2020) where he focuses on nations of color and "their struggle for justice" (Prashad 2007, 60). Prashad provides narratives about "the economic exploitation and cultural suppression" of these so-called darker nations—accounts that are different from the official history and postulations of mainstream media. His work contains insights into media accounts that come from his firsthand experiences as a journalist. He is chief correspondent for the *Globetrotter* (a project of the Independent Media Institute), a columnist for *Frontline*, and contributor to *The Hindu* and *BirGun*.

In 2015, Prashad joined the New Delhi–based LeftWord Books as chief editor, publishing two of his own books with them (*No Free Left: The Futures of Indian Communism* 2015a; and *Washington Bullets* 2020a). A prolific writer, he produced five books between 2012 and 2014, including *Arab Spring, Libyan Winter* and *Uncle Swami: South Asians in America Today.* His 2007 book, *The Darker Nations: A People's History of the Third World*, was selected as the best nonfiction book by the Asian American Writer's Workshop in 2008 and, in 2009, it won the Muzaffar Ahmed Book Award. Verso published his 2013 book, *The Poorer Nations: A Possible History of the Global South*, and a collection he edited, *Letters to Palestine* (2015b). This collection contains writings by Teju Cole, Sinan Antoon, Noura Erakat, and Junot Díaz.

While his multifaceted career includes stints both in journalism and the academy, sometimes concurrently, Prashad's work has always been founded on the principles of Marxism. His views on capitalism are encapsulated in *Fat Cats and Running Dogs: The Enron Stage of Capitalism* (2002), which comes with illustrations. In this book, Prashad criticizes the US-based multinational company, Enron, which set an example in making money from merely trading, without actually producing anything. According to Prashad, such neoliberal capitalist phenomena go hand in hand with government policies that are crafted to control the economy and resources that rightfully belong to the masses. His website, thetricontinental.org, features scathing commentaries on US foreign policy and the effects of what he calls "American hegemony and imperialism." He also analyzes global news in light of the people's struggles against capitalist forces. His post, dated June 17, 2021, refers to farmers' protest in India against three agriculture-related laws passed by the Bharatiya Janata Party government in September 2020. These laws, according to him, "delivered Indian agriculture to a handful of mega-corporate houses" (Prashad 2021b). Seen through the eco-critical discourse analysis lens, Prashad's critiques explain how governments use the "megarhetorics of development" (Scott and Dingo 2012) to facilitate global trade agreements, which ultimately help corporations.

THEORETICAL CORE OF PRASHAD'S
LITERARY WRITINGS

Prashad, as a Marxist historian, provides critical insights into the ways power preponderant nation-states, motivated by vested material interests, continue to intervene and crush nations that attempt to build their own destiny. Whenever a developing nation has refused to succumb to Western hegemony, it has been subjected to severe sanctions by the West. Prashad exemplifies a deep commitment to an increasingly rare form of scholarship that is both radical and transformative. He has not only sought to reveal material drivers of militarism, war, exploitation, oppression, poverty, and inequality, but also has worked in solidarity with social and political movements to strive for a more just and humane world. Similar to W. E. B. Du Bois's ideas, masterfully elaborated in "The African Roots of War" (1915), Prashad's academic pursuits have exposed the aggressive tendencies of the imperialist forces, using extreme forms of violence, including wars, to expand their capitalist interests. As Du Bois said, "How can love of humanity appeal as a motive to nations whose love of luxury is built on the inhuman exploitation of human beings, and who, especially in recent years, have been taught to regard these human beings as inhuman?" (1915, 25).

Prashad's scholarship also has attempted to counter hegemonic cultural ideologies developed by colonizers in order to legitimate the subjugation and exploitation of people in the Global South. For example, his insights on the current COVID-19 pandemic critically reflect on the long arm of imperialism. He states that the so-called "Spanish flu" actually originated in a military camp in Kansas and was later brought to British India by American soldiers. India suffered 60 percent of the casualties, yet the U.S. government never offered to help pay to recover the costs. Similarly, in 1832, a cholera outbreak started in Britain and moved from there to the other parts of Europe, yet it was labeled as "the Asiatic cholera" (Prashad 2020c).

The organization of this theoretical section begins with addressing the dynamics of historical and contemporary approaches to power struggles. The later sections underscore the formation of neoliberalism, neocolonialism, and collective agency leading to social movement and change.

Historical Accounts of Power Struggles

Prashad's theoretical approach explicates historical and contemporary forms of conflict across social, political, and economic realms. His core theoretical works attempt to ground Marxist philosophy that broadly divides feudal, industrial, modern, and postmodern societies from within, in terms of class as Bourgeoisie and Proletariat. Across time and space, this division highlights a continuum of conflict, shedding light on the histories (time) of the countries (space) of the Global South that were subjugated by old empires such as the British, French, and Portuguese. The Global South includes the people, ideologies and actions of Asian, African, Latin American, Middle Eastern, and other nations, significantly concerned with human rights issues. Prashad's Marxist approach explicates the structural mechanisms that underlie contemporary Western imperialism. In *The Poorer Nations* (2013) he defines imperialism as a behavioral process that maximizes the theft of resources, labor, and wealth. Additionally, this work attempts to understand the social history of the demise of the *Third World* project.

Prashad's theoretical stance includes multiple dimensions. Ideological hegemony is one such dimension, vested in power that is dynamic and accumulative in nature across time among Western nations: imperialism has turned into neo-imperialism and old colonies are experiencing neocolonial forms of dehumanization. Other dimensions contained in Prashad's writing include ideology, time, and space. For instance, Prashad says that during the feudal system the idea of hegemony emerged from an ideological standpoint, claiming that the ruler was the self-defined bearer of supernatural powers. For instance, using historical evidence, Prashad notes that at the end of the sixteenth century, under conscious ruling in Delhi, the Mughal Emperor Akbar began to have doubts about the idea of "divine rights" possessed by the empire. Henceforth, he announced that the idea of sovereignty needed to be brought onto the monarch to rule the people, surpassing autocratic God-given rights. In contrast, a generation later, Louis XIV of France said, "the state is Me" (Prashad 2020, 23). This conception of power did not end with the monarchy in the Western epiphany; more overt moments of power were manifested following technological development, but in different structural forms. One worth noting is when the United States dropped atomic bombs containing sixty-four kilograms of uranium-235 on Japan.

The Power Struggle during the Postcolonial Period

The postcolonial period witnessed the imposition of power across the globe by the United States and its allies, although the colonization process was covert in this period. Following the dissolution of the Soviet Union, the

United States rose to become the sole hegemonic, global power. Furthermore, neoliberal policies and the development of new technologies increased power among the Washington bureaucrats. An even further appetite for power has created a tendency among US policy makers to resist settling for anything less than all they want to serve their vested interests. This attitude steered international policy in the post–World War II period as the colonial masters claimed to be looking for ways to spread the message of peace and civilization. They swamped the world with their messages of peacemaking. The motive behind this decision to bring peace to the colonies was to show that the imperialists were selflessly promoting peace and civilization around the world. Prashad's scholarship upends these attempts by exposing massacres such as the Jallianwala Bagh and the Nicaraguan federal unity, and the brutal seizure of land in Africa, carried out to suppress the people's aspirations. These oppressive practices were carried out to serve the needs of Europe and the United States through legal manipulations to conceal their effort to loot and exploit the people of the Global South across Asia, Africa, and Latin America. Rapid globalization and unequal transnational relations between the United States, its core allies, and the peripheral countries facilitated resource exploitation of the historical colonies without providing social programs to their people who needed them.

Imposing military incursions and supporting internal military sources in targeted countries are just a few examples of how the imperialist countries maintain their hegemony. These operations obliterate any chance of political leaders in Asia, Africa, and Latin America to successfully implement reforms aimed at elevating their citizens' human dignity and providing for their basic survival needs. For example, the CIA's participation in the 1954 coup d'etat against the democratically elected president of Guatemala, Jacobo Arbenz Guzman, was a result of his opposition to the United Fruit Company. Similarly, when Chile's leadership refused to bow to American economic interests, the American government poured millions of dollars into the country to finance a successful coup against their president, Salvador Allende. In Prashad's work, these coups are regarded as a visible weapon of terrorism that annihilates the united communist front. Prashad cites numerous other examples of similar coups in various countries in the Global South whenever United States interests were endangered, including Bangladesh (1975), Chad (1975, 1978), Pakistan (1977), Iraq (1978), South Korea (1979), and Turkey (1980).

Prashad (2007) introduces *Third World* as a "project," which promoted collective consciousness and agency against an array of conflicts. It was a continuous struggle to build this project by Third World peoples since colonial times. Gradually, this carried into the post-colonial period. He states that the *Third World* project was undertaken by organized reformers and leaders alike to end the cycle of deconstructed identity fostered in the colonial period. Emerging among the oppressed and subjugated people in nations under Western colonial rule, the *Third World* project was deliberately multidimensional in its historical struggle to resist the tyranny of Western imperialism. This multidimensionality was defined by the interaction of multiple social forces across time and space, including ideology, race, ethnicity, and class. When the upsurge of demands began among oppressed and subjugated peoples in nations colonized by the West, the Western powers reacted with state violence through military invasion, counterinsurgency, and support for military dictatorships in order to weaken and secure compliant regimes in the periphery or, as Prashad says: "powerlessness . . . [grew] out of the barrel of a gun" (2013, 162). Whenever the Third World states fought back against the tyranny of western attack, they paid a high price in terms of defense and lack of investment in their nations' social welfare.

As depicted in Prashad's 2013 book, *The Poorer Nations*, additional reasons for the demise of the *Third World* project were due to CIA-funded cultural projects designed to malign and ultimately call for its ending in the developing nations. Imperialist intellectuals and institutions attacked the ideas of economic and trade development that culminated in the 1974 UN Resolution on the New International Economic Order (NIEO). The Group of Seven (G7), formed in 1973, confronted the NIEO directly and sought to undermine the Third World bloc's political authority. By the early 1980s, it had been snuffed out as a result of the severe debt crisis and the political maneuvers aimed at destroying it.

The Rise of Neoliberalism and Neocolonial Power

In Prashad's view, the neoliberal or, more specifically, postcolonial period, similar to the colonial and imperial era, saw power dominated by capitalist owners. Prashad's views here are consistent with those of Marx. The particularization of Marxist conflict states that the source of conflict in a society is based on historical materialism, which determines the historical and social formation of social interactions. Marx viewed the relationship between the bourgeoisie and proletariat in terms of class struggle: the history of all hitherto existing society is the history of class struggle. Entrenched in the class struggle are the driving forces of social formations.

The neocolonial period is marked by the rapid development of technology over time, from imperialism to multinational capitalism. Prashad affirms that technology in any form of power cannot build the trust between people. Interactions in person have a greater chance of establishing trust than those conducted via networks or social media. Technology-as-means-of-production came to be owned by the growing superstructure of power elites, a theoretical understanding that Frankfurt School critical theorists would readily accept. On the other hand, their conceptualization of substructures encompasses the fluidity of social formations. This view is evident in Prashad's writing and the exception here is Habermas, who concurs with Marx's emancipatory theory and views flexibility within substructures as necessary for protagonists rising against fascism to achieve their self-defined destiny, depicted by the "accelerated historical formation of modernization" (Habermas 1979, 370). As a result, Prashad observes that, while trust strengthens relationships, it is also a critical tool for establishing social forums to challenge hegemony.

Prashad highlights the chilling historical and contemporary accounts of American participation in the destruction of everyone who refuses to subsidize the diabolical business dealings of multinational corporations. As illustrated in his 2020 book *Washington Bullets*, obstructing American capitalist interests, based on greed and exploitation by multinational corporations, means facing bullets or dynamite. These bullets can come in barbaric forms, e.g., embargoes imposed during the COVID-19 pandemic against more than fifty countries, especially targeting Cuba, Iran, and Venezuela. Nonetheless, Prashad notes: "No international body dare tell the United States what to do, even in a time of a global pandemic" (2020a, 146). Any revolutionary step against US power and authority will end up forcing the "use of law as a weapon of war" (Prashad 2020a, 146).

When Prashad discusses nation-states in his 2015 book *No Free Left in India: The Future of Indian Communism*, he sees pre-independence social, political, and communal ties transformed into a contemporary alliance with insidious Western imperialism in the firm clutches of neoliberal policies and the global capitalist market economy. In India, Prashad argues, neoliberalism has ceded political autocracy and economic market hegemony to the West by adopting neoliberal social and economic policies through the full integration of capital's neoliberal authoritarianism in the domain of political economy and state power. Prashad believes that the inauguration of non-Left parties brought apparent stability to bourgeois rule in India in exchange for a closer external alliance with imperialism and the imposition of a neoliberal order on the domestic front. The bourgeoisie in the form of new landlords, expelled the peasants from their land through an alliance with multinational corporations via the mechanization of power.

The products of neoliberal cultural transformation, such as malls, entertainment centers, even disenfranchisement, hold infinite power in their development. These aspects of cultural change were, however, claimed as the core of the Left, yet they demanded the transference of ownership from corporations to the public. Hostile experiences in the case of India, such as the displacement and loss of sustainability for local farmers, loss of freedom of speech and expression, and threats against cultural and religious differences resulted from this global capitalist trade order. In *No Free Left* (2015a), describing the effects of capitalist ownership of agriculture, Prashad points out that over half of 1.3 billion lives were plunged into deprivation. He further underscores the demise of people's freedom regarding speech, cultural, and religious practices.

Agency and the Power of the Collective to Bring Social Change

Prashad's 2017 book *Red Star over the Third World* and the *Third World* project equally highlight ways to strengthen liberation and the communist movement. In *Darker Nations* (2007) he employs a model of racial, ethnic, and class conflict to describe how Western nations accumulate power. He argues that the rhetorical use of racism and classism is implied in racist stereotypes, such as labeling the Chinese as an inferior race, along with other forms of racial subjugation against Chinese laborers, to maintain the West's power. Using this "othering" or "blaming" tactic, Chinese laborers were racialized to serve the self-fulfilling prophecy of Western dominance. This parallels the history of the great migration in the United States, when White flight occurred in the north to justify the claim that Blacks are inferior. To resist African Americans' assimilation, the route to blame was a significant validation of White privilege.

Throughout his oeuvre, Prashad describes how communism has demonstrated the ability to liberate democracy whenever Western imperialism led to its demise in the sovereign nations of the Global South. He believes in the universal emancipatory ideals of Marxism. He is, however, cautious about his views on regaining power by the colonies; one-dimensional bottom-up agency is insufficient. Differences here between Marx and Prashad can be noted in the latter's speech at Bard College on social justice. He asserts that the power of the Global South must be implemented both from the top and the bottom to contest the imperialist power of American hegemony. In other words, unlike Marx, for Prashad the proletariat must be liberated both above and below, that is, through both ideology and action.

The ideological differences between communism and capitalism since the Cold War continue unabated. More than ever, the boundaries of the conflict have widened across different socialist and capitalist nations. The postindependence nations who saw their future in terms of socialist ideologies have been brought to their knees by American power, as the inherent values of the communist manifesto differ radically from those of capitalist societies. Prashad concurs with Marx that the dominant class ideology serves its own interests, in contrast to those of the proletariat, whose agency and praxis are based on universal principles.

Prashad also idealizes speech theory as another step toward achieving social justice—amplifying a postmodern imagination of intellectualism. In his speech at a Bard College symposium on social justice, Prashad argues that language contains power. This is similar to Habermas's theory of the ideal speech situation (Bohman and Rehg 2017) in his *Communication and the Evolution of Society* (1979). Prashad insists that instead of saying "Vietnam War," which implies shifting the blame to Vietnam, we must use the phrase, "American war on Vietnam." The characteristics of speech socialization correlate with multiple agencies: the conscious mind, developing a collective agency and mobilizing resources for social movements to achieve social justice. He endorses communism to curtail the historically rooted power of the bourgeoisie that continues to exploit the people of the Global South. The collective, organized under the ideology of communism, advances a multifaceted struggle against pre– and post–World War II colonizers, such as the United States, the United Kingdom, France, Portugal, and the other Western powers.

Towards the end of the *Darker Nations* (2007), Prashad advocates combining imagination with praxis to envision a just society. He emphasizes the potential power of investing in communism to thwart the imperialist agenda, which is based on the development of neoliberal policies through the IMF and the World Bank, which greatly reduce the range of options available to the left for overcoming imperialism in the nations of the Global South.

In the later sections of *Red Star Over the Third World*, Prashad (2017) extols the Third World, including the former USSR, as spaces for advancing the Left's ideology and agenda to bring about socialist and Marxist revolution. However, communist and revolutionary formations are portrayed as complex. For example, the imperialists' role is seen as both functional and antagonistic in facilitating social movements and change on the part of the commune. He asserts Lenin's view that communism is more likely to be successful in the West than in the colonies because Western imperialism forces the establishment of communism. He also claims that the left movement did not fail, it achieved its success among Third World leaders, implying that the West was created by the East and not the other way around. By making this claim, Prashad is expressing hope for communist success in overturning the West's neocolonial agenda. The revolutionary movement's central agenda includes not only political liberation, but also the general ascension of humanity.

One way is to envision the rise of humanity is juxtaposed at the intersection of race, class, gender, space, and time institutionalized in communist reforms. Prashad sheds light on the meaning of space in Christopher Lee's (2019)

Making a World After Empire: The Bandung Moment and Political Afterlives.
Bandung's space is transformed into sentiments of imperial exigency in
"post" colonialism. In response, historical tenets have documented the voices
of Dalits, peasants, and the awakening of women taking to the streets during
British rule in Punjab, West Bengal, Andhra Pradesh, and Rajasthan. The
socialist movement's success here was demonstrated by the implementation
of numerous programs addressing human rights concerns.

In *No Free Left*, Prashad (2015) analyzes the case of the Indian republic
from 1947 to 1991, where the Left parties in power at the provincial level provided the significant land reform and agricultural worker tenancy programs,
enacted deep local self-government schemes, and provided a safe haven from
the toxic social agenda of politicized (Hindu) religion. Outside the government, the Left participated in a wide range of other struggles, for the rights of
workers and peasants, and for the defense of the good side of history against
the bad. Religion undermined the agency of communism because it taught its
followers to accept poverty with conviction in faith, as opposite to the Left's
agenda, which was to end poverty by transforming the social system. In *Red
Star over the Third World,* borrowing from Marx, Prashad notes that "the
commune declared an end to private property" (2017, 234). As the hegemony
of global financial capital continues, the bedrock of Left praxis lies in its
political formations, or mass organizations, including running the state's gov-
ernmental apparatus to bring about social justice and freedom for the people.

SIGNIFICANCE OF PRASHAD'S COLLECTED
WORKS IN CONTEMPORARY SOCIETIES

Prashad engages in a strand of scholarship that not only enhances our understanding of the social world, but also shows how to work in solidarity with
social and political movements to change that world. The latter is critically
important if we hope to marshal our collective resources to reverse the
impending catastrophe from ongoing climate change and ever increasing
massive social and economic inequalities. The richest 1 percent of the global
population have extracted more than double the income of the bottom half of
the population over the last forty years. Women, racial/ethnic minorities, and
lower caste groups have experienced a disproportionate impact of these neoliberal economic systems. For instance, men possess 50 percent more wealth
than women. Differences in wealth among intersecting social groups (e.g., of
race, gender, caste, and sexuality) are likely to intensify due to the COVID-19
pandemic (Berkhout et al. 2021; Lawson et al. 2019). As neoliberal economic
policies regarding public institutions (e.g., cuts to education and health care,

erosion of job security, stagnant wages) continue to erode human solidarity in favor of hyper-materialism, individualism, and consumerism, widespread unemployment, poverty, depression, anxiety, and loneliness have become the norm. The disillusionment with existing political and economic arrangements is also giving rise to support for neofascism. Theoretical frameworks that are oblivious to imperialist political and economic contexts and are not "rooted in the experiences of workers, peasants and the unemployed" (Prashad 2018) are inadequate for explicating the mechanisms that have led to devastating material consequences for a large segment of the population in the Global South,

Prashad's work also highlights the need for scholars to center the victims of imperialist neoliberal economic policies in their studies of the Global South. He offers much needed historical and contemporary context to understand various social problems such as poverty, unemployment, and inequality in the Global South. His works remind us that scholarship on poverty and inequality is inadequate without questioning the role of the "underlying structures of property and power" that form the foundational basis of unequal material conditions. Scholarship on the origins of those problems in the Global South requires consideration of the devastating impacts of neoliberal economic policies advanced by the imperial powers. The failure to do so inadvertently blames the victims of poverty and inequality in the countries of the Global South. For example, the sources of various forms of contemporary inequalities in countries such as Chile and Burkina Faso cannot be understood without considering the historical context of the assassinations of their political leaders who were trying to chart a destiny different from that of imperialism. Salvador Allende, who was democratically elected president of Chile in 1970, initiated the nationalization of large-scale industries (such as those of the American-owned copper mining corporations) and pursued reforms to raise the minimum wage, redistribute land and wealth, and increase access to education and health care. He was assassinated in a CIA-backed coup within three years, leading to the dictatorial rule of General Augusto Pinochet and, subsequently, the implementation of neoliberal economic policies. Similarly, Thomas Sankara, popularly known as Africa's Che Guevara, instituted major reforms, such as land redistribution and the advancement of education and health care in Burkina Faso. His ascendency to power in 1983 represented an attempt to assert political and economic sovereignty, and, thereby, to chart a destiny that deviated from the dominant neoliberal world order. During his four-year tenure as the president of Burkina Faso, he was able to increase school attendance from 6 percent to 22 percent. He built thousands of health centers and vaccinated 2.5 million children. However, he met a fate similar to Allende, and was assassinated in a coup supported by France, the UK, and the United States (Prashad 2020a; Smith 2015).

An attempt to chart a similar coup also took place in Bolivia when Evo Morales was elected president. He too enacted redistributive policies that entailed the nationalization of large industries (e.g., the hydrocarbon industry) and the distribution of 134 million acres of land to indigenous families. The funds accrued from the nationalization of large-scale industries were used to build almost 4,500 educational facilities since 2006. Other initiatives included nutrition programs, which reduced child malnourishment from 27 percent in 2009 to 16 percent, and child mortality by almost half during the same period (Falach 2020). Similarly, poverty declined from 60 percent in 2006 to 35 percent in 2017 (Balch 2019). The unemployment rate almost halved (from 7.7 to 4.4 percent) by 2008, which remained resilient even during the global financial crisis at that time (Arauz et al. 2019). Though he was in power longer than Allende and Sankara, his government was also overthrown in 2019 through a military coup generally supported by the Western countries.

Prashad's scholarship has been motivated by a belief that "the right ideas aren't enough" to transform the world. This has propelled him to Marxist ideology and to strive to transform ideas and discourses into social and political movements in support of a just and peaceful world. He considers these engagements as necessary for understanding the social world, arguing that we "can't know the world unless we are trying to change" it. He continues his movement-driven scholarship via the Tricontinental Institute for Social Research, which he directs. Tricontinental was named after the 1966 conference of the Non-Aligned Movement (NAM). According to Prashad, the goal of the conference was to offer space for conversations among nations that looked to chart an anti-imperialist and socialist path. The process of confronting imperialism entailed going beyond winning political power (i.e., the power to govern), to challenge the world system that allows a minority of countries to extract material and intellectual resources from everyone else. This involves the power of independent nations to imagine an alternative world system based on the political sovereignty to shape their own economy and culture. As a remarkable example of internationalism and international solidarity, Prashad has used his scholarship (such as his 2020a book, *Washington Bullets*) and journalism to actively expose right-wing forces that were instrumental in plotting the coup against Morales. This coup was ultimately defeated through a democratic process, bringing Morales's MAS (Movement for Socialism) party back to power under the leadership of a new president, Luis Arce, in 2020.

Prashad encourages a close collaboration between intellectuals and political and social movements to formulate "a theory of the future." The process of developing such a theory should inspire conversations among intellectuals and movement leaders to envision ways to affect the social and economic transformation of the existing world order. It is critically important for such scholarship to value emancipation that advances ideals that "the present is not eternal and that a transformation is possible" (Prashad 2018). This approach to scholarship radically deviates from traditional and mainstream research, which is mostly detached from concrete social movements. Additionally, the understanding of social movements in American mainstream scholarship is viewed as activism and construed with the fear of socialism. Working closely with social and political movements helps identify "contradictions in our social system," which fuel movements in their struggle for social and economic transformation.

The longtime neglect of scholarship that focuses on real social movements has influenced the US economy immensely; it has nonunionized our workforce, leading to a monopoly of power among employers and the exploitation of laborers. Policies such as "at-will employment" have created havoc in the lives of workers, leading also to a diminishing middle class.

Prashad argues for the need to "bridge the increasing gap between intellectuals and movements," so that both of them can learn from the other (Whittall 2018). Scholarship of this kind, according to Prashad, also should recognize the hierarchies of race, caste, sexuality, and gender. Prashad believes in class analysis that considers such hierarchies, similar to an observation Marx made in *Capital*, where he argued that "labor cannot emancipate itself in the white skin when in the black it is branded" (Polychroniou 2018). So, ending hierarchies based on caste and gender in India will not be achieved by just ending the hierarchy based on class, or vice versa. Social and political movements that aim to elevate the status of working-class people should, therefore, also recognize their varying life experiences due to their multiple social identities (Govan 2018).

REFERENCES

Arauz, Andrés, Mark Weisbrot, Andrew Bunker, and Jake Johnston. 2019. "Bolivia's Economic Transformation: Macroeconomic Policies, Institutional Changes, and Results." Washington DC: Center for Economic and Policy Research (CEPR). Accessed June 20, 2021. https://www.cepr.net/images/stories/reports/bolivia-macro-2019-10.pdf.

Aziz, Rana. 2014. "Break the Silence: An Interview with Vijay Prashad." *Asian American Writers' Workshop*. Accessed July 16, 2019. https://aaww.org/break-the-silence-vijay-prashad/.

Balch, Oliver. 2019. "How a Populist President Helped Bolivia's Poor—but Built Himself a Palace." *The Guardian*. Accessed June 15, 2021. https://www.theguardian.com/world/2019/mar/07/how-a-populist-president-helped-bolivias-poor-but-built-himself-a-palace.

Berkhout, Esmé, Nick Galasso, Max Lawson, Pablo Andrés Rivero Morales, Anjela Taneja, and Diego Alejo Vázquez Pimentel. 2021. "The Inequality Virus: Bringing Together a World Torn Apart by Coronavirus Through a Fair, Just and Sustainable Economy." Oxfam International: Oxfam Briefing Paper. Accessed June 20, 2021. https://webassets.oxfamamerica.org/media/documents/the-inequality-virus-report .pdf?_gl=1*kapw30*_ga*MjA2Nzc1MzExNi4xNjI0Njg1NzA0*_ga_R58YETD6 XK*MTYyNDc3NjIzOC4yLjEuMTYyNDc3NjI1MC4w.

Bohman, James, and William Rehg. 2017. "Jürgen Habermas." In *The Stanford Encyclopedia of Philosophy*, edited by Edward N. Zalta. Stanford, CA: Stanford University Press. https://plato.stanford.edu/archives/fall2017/entries/habermas/.

Buhle, Paul. 2014. "Prashad at Large." *Monthly Review*. January 1. Accessed June 20, 2021. https://monthlyreview.org/2014/01/01/prashad-large/.

Du Bois, W. E. B. 1915. "The African Roots of War." *The Atlantic*. May 1915 Issue. Accessed June 26, 2021. https://www.theatlantic.com/magazine/archive/1915/05/ the-african-roots-of-war/528897/.

Falach, Maya. 2020. "How Former President Morales Transformed Bolivia." *The Borgen Project Blog-Latest News*. Accessed June 26, 2021. https://borgenproject .org/morales-transformed-bolivia/.

Govan, Dexter. 2018. "Doubt Everything: An Interview on the State of Marxist History with Vijay Prashad and Ewan Gibbs Part I." Interviews: Toynbee Prize Foundation. Accessed on June 20, 2021. https://toynbeeprize.org/posts/vijay -prashad-and-ewan-gibbs-i/.

Habermas, Jürgen. 1979. *Communication and the Evolution of Society*. Boston, MA: Beacon Press.

———. 1984. *The Theory of Communicative Action: Reason and the Rationalization of Society*. Vol. I. Translated by Thomas McCarthy. Boston, MA: Beacon Press.

Lawson, Max, Chan, M. K., Rhodes, F., Butt, A. P., Marriott, A., Ehmke, E., and Gowland, R. 2019. "Public Good or Private Wealth? Universal Health, Education and Other Public Services Reduce the Gap between Rich and Poor, and between Women and Men. Fairer Taxation of the Wealthiest can Help Pay for Them." Oxfam GB, UK: Oxfam Briefing Paper. Accessed June 20, 2021. https: //s3.amazonaws.com/oxfam-us/www/static/media/files/bp-public-good-or-private -wealth-210119-en.pdf.

Lee, Christopher J., 2nd ed. 2019. *Making a World After Empire: The Bandung Moments and Its Political Afterlives*. Athens: Ohio University Press.

Marx, Karl. 1976 [1867]. *Capital: A Critique of Political Economy*. Translated by Ben Fowkes. New York: Penguin Books.

Najmi, Samina, and Rajini Srikanth, eds. 2002. *White Women in Racialized Spaces: Imaginative Transformation and Ethical Action in Literature, Mother Teresa as the Mirror of Bourgeois Guilt*. Albany: SUNY Press.

Polychroniou, C. J. 2019. "To Be Effective, Socialism must Adapt to 21st Century Needs." GP Opinion: Global Policy. [published in Truthout 2019 first]. Accessed June 26, 2021. https://www.globalpolicyjournal.com/blog/13/06/2019/be-effective -socialism-must-adapt-21st-century-needs.

Prashad, Vijay. 1994. "Native Dirt/Imperial Ordure: The Cholera of 1832 and the Morbid Resolutions of Modernity." *Journal of Historical Sociology* 7 (3): 243–60.

———. 1997. "Mother Teresa: Mirror of Bourgeois Guilt." *Economic and Political Weekly.* 32 (44/45): 2856–58.

———. 1998. "Mother Teresa: A Communist View." *Australian Marxist Review: Journal of the Communist Party of Australia.* August 1998. Accessed July 16, 2021. https://archive.cpa.org.au/amr/40/amr40-10-mother-teresa.html.

———. 2002. *Fat Cats and Running Dogs: The Enron Stage of Capitalism.* London: Zed Books

———. 2007. *The Darker Nations: A People's History of the Third World.* New York: The New Press.

———. 2012. *Arab Spring, Libyan Winter.* Edinburgh, Oakland, Baltimore: AK Press.

———. 2013a. "Questioning the Underlying Structures of Property and Power is Off the Table- Vijay Prashad Pt2/4," edited by Paul Jay. The Analysis. Accessed July 16, 2021. https://theanalysis.news/questioning-the-underlying-structures-of-property-and-power-is-off-the-table-vijay-prashad-pt-2-4/.

———. 2013b. *The Poorer Nations: A Possible History of the Global South.* New York: Verso.

———. 2014. *Uncle Swami: South Asians in America Today.* New York: The New Press.

———. 2015a. *No Free Left: The Futures of Indian Communism.* New York: LeftWord Books.

———. 2015b. *Letters to Palestine: Writers Respond to War and Occupation.* New York: Verso.

———. 2017a. *Red Star Over the Third World.* New Delhi, India: LeftWord Books.

———. 2017b. "The World of Du Bois and Our World of Fascism and the Possibility of Humanity." https://simons-rock.edu/news/vijay-prashad-symposium-keynote.php.

———. 2018a. "Confronting Imperialism Means Winning Back the Power to Imagine Alternatives: An Interview with Vijay Prashad." Interview by Daniel Whittall. *Red Pepper.* https://www.redpepper.org.uk/confronting-imperialism-means-winning-back-the-power-to-imagine-alternatives-an-interview-with-vijay-prashad/.

———. 2018b. "In the Ruins of the Present." *Tricontinental.* Accessed June 26, 2021. https://thetricontinental.org/working-document-1/.

———. 2019a. "Forward." In *Making a World After Empire: The Bandung Moments and Its Political Afterlives*, edited by Christopher J. Lee, x–xv. Athens: Ohio University Press.

———. 2019b. "Not Backing Down: What it Means to Speak for Palestine." *Daily Hampshire Gazette*, May 9. Accessed 30, 2022. https://www.gazettenet.com/Columnist-Vijay-Prashad-25411541.

———. 2019c. "The Right Ideas Aren't Enough: Interview with Vijay Prashad" Interview by Katelyn Hemmeke. Yeongdeungpo, Seoul: International Strategy Center, September 8, 2019. https://www.goisc.org/englishblog/2019/9/8/the-right-ideas-arent enough.

———. 2020a. *Washington Bullets*. New Delhi, India: LeftWord Books.

———. 2020b. "Vijay Prashad: You Can't Know the World Unless You're Trying to Change It." YouTube video, 1:58. September 25, 2020. https://www.youtube.com/watch?v=vSk_MXUgtEs.

———. 2020c. "Truth and Propaganda About Coronavirus." Independent Media Institute. Accessed June 26, 2021. https://independentmediainstitute.org/growing-xenophobia-against-china-in-the-midst-of-coronashock/.

———. 2021a. "'Doubt Everything': An Interview on the State of Marxist History, Part I." Interview by Ewan Gibbs. Toynbee Prize Foundation, June 6, 2018. https://toynbeeprize.org/posts/vijay-prashad-and-ewan-gibbs-i/.

———. 2021b. "The Kisan [Farmers'] Commune in India: The Twenty-Fourth Newsletter." *Tricontinental*. Accessed June 17, 2021. https://thetricontinental.org/newsletterissue/24-kisan-comune/.

Prashad, Vijay, and Brinda Karat. 2020. "For the Ruthless Abolition of the Caste System: An Interview with Brinda Karat, Politburo Member of the Communist Part of India (Marxist)." Interview by Brinda Karat. MROnline, December 29, 2020. https://mronline.org/2020/12/29/for-the-ruthless-abolition-of-the-caste/.

Raines, John, ed. 2002. "Critique of Hegel's Philosophy of Rights (1844)." In *Marx on Religion*, edited by John Raines, 170–82. Philadelphia, PA: Temple University Press.

Scott, J. Blake, and Rebecca Dingo. 2012. "Introduction: The Megarhetorics of Global Development." In *The Megarhetorics of Global Development*, edited by J. Blake Scott, and Rebecca Dingo, 1–25. Pittsburgh, PA: University of Pittsburgh Press.

Smith, David. 2015. "Burkina Faso's Revolutionary Hero Thomas Sankara to be Exhumed." *The Guardian*, US Edition. Accessed June 26, 2021. https://www.theguardian.com/world/2015/mar/06/burkina-fasos-revolutionary-hero-thomas-sankara-to-be-exhumed.

Chapter 10

Psychological Errors and Digital Rumors

Revisiting Two of Shibutani's Contributions

Simon Gottschalk

Let me start by saying that I am a bit ambivalent about including Tamotsu Shibutani in a list of neglected or ignored theorists. On one hand, his contributions have been translated into several languages, are discussed in a celebratory volume edited by Kian Kwan (1996), and in numerous essays about his scholarship (Baldwin 2006, 1990; Helle 2008; Inouye 2012; Miller 2006; Shay 2006; Turner 2006). Shibutani was elected Fellow of the American Association for the Advancement of Science in 1984, was awarded the George Herbert Mead Award by the Society for the Study of Symbolic Interaction in 1986, and the ASA Distinguished Career Award in 2004. As his many articles published in *Symbolic Interaction* and other top tier American and international journals attest, his contributions continue to inspire scholars working in a wide variety of disciplines as well as practitioners working outside of academia. On the other hand, his name barely appears in the 1,057-page long *Handbook of Symbolic Interaction* (Reynolds and Herman-Kinney 2003). His near absence in this massive volume is a bit disappointing, especially in light of Shibutani's important contributions to the many topics reviewed therein, and in light of his position on the Symbolic Interactionist family tree. He was, after all, Blumer's "prize student" while attending the University of Chicago (Davis 1991, 2).

The purpose of this essay is to offer neither grand review, nor genealogy, nor synthesis, as much more knowledgeable scholars than me have already produced those. Rather, after a brief overview of Shibutani's biography, main work, and approach, I discuss two of his contributions in light of contemporary social conditions. The first concerns the irrational dimension of self-concept and perception; the second concerns rumors in the digital era.

BIOGRAPHY

Tamotsu ("Tom") Shibutani was born in 1920, in Stockton, California. Both his parents were educated and well-to-do Japanese immigrants who encouraged Tom to read and to pursue a higher education (Inouye 2012). Although Tom identified as American, he became acutely aware of anti-Japanese racism while growing up. In 1939, he joined Stockton Junior College where he studied English. Inspired by John Steinbeck's *Grapes of Wrath*, he wanted to write a similar book about Japanese Americans' experiences in California. Following his father's advice, Tom decided to major in sociology and, in 1940, began attending the University of California at Berkeley, where he studied under Dorothy Thomas. His progress was interrupted in 1942 by Executive Order 9066, which ordered the forced relocation of Japanese and Japanese Americans to internment camps. While at the Tule Lake camp, Tom conducted sociological research with Frank Miyamoto and others, under the direction of Dorothy Thomas, who had established the *Evacuation and Resettlement Study*—a large-scale investigation of four Japanese American relocation centers and the resettlement of evacuees. After concluding his undergraduate degree at UC Berkeley, Tom enrolled at the University of Chicago, where he studied under Louis Wirth, Everett Hughes, and Herbert Blumer, among others. In 1944, Tom was drafted into the army, an experience that inspired his book *The Derelicts of Company K* (1978). He earned his PhD from the University of Chicago in 1948, and taught there until 1951. That same year, he accepted a position at UC Berkeley, from which he resigned in 1957 because of the conflicts marring that department. In 1961, Tom joined the Sociology faculty at UC Santa Barbara, where he taught until his death in 2004.

Baldwin (1990, 119–20) summarizes Shibutani's approach by remarking that "both macro and micro problems are among the things that stimulate people, individually or collectively, to think creatively and to search for solutions to problems." At some level, Tom's intelligent and creative adaptation to the events unfolding around him—some of which were quite disheartening and threatening—both articulated this approach and contributed to the development of his scholarship. Throughout his writings, he shows a remarkable optimism about the fate of American society and humanity in general. For example, he concludes *Ethnic Stratification* with the hopeful statement:

Whenever men interact informally, the common human nature comes through. It would appear, then, that it is only a matter of time before a more enlightened citizenry will realize this. Then, there will be a realignment of group loyalties, and ethnic identity will be a thing of the past. (1965, 589)

One cannot help but wonder how he would explain the multiplying incidents of vicious anti-Asian violence that we witness today, as well as the growing polarization of our society around issues of racial justice, culture wars, and immigration.

While I did not take classes with Shibutani when I was a graduate student at UCSB, I lived with students who did. Talking to me about his classes, the assigned readings, and his teaching style, the affection and respect they had for him were unmistakable. In my own interactions with him, I always found him to be sharp and modest, kind and respectful.

SCHOLARSHIP AND APPROACH

Shibutani's contributions include books about social psychology, ethnic stratification, communication, general sociology, and a number of important articles where, among others, he presents a sharp review of *The Authoritarian Personality* (1952), refines the concept of reference groups (1955), explains Mead's theory (1968a), develops symbolic interaction theory as a cybernetic model of motivation (1968b), and discusses Blumer's approach to research (1988). In all these writings, he combines a strong commitment to pragmatism, symbolic interaction theory, and a scientific approach. Whether writing about ethnic relations, developing a theory of rumors, or explaining the connections between personality and society, he finds across eras, continents, and social groups examples that illustrate recognizable and essentially pragmatic patterns of human behavior.

Shibutani's approach is scientific in content, organization, and style. Both precise and meticulous, he organizes the relevant scholarship to develop clear hypotheses that explain the phenomena under consideration. Throughout his various books, he reminds readers that the sociologist's task is not to guess or advocate but to find out, analyze, explain, and develop general principles about human behavior. Of course, as social beings we have subjective biases borne out of physical habits, biographical experiences, and cultural orientations, but he cautions against letting these contaminate the research process and the sociological project. Though subjective experiences can be useful catalysts for research, they are not appropriate criteria to guide it or evaluate its results. Questions informed by theory, careful observations, rigorous analysis, and a commitment to facts are.

While he experienced anti-Japanese racism, both growing up in Stockton and managing his everyday life and studies at the Tule Lake internment camp, Shibutani's book on ethnic relations contains very few mentions of Japanese Americans and none about internment camps. On the other hand, in *Ethnic Stratification* (1965), he and Kian Kwan write at length not only about the experiences encountered by various minority groups but also about the varieties of subgroups within them. In so doing, their analysis suggests both recognizable patterns across minority groups and heterogeneity within them, as members of various subgroups have different experiences, interests, and demands. For example, they note the patterned conflicts of generations between immigrant parents and their native-born children, the distinctive orientations towards assimilation among upper-class and lower-class members of particular minority groups, the various causes for resentment among differently educated layers of a minority group, and the class origins of minority group members who are most likely to join nationalistic political movements or express racist sentiments against dominant group members. And while Shibutani and Kwan do not discuss issues of gender and sexuality in great detail, their attention to class and status differences within minority groups anticipates the concept of intersectionality.

Shibutani also advises social scientists to keep their political inclinations in check while conducting research. Researchers can of course be activists and develop projects that will improve the conditions of disadvantaged groups and of society as a whole. To wit, he was a leading member of the "Berkeley radicals" "who worked furiously to document the aftermath of Pearl Harbor and its impact on Asian Americans in the San Francisco Bay area" (Shay 2006, 522). However, when a researcher replaces scientific guidelines with political agendas, the research risks becoming weaker scientifically, and hence less likely to motivate people to act in successful ways or to intervene strategically when the need arises. For example, his analysis of "extemporaneous rumors" and crowd behavior points to the disastrous consequences that result when individuals no longer rely on their capacity to critically evaluate information, neglect their responsibility as communicators, and let intense emotions and selective perception displace facts. This stance does not absolve sociologists from addressing the ethical and political aspects of their research. As he (1961) reminds readers, sociological knowledge can be used to improve the human condition and enlighten people, but also to manipulate them.

While this is not the place to discuss the politics, weaknesses, failings, complicities, and cultural encodings of the scientific enterprise (see Carey 2009), science is still the knowledge-system that "maximizes the chances of accuracy" (Baldwin 2006, 489) and therefore the chances of successful human action. Accordingly, Shibutani's insistence that sociologists conduct rigorous research seems especially relevant in a contemporary moment that witnesses both an increasing defunding of academic resources and de-founding of its raison d'être.

In the following paragraphs, I revisit two of Shibutani's contributions in light of contemporary debates and societal conditions. The first concerns the irrational dimension of self-concept and perception; the second concerns rumors in the digital era.

PSYCHOLOGICAL ERRORS:
EGO DEFENSE MECHANISMS,
SELF-CONCEPT, AND ETHNIC RELATIONS

In contrast to orthodox symbolic interactionists, who assume that individuals typically interpret others' (and their own) interactions correctly and respond rationally, Shibutani proposes a number of qualifications that are partially informed by his encounter with psychoanalytic theory, an encounter that would have a lingering effect throughout his life. For example, Jonathan Turner remembers reading Freud's *The Interpretation of Dreams* in Shibutani's class in the 1960s, and regularly returning to Freudian ideas in his conversations with Shibutani (2006). In an informal interview he gave during his visit at the University of Munich toward the end of his life, Shibutani indicated that the two domains he wanted to develop were individuality and unconscious behavior (Helle 1988). Especially noteworthy is Shibutani's treatment of ego defense mechanisms. Calling them "perceptual defenses," he explains that they are "spontaneous reactions which protect each person from recognizing certain facts about himself which are obvious to almost everyone else" (1961, 439). Rather than locating the causes of such patterned misinterpretations in a repressed sex drive, a tumultuous anal stage, or a rowdy tête-à-tête between id, ego, and superego, Shibutani traces them to interactions individuals experienced in early socialization with significant others. As he remarks, "some people are deeply hurt during childhood and devote a lifetime to improving their lot" (1961, 465). As a result, "we may go all through life acting as if we were the kind of people we were when we were children" (Helle 1988). Discussing the various types of ego-defense mechanisms and the role of self-concept in mental disorders, Shibutani shows that adult actors neither necessarily interpret how others reflect them correctly nor develop a self-concept that corresponds to others' reflections. As deeply held irrational beliefs may systematically distort these cognitive-emotional processes (Turner 2006), self-concept can be completely erroneous, misaligned with everyday encounters, and (mis)informed more by childhood experiences than by adult interactions. Following Sullivan's theory, he concludes that "the limits of conscious awareness . . . are set by security operations. If a person cannot face his glaring faults and still maintain his self-respect, the painful experiences are repressed; life goes on as if the events did not occur" (1961, 439).

Shibutani's discussion of ego-defense mechanisms illustrates the central importance he assigns positive self-concept and self-respect, which, among humans, are necessary for self-preservation (1961, 465). And because self-concept emerges in social interactions, individuals need to be assured they will be "treated with reasonable respect in their community." Anticipating Axel Honneth's "struggle for recognition" (1995), Shibutani concluded that "men struggle for personal status, to keep up their reputation for integrity; they also struggle for self respect" (1961, 466).

This attention to positive self-concept and self-respect also appears in *Ethnic Stratification,* which he coauthored with Kian Kwan. As they note:

> The fundamental problem in the contact of peoples is the preservation of the individual's moral worth in his own eyes. . . . Although unfair employment practices and residential segregation are condemned by members of minority groups who seek advancement, what is resented most of all is lack of respect. . . . Unless men can have self-respect, they will always be discontented, no matter what else they have. Men are willing to fight and even to die for it. Without it they can neither look themselves in the face nor stand before their children without a sense of shame. Many who oppose segregation have no desire to associate with members of the dominant group, they just want to be able to live with themselves—with a sense of dignity. (1965, 585)

In their approach, "what is commonly called 'race relations' is essentially a psychological problem" (1965, 81) that can be understood in terms of how members of the dominant group construct members of the minority group and the consequences of such constructions for the latter. It goes without saying that these consequences include real material and objectively measurable inequalities in minority group members' life-chances. However, I will focus here on their social psychological consequences.

Shibutani and Kwan suggest that members of the dominant group categorize members of minority groups as either "valuable," "frustrating," "feared," "dangerous," "useful," or "esoteric" objects (1965, 95–109). Because dominant group members impose such constructions on minority group members and treat them accordingly, they exercise considerable power over minority group members' self-concept and therefore their access to the essential social psychological resource that is self-respect. Members of minority groups have historically both internalized and resisted such impositions, and this resistance takes various forms in different historical periods. Importantly also, minority group members who resist often reconstruct their self-concept as "valuable objects" (1965, 518) by self-reflecting though the eyes of their peers, and not those of the dominant group. However, regardless of its forms, this resistance typically takes enormous and continuous effort and is socially, psychologically, and physically perilous and inherently stressful.

Freudian Slips and Microaggressions

Combining Shibutani's treatment of ego-defense mechanisms with his micro-level approach to interethnic relations, it seems that if some individuals struggle to develop a positive self-concept in spite of contradictory evidence and because of irrational beliefs fixated in childhood, minority group members must struggle to develop a positive self-concept because of irrational constructions that are daily enforced on them by dominant group members and by the routine operations of key social institutions. These constructions evoke patterned emotional responses among dominant group members that are especially visible when minority groups members are attacked, try to sexually seduce a member of the dominant group (or are perceived to do so), are in positions of power, or claim equal status (1965, 99–105). At the same time, and not unlike Freudian slips and *actes manqués*, dominant group members also manifest these constructions when they routinely interact with minority group members in spontaneous, unconscious, and accidental behaviors. Accordingly, if ego-defense mechanisms are manifestations of an individual's irrational negative self-concept, microaggressions are manifestations of dominant group members' irrational beliefs about minority group members. But, while individuals seeking to correct their own irrational beliefs about themselves might decide to undertake the difficult work of therapeutic introspection, dominant group members de facto delegate this work to minority group members, who must now expand their own emotional energy to manage these microaggressions. In so doing, they are relieving dominant group members from performing this necessary work on their own psyche.

Encounters that threaten a person's positive self-concept or "face" are likely to induce shame (Goffman 1955), an emotion that is often bypassed or repressed because of the intense negative charge it conveys and the threats to the self it evokes. However, these ego-defense mechanisms both intensify this emotion and transmute it into pathological and often violent manifestations (Scheff 2014, 2003, 2000, 1994, 1991). For Turner (2007), the experience of shame in key social institutions can trigger social-psychological processes that lead individuals to organize, mobilize, and, on occasion, perpetrate extreme violence against designated culprits. One motivation for this violence is the thirst for revenge, which is an important reaction—and antidote—to shame (Scheff 1994). According to Cota-McKinley, Woody and Bell, "the person seeking vengeance will often compromise his or her own integrity, social standing, and personal safety for the sake of revenge" (2001, 343). To push this argument to the extreme, if revenge has pragmatic aims (deterrence, elimination of perceived injustice, communication), Altman's analysis of suicide bombing calls our attention to the self-restorative psychological functions of such exceptionally violent acts:

> Extreme shame, extreme humiliation, can be experienced as psychological death. People will kill and die for their honor or their self-respect, because to lose their dignity can be experienced as a fate worse than death. The word "mortification," which has come to refer to states of humiliation, means, literally, to be rendered dead. Humiliation also leads to rage, the kind of blind rage that ignites a firestorm that feeds on itself and eventuates in a scorched earth in which everything is destroyed . . . by killing himself, the suicide bomber undoes the indignity of having been helpless to prevent his death at the hands of another and turns the tables by killing that other. (2005, 16–17)

By combining psychoanalytic theories and symbolic interactionism, Shibutani highlights the irrational and emotional aspects of self-concept, underlies its importance for the need for social psychological self-preservation, and points to the interactional dynamics by which it rises, falls, is sustained, contested, and reclaimed. In so doing, he suggests that this most abstract and seemingly trivial idea or *representation* is in fact critical to understand—let alone resolve—enduring and violent social conflicts.

DIGITAL RUMORS: ESSENTIAL TOOLS AND NEW DIRECTIONS

In the age of deepfakes, Zoom meetings, QAnon conspiracies, bots, and cyberbullying, Shibutani's *Improvised News* (1966) and other writings about communication are especially relevant and insightful. In this section, my purpose is not to criticize Shibutani's contributions to these topics in light of new communication and information technologies however. First, he could not have reasonably anticipated their emergence, accelerated development, and chaotic impact on all levels of society. Second, he was writing in a very different sociohistorical context. Rather, I use his analysis of mass-media technologies and rumors as guidelines to both examine their contemporary forms and to ask new questions.

Following Dewey, Shibutani maintained that "society exists in and through communication" (1955, 565) and that "*what characterizes the interactionist approach is the contention that human nature and the social order are products of communication*" (1961, 22—italics in the original). In an article where he proposes a cybernetic model of motivation, he notes that Mead "is primarily concerned with communication and control" (1968a, 331), and that the necessary self-control we are all called upon to exercise in order to participate in social life is itself "a communicative process . . . a continuous dialogue with oneself, an inner forum made up largely of subvocal linguistic communication" (1968b, 24). At a more macro-level, Shibutani saw the rapid development of new technologies and the ease of participating in them as distinctive and—in contrast to the Frankfurt School—promising aspects of contemporary society and its evolution to more sophisticated forms (1955, 565–66).

Shibutani's optimism must be partly explained by the kinds of communication channels that were multiplying around him at the time of his writing: radio and TV broadcasts, magazines, novels, and newspapers. In other words, the channels of communication on which he pinned his hopes were the mass media. They typically function according to a one-to-many model, where a few sources of information communicate to many dispersed audience members. Members talk to each other—and typically face-to-face—about that information but cannot talk back to the source or become themselves sources of mass-mediated information. In addition, while the channels of information Shibutani considered are pitched to specific audiences and celebrate particular tastes, dispositions, or subcultures, they generally tend to promote consensus and to integrate their respective audiences within the larger society. They can increase social distance between neighbors and extract culture from geographical location, but they can also evoke a sense of community among geographically distant individuals. In their book *Ethnic Stratification*, Shibutani and Kwan believed that, by facilitating the acquisition of a humanizing personalized knowledge about others, the media of mass communication would enlighten the citizenry about our shared humanity. As they put it,

> The development of the media of mass communication is likely to break down the walls of ethnocentrism. . . . As they become better able to understand the lives of people whose cultures are different, [audiences] will be able to appreciate that most of their preoccupations and motives are the same. If human nature is indeed universal, more efficient communication will eventually break down ethnic barriers. (1965, 588)

Unfortunately, although computer-mediated communication technologies are quite efficient in facilitating the synchronous circulation of information among millions of geographically dispersed individuals, their characteristics, dynamics, and sheer numbers seem to produce different outcomes than Shibutani hoped for. For example, as we saw above, he believed that a person's ability to correctly role-take and self-reflect from the perspective of others is key to effective participation in social life and, as his discussion of ego-defense mechanisms suggests, to a modicum of mental health. This ability in turn is central to the exercise of self-control—a topic that Shibutani found especially important in his analysis of the interplay between society and personality (1961; see also Hesse 1988, Turner 2006). However, while our advanced communication technologies multiply the number of people with whom we could potentially role-take and self-reflect, Turkle's research (2011) suggests that today's youth are decreasingly capable of role-taking and of finding much value in the ability to do so. This technologically induced incapacitation must be partly explained by the personalization of online communication channels. Rather than promoting an ever-more sensitive attention to others' perspectives and inclinations, this revolutionary affordance invites users to withdraw into "endless you-loops" where the only perception of reality that really matters is one's own. Rather than negotiating interpretations of social reality with others through intelligent, empathic, mutually perceptive, and complex interactions, individuals must now do so under conditions that prevent and distort the "expressive gestures" that are so necessary for such negotiations to succeed. To make matters worse, omniscient algorithms continually validate our solipsistic interpretations and "truths," reassuring us that those are indeed sound and sufficient.

In their analysis of ethnic relations, Shibutani and Kwan emphasized the importance of our ability to transmit and detect sentiments, as it "provides the initial crack through the walls of ethnocentrism. . . . Sentiments enable us to get inside of others" (1965, 582). As they saw it, if ethnic prejudice arose out of competition, it was "maintained in communication" (1965, 577) and could thus be reduced by more efficient communication. Accordingly, "anything that facilitates the acquisition of personalized knowledge about an ethnic other will tend to lower social distance" (1965, 574). In light of the opportunities provided by online communication channels to develop empathic knowledge with and about more people than was imaginable a mere few decades ago, across continents, and near-synchronously, one would have reasonably expected a significant improvement in intercultural relations, in mutual understanding, or at minimum, in the exercise of civility. Instead, online communication channels evidence a dehumanization of human relations (Gottschalk and Fuller, 2021; Gottschalk 2020, 2018). As a recent study conducted by the Pew Research Center finds, 66 percent of adult internet users have seen someone be harassed in some way online, 40 percent have personally experienced online harassment (Rainie et al. 2017), and 62 percent consider that it is a problem (Duggan 2017). To take an extreme but increasingly frequent example, while Shibutani acknowledged that the different "social worlds" enabled by the communication channels of his days could sometimes conflict with each other, he could not anticipate that in the *digital* social worlds of Twitter, Facebook, 8chan, Subreddits, and blogs, members could also call for the violent overthrow of the social order, spew vitriolic accusations, threaten perceived enemies, or celebrate hate crimes against them. Tragically, therefore, the most sophisticated channels of communication can also contaminate the global communication stream with the most regressive memes, at devastating speed. They seem to have cultivated neither a more enlightened public nor a more empathic one.

Rumors

Improvised News: A Sociological Study of Rumor (1966) provides an incisive analysis of rumors—a seemingly unremarkable phenomenon. In contrast to the dominant 1950s and 1960s models that explained rumors as resulting from distortions in communication and as pathological responses to uncertainty, Shibutani argued that rumors are typically rational and "collective transactions" individuals participate in when information is lacking (see also Miller 2006). As a verb rather than a noun, a rumor is

> a recurrent form of communication through which men caught together in an ambiguous situation attempt to construct a meaningful interpretation of it by pooling their intellectual resources. It might be regarded as a form of collective problem solving. (1966, 17)

This complex process typically features four distinctive types of actor (messenger, interpreter, skeptic, and auditor) whose roles are themselves dynamic over the life course of a rumor and across different contexts. Distinguishing between news and rumors, Shibutani noted that, although the formal media of communication that deliver news in a society (such as respected newspapers, TV and radio news programs) are not entirely objective, they typically have a high degree of accuracy. They are the first sources individuals turn to when they need important information, and the standard against which they test the informal reports they hear about. In typical conditions, "when 'grapevine' information conflicts with official news, the latter is generally accepted" (1966, 22).

Shibutani also distinguished between deliberative and extemporaneous rumors. In the first and most common type, "unsatisfied demand for news is moderate, collective excitement is mild, and rumor construction takes place through critical deliberation" (1966, 94) in auxiliary networks of information. Concerned about their reputation, individuals who occupy positions of authority in those networks tend to feel responsible for the information they share; they are accountable. In those networks also, audience members evaluate rumors for plausibility and for source reliability. They reject implausible reports and those communicated by unreliable or suspicious sources, so that the "interpretations that eventually emerge tend to be consistent with cultural axioms" (1966, 94) and tend to be pragmatic.

The dynamics are very different in extemporaneous rumors, which are much rarer and likely to emerge when the unsatisfied demand for news is excessive. As collective excitement intensifies, rumor construction occurs through spontaneous, informal, and weakly regulated interactions rather than through critical deliberation in auxiliary channels, or evaluation against official information channels. In extemporaneous conditions, the sources of rumors and those who transmit them tend to be anonymous and have a minimal sense of responsibility for sharing them. As excitement rises, thinking becomes more confused, participants become increasingly suggestible, and respond now more to other *participants' emotions* than to the *content of the information*. As these emotions intensify and become increasingly contagious, participants' perceptions, evaluations, and attention become almost exclusively focused on particular objects or people that can quickly become the targets of collective violence. In those conditions of intense physical arousal and heightened suggestibility, participants celebrate, amplify, and select those messages that confirm their emotions while dismissing, ignoring, or violently rejecting those that do not. Crowd behavior can thus be explained as an emotionally charged *shift in perspective* where cognitive processes are radically altered and where highly emotional and distorted perceptions become facts and guides for collective—and often disastrous—action (1966, 95–120). It is ignited by rumors, fueled by them, and generative of them in an increasingly intense and rapid "closed circuit."

While Shibutani recognized the danger of extemporaneous rumors, he remained overall optimistic that, through a process of natural selection, individuals would ultimately weed out bad interpretations and, guided by pragmatic criteria, would utilize those that enhance their intelligent adaptation to changing conditions:

> Regardless of their formal philosophies most men are pragmatic in their actual orientation toward their world; a premium is placed upon accurate knowledge, for the simple reason that errors in the long run lead to painful consequences. . . . As long as shared beliefs emerge through natural selection . . . perspectives are successively reconstituted to become increasingly more efficient instruments of adjustment. (1966, 213)

In *Improvised News*, Shibutani reviewed dozens of cases scattered across continents and eras to develop general hypotheses about rumors, their causes, components, variations, extreme cases, political uses, and social consequences. In so doing, he provided scholars of rumors with useful tools with which to examine their transformations in digital environments. Here, I focus especially on verification, messengers, and types and dynamics.

Verification

Shibutani suggested that, under normal conditions, individuals hearing rumors would naturally seek to verify them and ensure they make sense in order to put them to pragmatic use. In online communication channels, however, digital rumors compellingly invite readers to bypass this critical step. They do so by providing visual, dramatic and credible "proofs" that the false and constantly "updated" information they transmit is not only obviously true, but also shared and "liked" by a large number of people, especially famous ones (see Wardle and Derekhshan 2017; Woolley and Howard 2017). As Shibutani noted, currency enhances credibility. Similarly, while he believed that, in conditions of deliberative rumors, individuals compare the informal reports they hear with the information transmitted by official news channels, an increasing number of citizens worldwide distrust official news channels and, for all intents and purposes, have reversed this relationship. They now use propaganda claims as the standards against which they evaluate official information. While the wholesale distrust of official channels of information makes perfect sense in authoritarian regimes where citizens correctly per-ceive those channels as ventriloquists for the ruling party, it is more puzzling in democratic societies. One way to resolve this paradox is to suggest that the relationship between rumor-churning channels and the official ones has changed from competitive to parasitic. While hostile and alternative channels of information seek to successfully compete against official news channels to increase their persuasive power, they are now *using* official news channels to do the work for them. By merely *addressing* rumors (even if it is to deny them), official news channels are spreading deceitful messages (see Wardle and Derekhshan 2017; Woolley and Howard 2017).

During World War II, the French government in exile in London was transmitting radio communiqués to Resistance fighters about the course of the war, the landings in Normandy, and other critical information. On their end, the Germans were scrambling these transmissions by broadcasting loop-ing noise signals. In our society, digital rumors perform the same function: they scramble the transmission of potentially life-saving information (think of mask-wearing, social distancing, and vaccinating) with disinformation, accusations, and threats. However, in contrast to French citizens living under German occupation who could easily distinguish between the German jumbling radio signals and London communiqués, millions of people in our society can no longer do so—or no longer want to. Thus, recent research conducted by the *Survey Center on American Life* reveals that about 30 percent of the population (and 70 percent of Republican voters) think that the 2020 elections were illegitimate (Cox, 2021) in spite of repeated and bipartisan research proving otherwise. Camilia Domonoske's (2016) research at Stanford University finds that students have a dismaying inability to distinguish between fake and real news, and that this affliction is not limited to students. Adult Facebook users are more likely to share fake (but dramatic) news than real news, a finding that is especially worrisome when one considers that 62 percent of adult American users get their news from social media (Rainie, Anderson, and Albright 2017), that 44 percent of them get their news from Facebook, and that those who do are less engaged and knowledgeable than those who do not (Mitchell et al. 2020). Accordingly, it's no longer the lack of important information that prompts individuals to produce rumors, but the inability to select the most plausible, accurate, and trustworthy ones.

In contemporary society, online channels of communication have not simply multiplied, merged, and evolved beyond comprehension; they increasingly contradict one another on fundamental values, the nature of society, and its desired direction. The attempts by Russia and other hostile agents to infect the online communication stream with disinformation attest to the importance of these channels for the maintenance of social stability, the integrity of the public discourse, and the possibility of social solidarity. They also reveal their excessive fragility (Wardle and Derakhshan 2017; Woolley and Howard 2017).

Messengers

In deliberative rumors, members of auxiliary channels collectively evaluate information in terms of the source's "reputations for honesty, knowledge, sound judgment, and 'connections'" (1966, 23). In those conditions, those who disseminate rumors must ensure accuracy and exercise self-control and moderation because their reputations are at stake. However, such criteria seem to have significantly weakened in the transmission of digital rumors. While Shibutani emphasized the importance of primary groups in the management of rumors, many members of online communication channels are known to each other as avatars rather than as real individuals, and some are even bots—nonhuman agents that know more about human sentiments than we do ourselves. Thus, Ferrara et al. report that, increasingly, minded bots can engage users in conversations, comment on their posts, and answer questions. Some can search a social network to locate influential people and capture their attention. They can infiltrate popular discussions, zero in on topics, and participate in them. Others can "'clone' the behavior of legitimate users, by interacting with their friends and posting topically coherent content with similar temporal patterns" (2016, 99–100). As some suspect, those bots will become increasingly personalized to users (Donnath 2017; see also Wardle and Derakhshan 2017; Woolley and Howard 2017). To wit, millions of otherwise rational individuals living in vastly different societies angrily dismiss the scientific evidence developed by world-renowned experts on behalf of depraved delusions "dropped" by an anonymous Q (Rauhala and Morris 2020), who/which, as far as we know, could be a bot. Rather than assessing the plausibility and pragmatic usefulness of these delusions, millions organize those as ideology, social movements, and justification for violent action. In contrast to Shibutani's analysis, therefore, contemporary researchers must also contend with the fact that those who circulate rumors, incite violent emotions, or sow confusion may be nonhuman agents that are increasingly autonomous, minded, and intelligent.

Types and Dynamics

In Shibutani's model, most cases of rumors are of the deliberative kind. In other words, they emerge in conditions where "unsatisfied demand for news is moderate, collective excitement is mild, and rumor construction takes place through critical deliberation" (1966, 94) in auxiliary networks of information. Extemporaneous rumors can of course emerge and radically transform the people's behavior, but those are rare and necessitate the presence of a large number of interrelated conditions. Key among those is physical co-presence.

Physical co-presence is already implied in the production of deliberative rumors, as those consist of concerned actors interacting with others in auxiliary networks of communication that are sometimes only available in certain places, at certain times, and through certain connections. In contrast, access to digital rumors is guaranteed 24/7, worldwide, remotely, and from one's pocket to all those who seek them, and even to those who do not. Similarly, the crowd behavior that is ignited by extemporaneous rumors necessitates physical co-presence and the contagious effects of participants' *expressive movements*. In those conditions, "the flash of the eyes, the whisper of a syllable, or the glance of a shoulder may be far more revealing than verbal content" (Shibutani 1966, 98). However, if angry physical crowds increase adrenaline, Facebook "likes" trigger dopamine. When extemporaneous rumors are spread by physically copresent and emotionally aroused individuals, they may detonate into violent crowd behavior. When digital rumors are spread online by isolated individuals, they may detonate into "swarms" (Bauman 2000) and lone-wolf terrorism (Cohen et al. 2014). Under conditions of emotional contagion among physically co-present others, participants' reality testing is impaired as they are swept away by crowd psychology. Under conditions of virtual contagion, participants' reality testing is impaired because they no longer distinguish between virtual representations and facts. The rise of deepfakes further accelerates this process. Similarly, while the anonymity participants experience in crowd behavior induces a loss of self or identity, participants in online communication networks can choose to be completely anonymous or completely visible and identifiable. One puzzling example of this type of participation was demonstrated by the January 6 rioters who proudly transmitted "live" their criminal behavior on their social media networks.

In Shibutani's model, the energy necessary to sustain rumor circulation is typically limited; rumors run their courses. Thus, if organizations can and do manufacture rumors in order to frighten, discredit, confuse opponents, or incite particular emotions against them, such efforts are typically targeted to time, place, and audience, and are thus limited. In contrast, however, as shrapnel of the "Information Bomb" (Virilio 1999, 87), digital rumors circulate ceaselessly, without necessitating much physical effort or other resources, in a communication ecology saturated with information that is constantly updated by contradictory and horrifying "breaking news." Similarly, while rumors typically followed particular events and were created as a response to ambiguous conditions and to reduce confusion, digital rumors *create* the events where none existed for the purpose of creating confusion.

CONCLUSIONS: DIGITAL RUMORS
AND EMOTIONAL VECTORS

Applying Shibutani's discussion of the irrational aspects of social life to our understanding of digital rumors should prompt us to temper our belief in the pragmatic and rational dispositions he optimistically envisioned. More concretely, we should acknowledge that even in nonauthoritarian regimes and in conditions where accurate information is plentiful, sophisticated, free, instantly and constantly accessible, seemingly rational citizens will systematically reject it on behalf of disinformation whose unique advantage is that it validates their (typically negative) feelings—even if it literally kills them and their loved ones.[1]

Perhaps one perspective that can complement Shibutani's pragmatic approach to rumors and help us shed light on the current state of extreme political polarization is Carey's (2009) ritual view of communication. In his view, individuals do not process information solely to establish plausibility, accuracy, source reliability, or concrete usefulness, but to gratify societal psychological needs. Communication is more than just the act of imparting information or influence, it is "the creation, representation, and celebration of shared even if illusory beliefs" (33). Online communication channels are especially hospitable to such functions, as rituals where individuals publicly proclaim commitment to a collective identity, solidarity, and shared "truth" are plentiful there. Finding them is easy and using them is free and facile. In contrast to the channels of communication where people fabricate and circulate deliberative rumors, the verbal discharge of intense negative emotions is not incidental to the digital rumor but its very purpose. And as participants express and experience intense negative emotions, they are validated and encouraged to amp those up. Few other social spaces are as reliably rewarding, so fast, so constantly, and so cheaply.

In online channels of communication, digital rumors are not just carriers of information but also vectors of intense negative emotions. In some channels, that is perhaps their sole purpose. Accordingly, researchers seeking to interpret the meanings of digital rumors should perhaps complement their analyses of their content with analyses of their effects—both online and offline, as these domains are completely intertwined. By calling our attention to the importance of rumors and analyzing them in systematic ways, Shibutani provides today's researchers with the tools that can help them understand the power new communication technologies wield in shaping the dynamics of digital rumors and in intensifying their risks. Developing this understanding has never been more urgent.

REFERENCES

Altman, Neil. 2005. "On the Psychology of Suicide Bombing." *Tikkun* 20 (2): 15–17.

Baldwin, John D. 2006. "Shibutani and Pragmatism." *Symbolic Interaction*, 28(4): 487–504.

———. 1990. "Advancing the Chicago School of Pragmatic Sociology: The Life and Work of Tamotsu Shibutani." *Sociological Inquiry* 60 (2): 115–26.

Bauman, Zygmunt. 2000. *Liquid Modernity.* Cambridge: Polity Press.

Carey, James A., 2nd ed. 2009. *Communication as Culture: Essays on Media and Society.* New York: Routledge.

Cohen, Katie, Fredrik Johansson, Lisa Kaati, and Jonas Clausen Mork. 2014. "Detecting Linguistic Markers for Radical Violence in Social Media." *Terrorism and Political Violence* 26 (1): 246–56.

Cota-McKinley, A. l., William D. Woody, and Paul A. Bell. 2001. "Vengeance: Effects of Gender, Age, and Religious Background." *Aggressive Behavior* 27: 343–50.

Cox, Daniel A. 2021. "After the Ballots are Counted: Conspiracies, Political Violence, and American Exceptionalism." *Survey Center on American Life.* Feb 11, 2021. https://www.americansurveycenter.org/research/after-the-ballots-are-counted conspiracies-political-violence-and-american-exceptionalism/.

Davis, Fred. 1991. "Herbert Blumer and the Study of Fashion: A Reminiscence and A Critique." *Symbolic Interaction* 14 (1): 1–21

Domonoske, Camilia. 2016. "Students Have 'Dismaying' Inability To Tell Fake News From Real, Study Finds." *KNPR*. Accessed November 23, 2016. http://www.npr.org/sections/thetwo-way/2016/11/23/503129818/study-finds- students have-dismaying-inability-to-tell-fake-news-from-real.

Donnath, Judith. 2017. "The Robot Dog Fetches for Whom?" *Medium*. Accessed June 15, 2017. https://medium.com/berkman-klein-center/the-robot-dog-fetches -for-whom-a9c1dd0a458a.

Duggan, Maeve. 2017. "2017 Online Harassment." Pew Research Center. https://www.pewresearch.org/internet/2017/07/11/online-harassment-2017/.

Ferrara, Emilio, Onur Varol, Clayton Davis, Filippo Menczer, and Alessandro Flammini. 2016. "The Rise of Social Bots." *Communications of the Association for Computer Machinery* 59 (7): 96–104.

Goffman, Erving. 1955. "On Face-Work: An Analysis of Ritual Elements in Social Interaction." *Psychiatry* 18 (3): 213–31.

Gottschalk, Simon and Celene Fuller. 2021. "De-realization and Infra-humanization: A Theory of Symbolic Interaction with Digital Technologies." Forthcoming in the *Oxford Handbook of Symbolic Interaction*, edited by Wayne Brekhus, Thomas Degloma, and William Force. Oxford: Oxford University Press.

Gottschalk, Simon. 2020. "Accelerators, Amplifiers, and Conductors: A Model of Tertiary Deviance in Online White Supremacist Networks." *Deviant Behavior* 21 (7): 841–55.

———. 2017. *The Terminal Self: Everyday Life in Hypermodern Times*. London: Routledge.

Gottschalk, Simon, Daniel Okamura, Jaimee Nix, and Celene Fuller. Forthcoming. "From Insult to Injustice to Injury: Frame Amplification in Virtual White Supremacist Networks." In *All American Massacre: The Tragic Role of American Culture and Society in Mass Shootings*, edited by Eric Madfis and Adam Lankford. New York: New York University Press.

Honneth, Axel. 1995. *The Struggle for Recognition: The Moral Grammar of Social Conflicts.* Cambridge, UK: Polity Press.

Inouye, Karen M. 2012. "Japanese American Wartime Experience, Tamotsu Shibutani and Methodological Innovation 1942–1978." *Journal of the History of the Behavioral Sciences* 48 (4): 318–38.

Knight, Will. 2018. "Fake America Great Again." *MIT Technology Review* 121 (5): 36–41.

Kwan, Kian M. 1996. *Individuality and Social Control: Essays in Honor of Tamotsu Shibutani*. Greenwich, CT: JAI Press.

Miller, Dan E. 2006. "Rumor: An Examination of Some Stereotypes." *Symbolic Interaction* 28 (4): 505–19.

Mitchell, Amy, Mark Jurkowitz, J. Baxter Oliphant, and Elisa Sharer. 2020. "Americans Who Mainly Get Their News on Social Media Are Less Engaged, Less Knowledgeable." Pew Research Center, July 2020. https://www.journalism.org/2020/07/30/americans-who-mainly-get-their-news-on- social media-are-less-engaged-less-knowledgeable.

Rainie, Lee, Janna Anderson, and Jonathan Albright. 2017. "The Future of Free Speech, Trolls, Anonymity, and Fake News Online." Pew Research Center, March 2017. http://www.pewinternet.org/2017/03/29/the-future-of-free-speech trolls-anonymity-and-fake-news-online/.

Rauhala, Emily, and Loveday Morris. 2020. "In the United States, QAnon is struggling. The conspiracy theory is thriving abroad." *Washington Post*, November 13, 2020. https://www.washingtonpost.com/world/qanon-conspiracy-global-reach /2020/11/12/ca312138-13a5-11eb-a258-614acf2b906d_story.html.

Reynolds, Larry T., and Nancy J. Herman-Kinney, eds. 2003. *Handbook of Symbolic Interaction*. Walnut Creek, CA: Altamira.

Scheff, Thomas J. 2014. "Goffman on Emotions: The Pride-Shame System." *Symbolic Interaction* 37 (1): 108–21.

———. 2003. "Shame in Self and Society." *Symbolic Interaction* 26 (2): 239–62.

———. 2000. "Shame and the Social Bond: A Sociological Theory." *Sociological Theory* 18 (1): 81–99.

———. 1994. *Bloody Revenge: Emotion, Nationalism, and War*. Boulder, CO. Westview Press.

Scheff, Thomas, and Suzanne Retzinger. 1991. *Emotion and Violence: Shame and Rage in Destructive Conflicts*. Lanham, MD: Lexington Books.

Shay, William L. "Reflections on Tamotsu Shibutani: On a Biography and Sociology of America." *Symbolic Interaction* 28 (4): 505–19.

Shibutani, Tamotsu. 1952. "Review: The Authoritarian Personality." *American Journal of Sociology* 57 (5): 527–29.

———. 1955. "Reference Groups as Perspectives." *American Journal of Sociology* 60 (6): 562–69.

———. 1961. *Society and Personality: An Interactionist Approach to Social Psychology*. Englewood Cliffs: Prentice Hall.

———. 1966. *Improvised News: A Sociological Study of Rumor*. Indianapolis: Bobbs-Merrill.

———. 1968a. "A Cybernetic Approach to Motivation." In *Modern Systems Research for the Behavioral Scientist: A Sourcebook*, edited by Walter Buckley, 330–36. Chicago: Aldine.

———. 1968b. "Mead, George Herbert." In *International Encyclopedia of the Social Sciences*, edited by David L. Sills, 83–87. New York: McMillan.

———. 1978. *The Derelicts of Company K: A Sociological Study of Demoralization*. Berkeley: University of California Press.

———. 1988. "Herbert Blumer's Contributions to Twentieth Century Sociology." *Symbolic Interaction* 11 (1): 23–31.

Shibutani, Tamotsu, and Kian M. Kwan. 1965. *Ethnic Stratification: A Comparative Approach*. New York: Macmillan.

Turkle, Sherry. 2011. *Alone Together: Why We Demand More of Technology and Less of Each Other*. New York: Basic Books.

Turner, Jonathan. 2007. "Self, Emotions, and Extreme Violence: Extending Symbolic Interactionist Theorizing." *Symbolic Interaction* 30 (4): 501–30.

———. 2006. "Social Control and Emotions." *Symbolic Interaction* 28 (4): 475–85.

Virilio, Paul, Friedrich Kittler, and John Armitage. 1999. "The Information Bomb: A Conversation." *Angelaki: Journal of the Theoretical Humanities* 4 (2): 81–90.

Wardle, Claire, and Hossein Derakhshan. 2017. "Information Disorder: Toward and Interdisciplinary Framework for Research and Policymaking." Council of Europe. Strasbourg: Editions du Conseil de l'Europe. https://edoc .coe.int/en/media/7495-information-disorder-toward-an-interdisciplinary framework-for-research-and-policy-making.html.

Woolley, Samuel C., and Philip N. Howard. 2017. "Computational Propaganda: Worldwide Executive Summary." Working Paper No. 2017.11. Oxford: Oxford University Press. http://comprop.oii.ox.ac.uk/wp-content/uploads/sites/89/2017/06 /Casestudies ExecutiveSummary.pdf.

NOTE

1. I have in mind here especially individuals who refuse to be vaccinated, to wear a mask, or to maintain social distance.

Index

before World War II, 23–24
Black Feminist Thought
  (Collins), 55–56, 99
Black Lives Matter movement, 105, 123
Blackness, 11–15, 68
Black public sociology, 4, 48, 51, 53–59
Black-White binaries, 90–91
Black women, 10, 86
Blauner, Robert, 85–86
Blumer, Herbert, 5–6, 148–49
Bolivia, 140–41
Breton, André, 11, 14–15, 17n5
Britain, 111–12, 132, 138, 140, 159–60
Broaddus, Mary Dill, 52
The Brownies' Book (magazine), 51
Buggs, Shantel, 107
Burkina Faso, 140

Capital (Marx), 142
capitalism, 5, 20–22, 129–30,
  131, 136–37
Capitalism and American Leadership
  (Cox), 20, 22
Capitalism as a System (Cox), 20
Capra, Fritjof, 40–41
Caste (Wilkerson), 26–27
Caste, Class, and Race (Cox), 20, 22–24
caste system:
  for Dalits, 26–27, 112–
    20, 123–24;
  discrimination in, 121;
  "Downward Filtration"
    in, 113–14;
  in education, 111–12;
  gender in, 115–16, 126n2;
  marginalization in, 116–17;
  philosophy of, 119–20;
  race relations and, 22–25;
  social justice in, 112–13;
  women in, 114–15
censorship, 7–8, 13
Central Intelligence Agency, 134–35
Césaire, Aimé, 2, 7–10, 15
Césaire, Ina, 8–10

Césaire, Suzanne (née Roussi), 2,
  7–15, 17n3
La Chicana (Enríquez and Mirandé), 86
Chicana/os: in education, 81–82,
  91–93; identity, 103–4; lesbians
  and, 107; Native Americans and, 85;
  in queer culture, 104–5; in social
  theory, 4, 84–87, 93–95; in United
  States, 82–84, 89–90; use of, 97n1;
  women, 100
The Chicano Experience
  (Mirandé), 85–86
children, 15, 34, 51, 108,
  111–12, 151–52
Chile, 140
China, 137
Christianity, 31–33, 35, 111–12
Circle in the Dirt (Moraga), 102
class, 5, 20–23, 55, 102–4,
  106–7, 121–22
Cold War, 22, 129, 137
collective unconscious, 12
The College Bred Negro American (Du
  Bois and Dill), 50
Collins, Patricia Hill, 55–56, 58, 99
colonialism:
  Blackness and, 15;
  Britain in, 111–12;
  decolonization, 13–14;
  education in, 113–14, 119–20;
  feminism in, 117–18;
  gender and, 86;
  history of, 12–13;
  imperialism and, 12–13, 24–25,
    108, 129–38, 140–41;
  in India, 114–15, 123;
  indigeneity and, 102–4;
  land acknowledgment after, 44;
  Native Americans in, 81;
  neocolonialism, 132, 135–37;
  postcolonialism, 133–37;
  tourism and, 14;
  in *Tropiques*, 12;
  in United States, 29

About the Editors

Korey Tillman is a PhD candidate in sociology at the University of New Mexico. His work focuses on race, policing, and empire by situating contemporary policing within its antiblack and colonial past. As an abolitionist, the goal of his work is to build upon the legacies of the Black feminist and radical traditions to assert Black humanity and move toward a world where African diasporic communities receive care, not criminalization. Korey's writings have been published in *Social Problems*, *Sociology Compass*, and *The Sociological Review*. In addition, his scholarship has been supported, in part, by the National Science Foundation Graduate Research Fellowship Program, and The Fulbright U.S. Student Program.

David R. Dickens is professor of sociology at the University of Nevada, Las Vegas. His primary areas of research and teaching specialization include classical and contemporary sociological theory, critical theories of culture, and qualitative research methods.

C. C. Herbison holds a PhD in American studies from the University of Kansas and is faculty emeritus at The Evergreen State College in Olympia, Washington. His teaching and research interests are American studies, African American studies, Asian/Pacific Islander American studies, disability studies, and carceral studies. His community-based activities include work with communities of disability and incarcerated populations.

About the Contributors

Tirth Bhatta is assistant professor in the Department of Sociology at University of Nevada, Las Vegas. Bhatta earned two master's degrees, one in statistics and one in gerontology, before receiving a doctoral degree in sociology from Case Western Reserve University. His primary area of research seeks to understand how life course socioeconomic status intersects with other forms of stratification (especially race/ethnicity and gender) to shape later-life health disparities in the United States and internationally. His second area of research has focused on the role of nonmaterial resources such as altruism, love, and spirituality in ameliorating the adverse influence of stressors on psychological well-being. His work has appeared in high-impact journals around the sociology of aging and life course (i.e., *Journal of Gerontology: Social Sciences*, *Journal of Aging and Health*, and *Ethnicity and Health*).

Moushumi Biswas is assistant professor of English at Langston University, Oklahoma. She is a rhetoric and composition scholar from India who earned her PhD from the University of Texas at El Paso in 2017. Her doctoral dissertation examines ecofeminist resistance to neoliberal corporate rhetorics of global development. Her current research areas are global rhetorics, transnational feminist rhetorics, and digital rhetorics. As a journalist-turned-academic, Dr. Biswas enjoys transferring her digital communication skills from the media industry to composition classrooms. She is particularly interested in the rhetorical principles of web design, which she incorporates into her Technical Writing curricula. She also teaches First-Year Composition, Advanced Composition, and Special Topics in English that include topics of interdisciplinarity. Since Dr. Biswas's pedagogical inquiries stem from a transcultural perspective of so-called standard English, she is engaged in implementing inclusive writing strategies for diverse student populations. She is a proponent of non-racist activism in composition, and her long-term goal is to develop theory and praxis involving translingualism to help incorporate global "Englishes" into writing instruction.

Marcus Brooks is assistant professor in the department of sociology and criminology at Western Kentucky University. His research examines how social media technologies mediate racial discourses and social understandings of race and racism. His work also explores how technologies, both historically and in the present, have and are used to advance racial justice. Marcus will be joining Western Kentucky University as an assistant professor in Fall 2022.

Manisha Desai is professor of sociology and Asian and Asian American studies at the University of Connecticut. Her areas of research and teaching include transnational feminisms, gender and globalization, human rights, and contemporary Indian society. As part of a global network on the new Eco-Social Contract, she is currently working on alternative movement imaginaries for social transformation that go beyond human rights, to rights for all. Her last book, *Subaltern Movements in India: The Gendered Geography of Struggle Against Neoliberal Development* (Routledge 2016) analyzed three subaltern movements by adivasis (indigenous people), farmers, and fishers against "development by dispossession." Her other books include *Gender, Family, and Law in a Globalizing Middle East and South Asia* (coedited with Ken Cuno, Syracuse University Press, 2010) and *Gender and the Politics of Possibilities: Rethinking Globalization* (Rowman & Littlefield, 2008) and (coedited with Nancy Naples) *Women's Activism and Globalization: Linking Local Struggles to Transnational Politics* (Routledge 2002).

Robert J. Durán is associate professor of sociology at Texas A&M University. His areas of research concern racism in the post–civil rights era and community resistance, from gang evolution and border surveillance to disproportionate minority contact and officer involved shootings. He is the author of *Gang Life in Two Cities: An Insider's Journey* (2013), *The Gang Paradox: Inequalities and Miracles on the U.S.-Mexico Border* (2018), and currently finalizing a book project tentatively titled *No Justice, No Peace: Police Shootings as Legalized Violence* with Oralia Loza. All three books have been, or will be, published by Columbia University Press.

Simon Gottschalk is professor of sociology at the University of Nevada, Las Vegas. As a critical social psychologist, he has published on topics as diverse as terrorism, the mass media, countercultural youth, environmental identity, acceleration, the senses, Las Vegas, the transmission of trauma, ethnography in virtual spaces, and qualitative research methods, among others. His most recent book *The Terminal Self* explores how our interactions with digital technologies shape our everyday lives and experiences.

About the Contributors 183

Julien Grayer is assistant professor in the Department of Sociology, Criminology, and Anthropology at the University of Wisconsin–Whitewater. He was born in New Orleans where he received his bachelor's in Sociology from Xavier University of Louisiana. He received his master's in Criminal Justice from the University of Alabama at Birmingham. His research focuses on racial criminalization, criminology, stigma, symbolic interaction and racial identity construction. He received his doctorate in sociology from the University of Missouri where he developed his dissertation project focused on exploring how Black undergraduate students navigate their identities and interactions in predominantly white environments where they are often coded as suspect or deviant.

Amanda D. Hernandez, PhD started her academic journey at San Antonio College before transferring to the University of Texas at San Antonio, where she earned her bachelor's degree in Women's Studies. She completed her graduate studies in sociology at Baylor University. Broadly, Amanda's research areas contend with how sexism and white supremacy shape everyday life. Her dissertation, *Feminism, Feminists, and Faith: Intersectional Identities* examined how whiteness shaped both feminist and Christian identities and how women of color navigate both spaces. She is currently the research director for South Alamo Regional Alliance for the Homeless.

Heather A. O'Connell graduated with a PhD from the University of Wisconsin–Madison. She is currently an assistant professor in the Sociology Department at Louisiana State University. Her research centers on understanding race and the persistence of racial inequality in the United States. While pursuing this objective, she has given notable attention to the enduring structural consequences of historical institutions, particularly slavery.

Moushumi Roy is assistant professor of sociology at Hampton University, Hampton, Virginia. Dr. Roy's research interests lie at the intersection of structural inequality, social conditions, social determinants, social processes and population health in the United States and India. She studies the way structure and systems of societies change the experiences of different groups of people—i.e., immigrants, migrants, race/caste/varna-system, ethnicity, gender, older people—to produce inequality (e.g., advantaged, disadvantaged, and ultra-disadvantaged) and health disparity among populations. Dr. Roy can be reached at Moushumi.roy@Hampton.edu or mroyc77@gmail.com.

Rianka Roy is a doctoral student in sociology at the University of Connecticut. Her research is on the Indian tech industry and tech workers' mobilization. Her research areas include labor and labor movements, social movements, migration, gender, and the political economy of digital technology. She completed her previous doctoral research in India, on social media surveillance. The author has presented her work at several conferences and invited lectures. Her research has been published in peer-reviewed journals, books, blogs, and newspapers.

Maya Singhal is a doctoral candidate in anthropology at Harvard University. Their dissertation, *Yellow Peril, Black Power*, demonstrates how crime works as a kind of mutual aid—a set of practices around which people collaborate to secure resources, protection, and social mobility—through a historical and ethnographic study of collaborations between African American and Chinese American people in New York City from the 1960s to the present.

Sonia Valencia is a doctoral candidate in the English department at the University of Texas in San Antonio. Her research focuses on contemporary Chicana/o and Latina/o cultural production, environmental criticism, and Chicanx feminisms. She currently works at the University of Colorado Denver, where she serves as the Director of TRIO Programs: McNair and Student Support Services (SSS). She received her master's degree in English from Georgetown University and a bachelor's degree in English and Women's Studies from the University of California, Riverside, where she first encountered the powerful work of Cherríe Moraga.

Daniel R. Wildcat is a Yuchi member of the Muscogee Nation of Oklahoma. His service as teacher and administrator at Haskell spans thirty-six years. In 2013 he was the Gordon Russell visiting professor of Native American Studies at Dartmouth College. Dr. Wildcat received an interdisciplinary PhD from the University of Missouri–Kansas City. In 1994 he partnered with the Hazardous Substance Research Center at Kansas State University to create the Haskell Environmental Research Studies (HERS) Center to facilitate 1) technology transfer to tribal governments and Native communities, 2) transfer of accurate environmental information to tribes, and 3) research opportunities to tribal college faculty and students throughout the United States. He is the author and editor of several books, including *Power and Place: Indian Education In America*, with Vine Deloria Jr., and *Destroying Dogma: Vine Deloria's Legacy on Intellectual America*, with Steve Pavlik. His book, *Red Alert: Saving the Planet with Indigenous Knowledge*, suggests Indigenous ingenuity—*Indigenuity*—is required to reduce the environmental damage in the Anthropocene. He is a coauthor of the Southern Great Plains chapter of the *Fourth National Climate Assessment*.

www.ingramcontent.com/pod-product-compliance
Lightning Source LLC
Chambersburg PA
CBHW022316280326
41932CB00010B/1126